Illustrated Record of German Army Equipment 1939–1945

ARTILLERY

PART TWO

Published by
The Naval & Military Press Ltd
Unit 10, Ridgewood Industrial Park,
Uckfield, East Sussex,
TN22 5QE England
Tel: +44 (0) 1825 749494
Fax: +44 (0) 1825 765701

www.naval-military-press.com

© The Naval & Military Press Ltd 2004

Reproduced by kind permission of the Central Library,
Royal Military Academy, Sandhurst

ILLUSTRATED RECORD
OF
GERMAN ARMY EQUIPMENT
1939-1945

FOREWORD

1. The issue of this publication, three years after the end of the war in Europe, is designed to put on record essential information on the armament of the German Land Forces during the war. It includes some of the more interesting equipments which were developed, but which, due to the conclusion of hostilities, or to production difficulties, did not come into general service.

   The publication is primarily a photographic record, supported by a brief specification, and in some instances a short description. The material has been drawn from the large collection of matter compiled by the Technical Intelligence Services during and subsequent to the war. Much of it has appeared in the various Technical Intelligence Summaries and Bulletins issued by the War Office, and by G.H.Qs. overseas, supplemented by photographs and details added from German sources after the collapse.

2. Handbooks have already been published on some of the more important equipments. The volume of material and the scope of the present publication, have precluded detailed descriptions. For any recipient officially requiring fuller information on any particular subject, the records available can be consulted through M.I.10, The War Office, up to 30 May 1949. Thereafter they will be disposed of.

3. This publication is laid out in the form of a reference album showing a photograph of each equipment, together with the specification or brief description. It has been divided into five separate volumes under the following subject headings:-

Vol.I	Infantry Weapons		
Vol.II	Artillery	Part I	- Anti-Tank, Field, Medium, Heavy and super Heavy Weapons.
		Part II	- Anti-Aircraft, Coast Defence and Railway Weapons.
Vol.III	Armoured Fighting Vehicles		
Vol.IV	Vehicles (other than A.F.Vs.)		
Vol.V	Mines, Mine Detectors, and Demolition Equipment		

4. It will be noted that the sections dealing with mines, mine detectors, and demolition Equipment have been written up rather more fully, but in no case do these sections claim to be exhaustive.

5. It should be noted that all figures quoted are taken from German sources. It is appreciated that in many instances these differ from the figures quoted in official British and American reports.

6. In conclusion it is hoped that this publication will serve a purpose as a brief permanent record of the major German Army weapons and equipments developed and used during the 1939-1945 war.

The War Office

Director of Military Intelligence

ILLUSTRATED RECORD OF GERMAN ARMY EQUIPMENT

1939 – 1945

VOLUME II

ARTILLERY

PART II

CONTENTS   Page

CHAPTER I

The Development of German Artillery 1

CHAPTER II

The Development of German Light Anti-Aircraft Artillery 3
    2 cm.   Flak. 30 3
    2 cm.   Flak. 38 6
    2 cm.   Flakvierling. 38 9
    2 cm.   Foreign Equipments 11
    3 cm.   Flak. 103/38 11
    3 cm.   Flakvierling. 103/38 14
    3.7 cm. Flak. 18 18
    3.7 cm. Flak. 36 18
    3.7 cm. Flak. 37 21
    3.7 cm. Flak. 43 21
    3.7 cm. Flakzwilling. 43 23
    4 cm.   Flak. 28 23

CHAPTER III

The Development of German Medium Anti-Aircraft Artillery 27
    5 cm.   Flak. 41 27
    5 cm.   Flak. 214 31
    5.5 cm. Flak Gerät. 58 31

CHAPTER IV

The Development of German Heavy Anti-Aircraft Artillery 39
    8.8 cm. Flak. 18
    8.8 cm. Flak. 36   40
    8.8 cm. Flak. 37
    8.8 cm. Flak. 37/41 44
    8.8 cm. Flak. 41 45
    10.5 cm. Flak. 38 51
    10.5 cm. Flak. 39 53
    12.8 cm. Flak. 40 57
    12.8 cm. Flakzwilling. 40 61
    15 cm.   Flak Gerät. 50 64
    15 cm.   Flak Gerät. 55 64
    15 cm.   Flak Gerät. 60 66
    15 cm.   Flak Gerät. 65 66
    24 cm.   Flak Gerät. 80 67
    24 cm.   Flak Gerät 85 67

CHAPTER V

The Development of German Coast Defence Artillery 71
    3.7 cm.   S.K. C/30. in Einheitslafette. C/34 77
    7.5 cm.   Pak. 40 M. in L.M. 39/43 78
    8.8 cm.   S.K. C/35. in Ubts L. C/35 79
    10.5 cm. S.K. C/32. n L. in 8.8 cm. M.P.L. C/30. D 83
    10.5 cm. S.K. L/60 83
    15 cm.   S.K. C/28. in Küst M.P.L. C/36 84
    15 cm.   S.K. C/28. in Zwillingslafette 85
    15 cm.   Tbts. K. C/36 87

CHAPTER V (CONTINUED)

		Page
15 cm.	S.K. L/40	89
15 cm.	Ubts u Tbts. K. L/45	92
17 cm.	S.K. L/40	96
20.3 cm.	S.K. C/34	96
24 cm.	S.K. L/40 in Drh L. C/98	99
24 cm.	S.K. L/35	100
28 cm.	S.K. L/40	103
28 cm.	S.K. L/45	106
28 cm.	S.K. L/50	107
30.5 cm.	S.K. L/50	107
38 cm.	S.K. C/34. (Siegfried)	110
40.6 cm.	S.K. C/34. (Adolf)	113

CHAPTER VI

		Page
The Development of German Railway Artillery		121
15 cm.	K. (E)	129
17 cm.	K. (E)	133
20 cm.	K. (E)	135
21 cm.	K. 12. (E)	137
21 cm.	K. 12. (V)	137
21 cm.	K. 12. (N)	144
24 cm.	Theodor Bruno K. (E)	145
24 cm.	Theodor. K. (E)	151
28 cm.	kurze Bruno. K. (E)	153
28 cm.	lange Bruno. K. (E)	153
28 cm.	schwere Bruno. K. (E)	155
28 cm.	Bruno neue. K. (E)	157
28 cm.	K. 5 (E)	159
Notes on the projectiles used in the 28 cm. K. 5. (E)		166
38 cm.	Siegfried. K. (E)	175
40.6 cm.	Adolf. K. (E)	180
80 cm.	K. (E)	180
Ammunition for the 80 cm. K. (E)		184

APPENDICES

		Page
Appendix "A"	Data for German Heavy A.A. Guns	189
Appendix "B"	Performance data of German A.A. Guns	190
Appendix "C"	Performance data of German A.A. Equipment	191
Appendix "D"	Data for German Coast Defence Guns	193
Appendix "E"	Comparative data for "R - Geräte" and other miscellaneous equipments as at July, 1942	195
Appendix "F"	Data for German Railway Guns	196

LIST OF PLATES

		Page
1.	2 cm. Flak. 30	4
2.	"	5
3.	2 cm. Flak. 38	7
4.	"	8
5.	2 cm. Flakvierling. 38	10
6.	3 cm. Flak. 103/38	12
7.	"	13
8.	3 cm. Flakvierling. 103/38	16
9.	3.7 cm. Flak. 18	17
10.	3.7 cm. Flak. 36	19
11.	"	20
12.	3.7 cm. Flak. 43	22
13.	3.7 cm. Flakzwilling. 43	24
14.	"	25
15.	4 cm. Flak. 28	26
16.	5 cm. Flak. 41	28
17.	"	29
18.	"	30
19.	5.5 cm. Flak. Gerät. 58	36
20.	"	37
21.	"	38
22.	8.8 cm. Flak. 18	41
23.	8.8 cm. Flak. 36	42
24.	"	43
25.	8.8 cm. Flak. 41	47
26.	"	48
27.	"	49
28.	"	50
29.	10.5 cm. Flak. 38	52
30.	10.5 cm. Flak. 39	54
31.	"	55
32.	"	56
33.	12.8 cm. Flak. 40	58
34.	"	59
35.	"	60
36.	12.8 cm. Flakzwilling. 40	62
37.	"	63
38.	15 cm. Flak Gerät. 55	65
39.	15 cm. Flak Gerat. 60. F.	69
40.	"	70
41.	10.5 cm. S.K. C/32 in. 8.8 cm. M.P.L. C/30 D.	80
42.	" " " "	81
43.	" " " "	82
44.	15 cm. S.K. C/28 in Zwillingslafette	86
45.	15 cm. Tbts. K. C/36.	88
46.	15 cm. S.K. L/40	91
47.	15 cm. Ubts u Tbts. K. L/45 .	95
48.	17 cm. S.K. L/40	97
49.	20.3 cm. S.K. C/34	98
50.	24 cm. S.K. L/40 in Drh L. C/98	101
51.	"	102
52.	28 cm. S.K. L/40	104
53.	"	105
54.	30.5 cm. S.K. L/50	111
55.	38 cm. S.K. C/34. (Siegfried)	114
56.	" "	115
57.	40.6 cm. S.K. C/34. (Adolf)	119
58.	" "	120
59.	15 cm. K. (E).	132
60.	17 cm. K. (E).	134
61.	20 cm. K. (E).	136
62.	21 cm. K. 12. (N)	146
63.	21 cm. K. 12. (V)	147
64.	"	148
65.	24 cm. THEODOR BRUNO. K. (E).	150
66.	24 cm. THEODOR. K. (E).	152
67.	28 cm. lange BRUNO. K. (E).	154
68.	28 cm. schwere BRUNO. K. (E).	156
69.	28 cm. BRUNO neue. K. (E).	158
70.	28 cm. K. 5. (E).	173
71.	"	174

LIST OF PLATES (CONTINUED)

		Page
72.	38 cm. SIEGFRIED. K. (E).	179
73.	80 cm. K. (E).	182
	(GUSTAV AND DORA)	
74.	"	183
75.	Ammunition for the 80 cm. K. (E).	188

CHAPTER I

THE DEVELOPMENT OF GERMAN ARTILLERY

A. **General**

Modern conditions have tended to link together more closely the spheres of Anti-Aircraft, Coastal and Railway Artillery. It is proposed to deal with these three types, in that order, in this second and final part of the volume.

Two factors have led to this closer linking of the three types of artillery, viz:-

1. The interweaving of coastal and air defence against combined operations attack.

2. The tendency to favour mobile coastal artillery, thus bringing railway artillery into the coastal artillery role.

B. **A.A. Artillery**

The German Anti-Aircraft Artillery was controlled by the Air Force. This led to much discord, because of the use by local Army Commanders of A.A. guns in other roles, such as anti-tank defence.

Although the German Anti-Aircraft Artillery, as a whole, was quite good, it was never "on top". Development was a continuous battle to obtain increased performance, in order to cope with the mounting weight of air attack and advances in aircraft design.

In the light anti-aircraft gun sphere of 20 mm to 40 mm weapons, increased rate of fire and speedier rates of elevation and traverse were a continuous demand.

Even at the end of the war, the Germans had not succeeded in putting into the field a medium calibre, 50 to 70 mm, A.A. gun, which adequately covered the gap between light and heavy A.A. weapons.

The German heavy A.A. weapons, consisting of the 8.8, 10.5 and 12.8 cm guns, were quite good, and at the end of the war the Germans were striving to develop an efficient 150 mm (6 inch) weapon. The mobile 12.8 cm weapon was considered by many sound judges to be of outstanding merit.

C. **Coastal Artillery**

Coastal Artillery was the responsibility of the German Naval Authorities and many of the weapons used were of similar design to those used aboard ship. The lighter guns aboard ship were sited in a manner enabling them to be used in a dual role, i.e. against air and sea targets. This was reflected in the German Coastal Artillery.

The coastal weapons and layout of defences were not outstanding, compared with the other major powers. It is thought that their fire control of coastal artillery was inferior to that of some other powers. It was proved that their layout of communications was very vulnerable, being quite easily destroyed by gun fire, owing to the lack of protection given to transmission cables.

D. Railway Guns

The German Railway Artillery equipment, except for a few models, consisted of railway mountings, fitted with naval guns, which happened to be available when the demand for railway weapons arose.

Although these equipments were used principally in a field role, they also performed yeoman service as coastal artillery.

It is was realised that railway tracks were very vulnerable to air attack, but these could be repaired quite quickly. The Germans reasoned that weapons, up to 38 cm in guns and 52 cm in howitzers, could be transferred rapidly from one area to another over quite long distances. Railway gauges, bridges and rolling stock dimensions permitted the rail transportation of artillery weapons up to a weight of 350 tons; two parallel sets of track allowed of weight up to 1300 tons, as witnessed by the development of the 80 cm gun. The mounting was divided longitudinally into two parts for travelling on the normal two-rail track, the gun having previously been dismounted on to a special gun sleigh.

In fact even the largest equipments could be catered for as a railway weapon. All round traverse could be supplied by the use of special turntables for weapons up to 24 cm. For the other weapons, and as an alternative, use of curved tracks and cross tracks provided the necessary traverse.

A further development provided a combination of tracked-cum-railway gun mounting. With this arrangement, the end railway bogies could be withdrawn at the same time lowering the superstructure (consisting of the gun, gun-mounting and tracked chassis) to the ground. The gun then travelled as a self-propelled weapon on the tracked chassis. This enabled the weapon to circumvent damaged railway track and also gave it additional operational mobility.

The German Railway Artillery will be remembered if only for the fact that it included that mammoth effort the 80 cm (31 inches) gun. This weapon, fired from a double-track railway, was commanded by a Major General, had a gun detachment 3000 strong, and fired a projectile 7 tons in weight to a range of 41,500 yards or a 4.7 ton projectile to a range of 51,500 yards.

CHAPTER II

THE DEVELOPMENT OF GERMAN LIGHT ANTI-AIRCRAFT ARTILLERY

A. **General**

1. One of the main features, which characterised German light A.A. Artillery weapon development during the recent war, was the continual effort to increase the rate of fire of each size of weapon. This was the result of a light A.A. policy which claimed that the most effective defence against low flying attacking aircraft was to put up as great a volume of fire as possible. The ballistic performance of the 2 cm. and 3.7 cm. weapons used operationally did not change and, although new types of ammunition were introduced as hostilities progressed, the different models of these guns all fired the same range of ammunition of their own calibre.

2. The question of accurate laying of light A.A. guns was constantly in the forefront of the minds of the German designers. At the outbreak of war, the 2 cm. and 3.7 cm. guns were equipped with reasonably efficient speed and course sights, which were designed for use by well trained layers. They were of delicate and complicated design and it was found that they did not stand up to the rigours of active warfare as well as had been expected. As the war progressed, the standard of trained layers deteriorated and in the heat of battle the layers fired and adjusted by observing the shell tracers, yet it was not until 1944 that a new type of sight was introduced. These new sights were simpler and less expensive to manufacture and were much easier to use, thereby not requiring such a high standard of training on the part of the gunlayers.

3. The designers were continually striving to increase the rates of traverse and elevation of these two light A.A. weapons, and the latest models of both the 2 cm. and 3.7 cm. guns showed that considerable progress had been made in remedying the defects in the earlier models.

4. Summing up, the latest models had the following essential improvements:-

   (a) Increased rates of fire.

   (b) Increased accuracy of gunlaying.

   (c) Increased speeds in traversing and elevating.

B. **2 cm. Flak. 30 (.79 in. A.A. Gun Model 30) See fig:- 1 and 2**

1. The original 2 cm. A.A. gun to be developed for operational use was the 2 cm. Flak. 30 - developed and produced by the firm of Rheinmetall-Borsig. The design of the gun has generally been associated with the firm of Solothurn and it was assumed that the patents of the gun and ammunition had been obtained from the Swiss firm by the Germans. This is, however, disclaimed by Rheinmetall-Borsig technicians, who state that the gun was developed entirely by their firm, although its design was undoubtedly influenced by Solothurn, since many of the automatic gun designers of Rheinmetall-Borsig had at one time or another been employed by the Swiss firm.

The 2 cm. Flak. 30 was introduced into service in 1935. It was a gas and recoil operated automatic gun, mounted on a triangular platform and transported on a light two-wheeled carriage.

Laying was performed by one man; the original A.A. sight employed was the Flakvisier 35. This sight consisted of a mechanical course and speed computer, connected by a linkage train to a sighting head, to which the necessary deflections were thus applied.

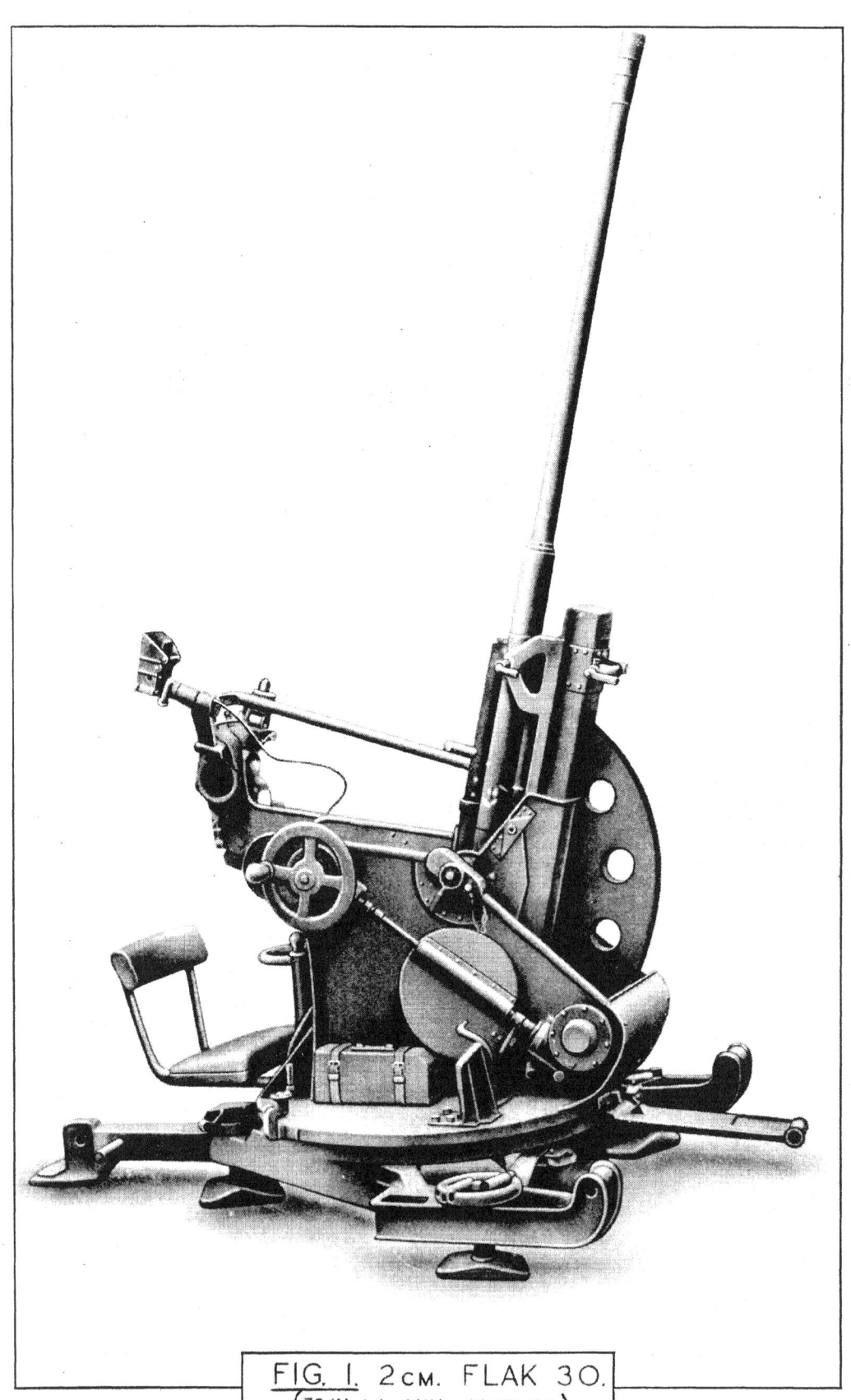

FIG. I. 2 CM. FLAK 30.
(·79 IN. A.A. GUN. MODEL 30)

FIG. 2. 2 CM. FLAK 30.
(·79 IN. A.A. GUN. MODEL 30.)

As such, the gun was employed during the opening stages of the war and, although it gave good service, it was considered necessary to have a higher rate of fire for the effective operation of a weapon of this calibre.

In pursuance of this policy, the original design of the Flak 30 was handed over to the firm of Mauser, who were instructed to redesign the breech mechanism to give a cyclic rate of fire of approximately 500 r.p.m.; the design of a new carriage and trailer was put in the hands of the firm of Gustloff. The new weapon, which appeared in service by 1940, was designated the 2 cm. Flak. 38.

2. **Data: 2 cm. Flak. 30.**

(a)
Calibre	.79 in. (20 mm.)
Length of ordnance	90½ in. (2300 mm.)
Rifling R.H. Uniform	
Rifling length	28 in. (720 mm.)
No. of grooves	8
Traverse	360°
Elevation	-12° to 90°
Recoil Normal	1.36 in. (33 mm.)
" Max	1.77 in. (44 mm.)
Overall length of equipment	13 ft. 1 in. (4000 mm.)
Overall height	4 ft. 11 ins. (1490 mm.)
Overall width	6 ft. 3 ins. (1900 mm.)
Wt. of equipment complete	1598 lbs (770 Kg.)
Type of carriage - Mobile, S.P., Static and Railway versions.	
Type of sight - Flakvisier 35 - Mechanical computer sight.	
" " " - Linealvisier 21 - Open aim-off sight.	
Rate of fire (cyclic)	280 r.p.m.
" " " (practical)	120 r.p.m.
Ceiling - Max.	12,460 ft. (3780 m.)
" - Effective	6,630 ft. (2200 m.)

(b)
Ammunition	M.V.	Wt. of projectile
H.E. tracer	2950 f/s (900 m.s.)	4.2 oz.
H.E. incendiary	2950 f/s (900 m.s.)	4.2 oz.
A.P./H.E. tracer	2725 f/s (830 m.s.)	5.2 oz.
A.P. tracer	2725 f/s (830 m.s.)	5.2 oz.
A.P. incendiary tracer	2725 f/s (830 m.s.)	5.2 oz.
A.P. 40 shot	3264 f/s (995 m.s.)	3.6 oz.

(c) **Fuze**

Percussion S.D.

C. **2 cm. Flak. 38. (.79 in. A.A. Gun Model 38). See Fig: 3 & 4.**

1. The 2 cm. Flak. 38 had the same ballistic performance as the Flak. 30 and fired the same range of ammunition. The redesign of the breech mechanism stepped up the rate of fire to 480 r.p.m. and the carriage was redesigned with double ring trunnions to give greater stability in action. The trailer was of similar construction to that used with the Flak. 30.

Whereas the Flak. 30 jammed frequently, the Flak. 38 functioned well. The chief disadvantage of the new model was that it lacked range. The original sight designed for use with this gun was the Flakvisier 38, consisting of an electric computer box and a reflector type sighting head. Rates of elevation and traverse were fed to tachy dynamos in the computer box, from which the output values, modified by a rheostat on the application of range, were transmitted to the sighting head and displaced the vertical and horizontal graticules according to the required deflections. A slightly modified version of this sight was produced and designated the Flakvisier 38A. Construction and principle of operation were similar to the Flakvisier 38, but the materials used for its manufacture were different and the separate electrical component parts were encased in dust and damp proof containers, as a protection against the weather and for ease of servicing in the field.

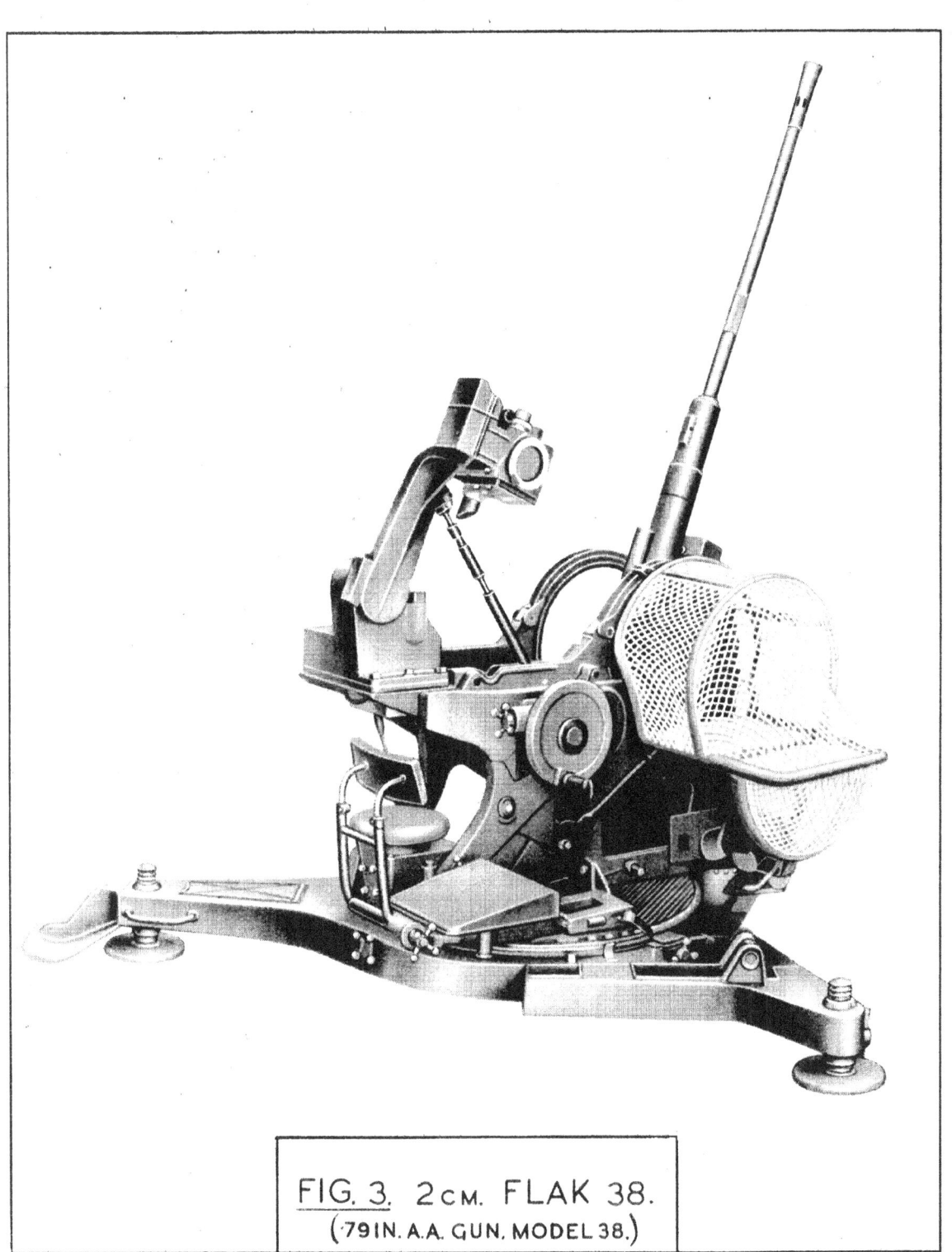

FIG. 3. 2 CM. FLAK 38.
(79 IN. A.A. GUN, MODEL 38.)

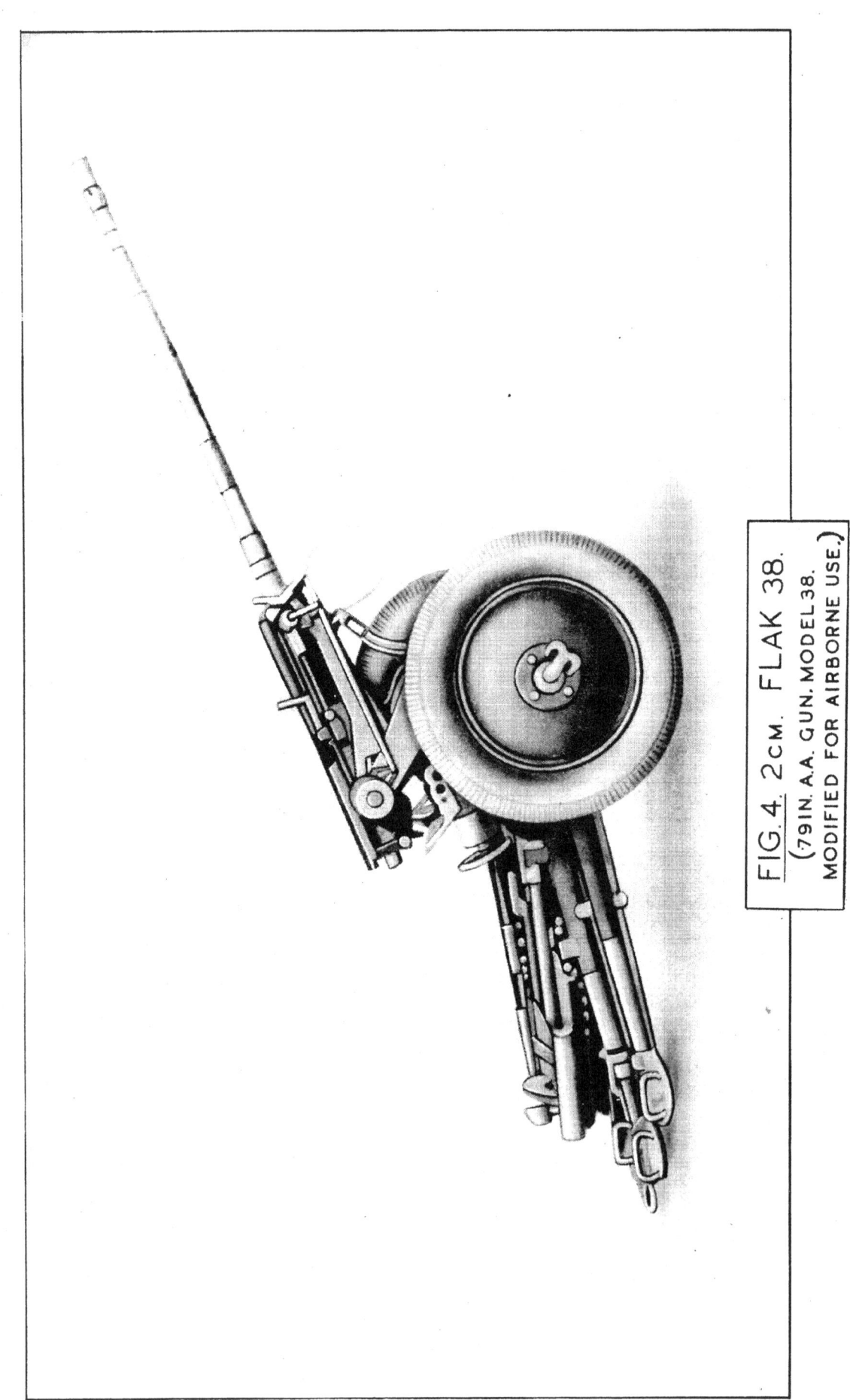

FIG. 4. 2cm. FLAK 38.
(79 IN. A.A. GUN. MODEL 38. MODIFIED FOR AIRBORNE USE.)

Both the Flakvisier 35 for the Flak. 30 and the Flakvisier 38 for the Flak. 38 gave a reasonably satisfactory answer to the light A.A. problem, but they were both complicated and of comparatively delicate design and, as such, required a high standard of manufacture and maintenance. This became all the more apparent when the equipments were used in the field under active service conditions and, by 1941, a complete change in policy took place with regard to the design and production of A.A. sights for 2 cm. guns. Instead of the early computer type sight, it was decided to introduce a simple open ring sight, which would be more easily operated and manufactured. The first of these to come into service was a simple course and speed sight, made of pressed steel and clamped on the sight bar of the gun, and was designated Linealvisier 21 when used with the Flak. 30 and Linealvisier 38 when used with the Flak. 38. A further development of this open type of sight was the Schwebekreisvisier 30 and 38, for employment with the Flak. 30 and Flak. 38 respectively. Eventually it entirely replaced the Linealvisier and was intended to replace the mechanical and electrical computer sights, as these became unserviceable.

2. **2 cm. Flakvierling. 38 (.79 in Quadruple A.A. Guns Model 38).** See Fig. 5.

In addition to the 2 cm. Flak. 38, a quadruple version of this gun was also brought into service at about the same time as the single mounted gun. The quadruple version designated "2 cm. Flakvierling. 38" consisted of four Flak. 38 guns mounted on a triangular platform and transported on a two-wheel carriage. The complete equipment was compact and effective and considered by German technicians to be the best 2 cm. A.A. equipment produced by any country. It was used intensively from the time of its introduction in 1940 until the cessation of hostilities and, during that time, only minor mechanical modifications were made to the original model used.

The standard sight used with this equipment was the Flakvisier 40, which was an electric techymetric sight, similar to the Flakvisier 38, but made for mounting on the four-barrel equipment. A Flakvisier 40A was also produced, embodying similar modifications to those in the Flakvisier 38A.

A later model of the 2 cm. Flakvierling. 38 incorporated a Radar laying device. The Radar scanning "bowl" was located on the centre axis of the four barrels and about 12 inches or so in rear of the four muzzles.

3. **Data: 2 cm. Flak. 38.**

(a) Calibre .79 in. (20 mm.)
Length of ordnance 88.6 in. (2252.5 mm.)
Rifling R.H. Uniform
Rifling length 28 in. (720 mm.)
No. of grooves 8
Traverse 360°
Elevation -20° to 90°
Recoil 2.07 in. (53 mm.)
Overall length of equipment 13 ft. 1 in. (4000 mm.)
Overall width 5 ft. 11 in. (1810 mm.)
Wt. of equipment complete 1654 lbs. (750 Kg.)
Type of carriage - Mobile, S.P. Static, and Railway versions.
Type of sight-Flakvisier 38 - Electric computer sight.
" " " -Linealvisier 21 - Open aim-off sight.
Rate of fire-max. 420 - 480 r.p.m.
" " " practical 180 - 220 r.p.m.
Ceiling - max. 12,460 ft. (3780 m.)
" - effective 6,630 ft. (2200 m.)

(b) | Ammunition | M.V. | Wt. of projectile |
|---|---|---|
| H.E. tracer | 2950 ft/sec. (900 m.s.) | 4.2 oz. |
| H.E. incendiary tracer | 2950 ft/sec. (900 m.s.) | 4.2 oz. |
| A.P./H.E. tracer | 2725 ft/sec. (830 m.s.) | 5.2 oz. |

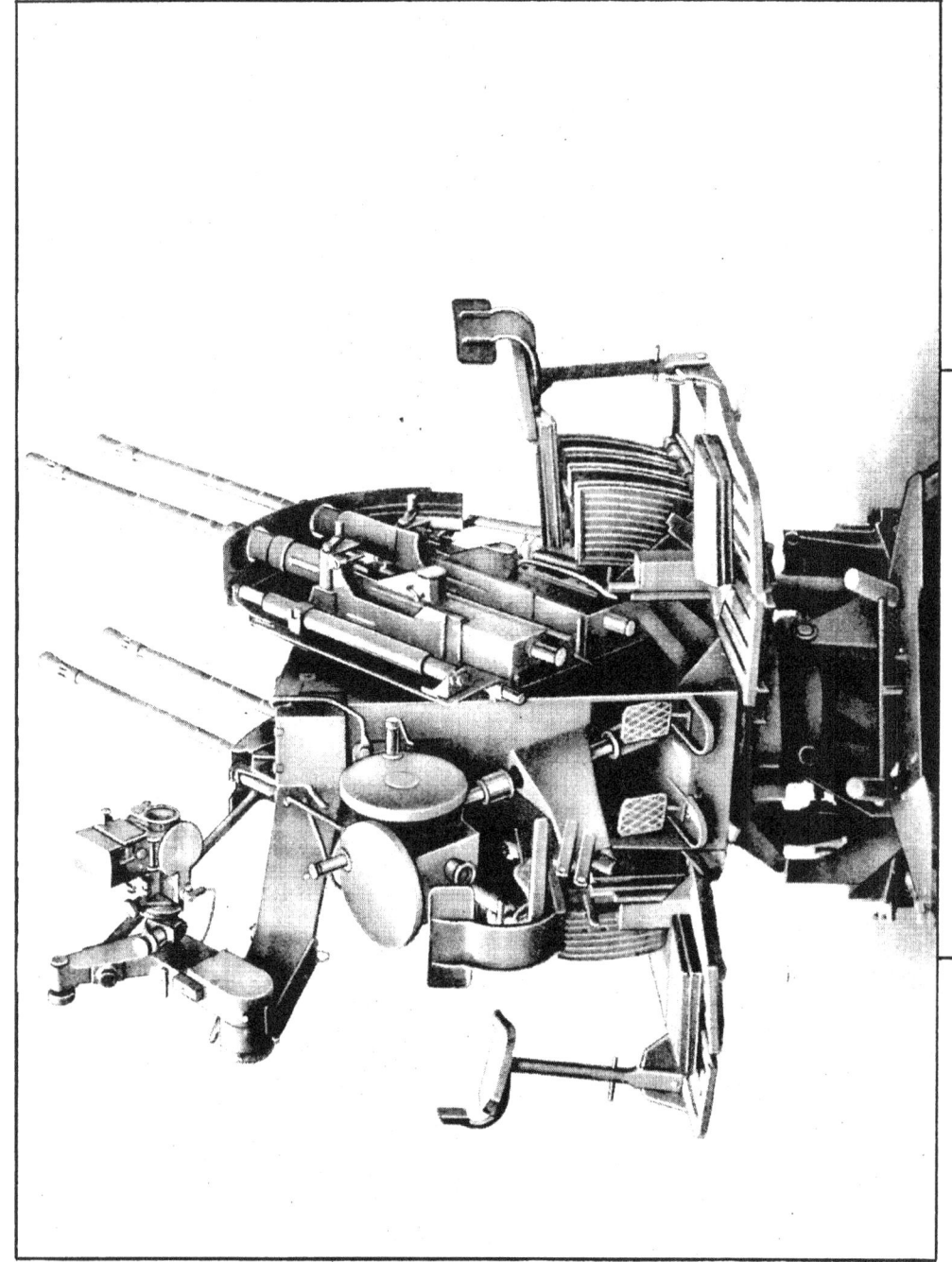

FIG.5. 2CM. FLAKVIERLING 38.
(.79IN. QUADRUPLE A.A. GUNS, MODEL 38.)

(b) Ammunition (contd.)

	M.V.		Wt. of projectile
A.P. tracer	2725 ft/sec.	(830 m.s.)	5.2 oz.
A.P. incendiary tracer	2725 ft/sec.	(830 m.s.)	5.2 oz.
A.P. 40 shot	3264 ft/sec.	(995 m.s.)	3.6 oz.

(c) Fuze

Percussion S.D.

4. Data: 2 cm. Flakvierling. 38.

The data for this four gun model is the same as that shown above, except for the following:-

Elevation	-10° +100°
Rate of Fire-	
Theoretical	1800 r.p.m.
" " " Practical	880 r.p.m.

D. **2 cm. Foreign Equipments**

Of the foreign 2 cm. equipments used by the German Army, the Swiss Oerlikon gun was employed on the largest scale. The German designation for this gun was <u>2 cm. Flak. 28</u>. There is little evidence of its employment to any extent in the field, but it was used on a comparatively large scale in a static role chiefly in coastal areas. The same applies to a more limited extent to the Danish Madsen gun.

E. <u>3 cm. Flak. 103/38. (1.18 inch. A.A. Gun Model 103/38). See Fig: 6 & 7</u>

1. (a) General

The story of the evolution of this equipment provides still further evidence that the German light A.A. defences were being strained to the limits of their capacity during 1944 by the increased Allied low level air attacks. It is a story of hurried improvisation in an effort to improve their harassed defences.

Briefly, the equipment consisted of the 3 cm. aircraft machine cannon 103 fitted into the 2 cm. Flak. 38 mounting. Both required modifications before the weapon could be completed, and documents show that there was much discussion between the representatives of Rheinmetall Borsig, who produced the gun, Gustloff-Werke (SUHL), who produced the mounting, and other armament officials during the autumn of 1944. A contract with special priority was placed for 1000 mountings to be delivered in numbers as follows:- 1944, NOV. - 79, DEC. - 185; 1945, JAN. - 230, FEB. - 250 and MARCH - 260. The Rheinmetall Borsig firm was ordered to deliver 2000 guns to Gustloff-Werke in sufficient numbers to enable the contract to be carried out as ordered, i.e. giving one spare barrel per equipment.

In addition to the standard towed weapon, which was to be transported on a special single Trailer No. 51, arrangements were also made to mount the equipment on a 2 ton STEYR unarmoured lorry.

(b) Characteristics

The weapon is an improvised makeshift. The heavy recoil power of the gun causes strong vibration in the light 2 cm. Flak mounting, which has a corresponding effect on the rigidity of the mounting and the rest position of the sight. In order to reduce to some extent the heavy recoil effect on the mounting, the gun is fitted with (apart from its own barrel muzzle brake) an additional casing muzzle brake on the mounting. For improving the stability, the undercarriage has been specially reinforced. For improving the rest position, the sight locking bracket is fitted with an oscillating sight, in which the sight is spring suspended in the direction of fire.

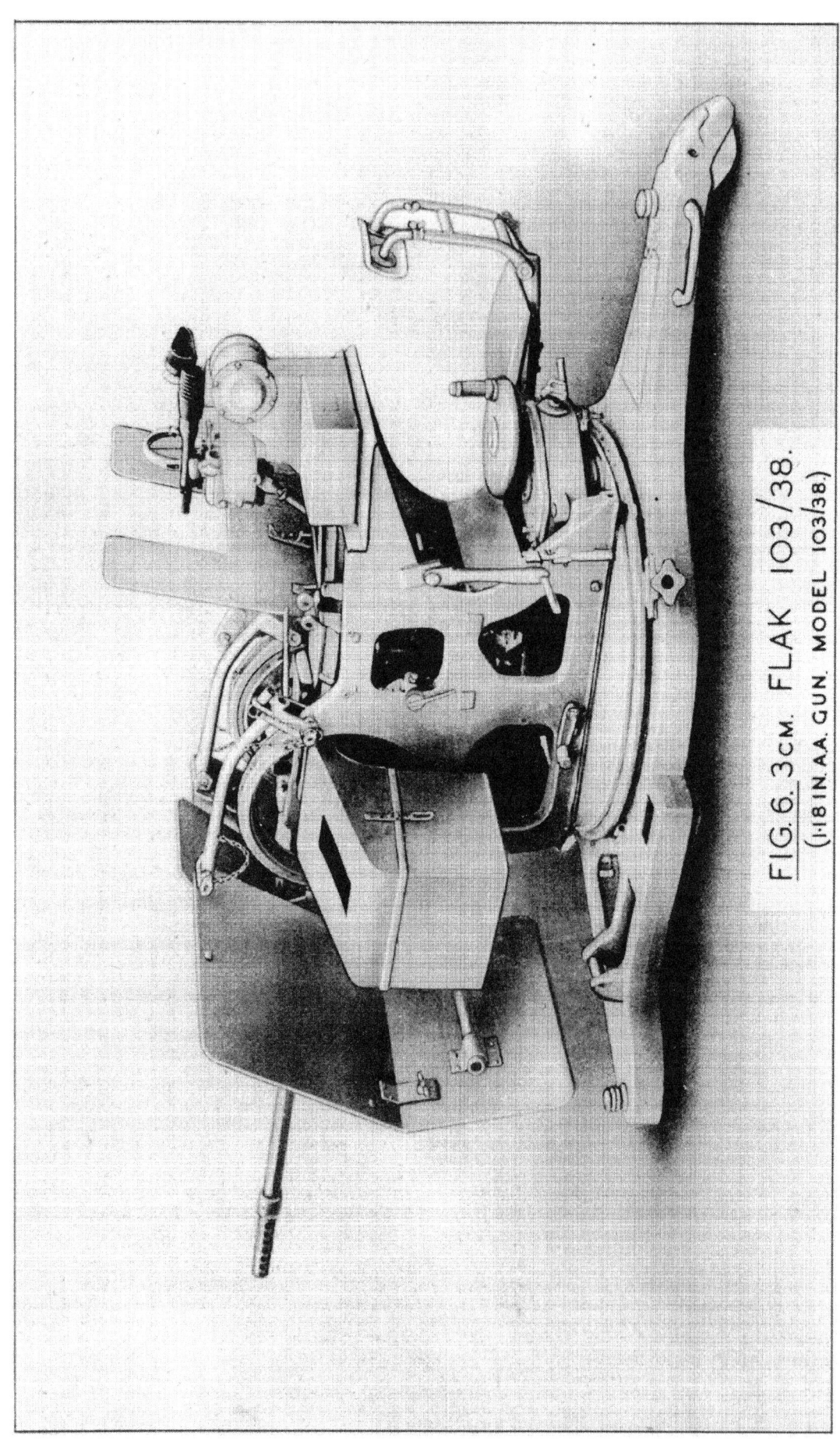

FIG. 6. 3CM. FLAK 103/38.
(1·18 IN. A.A. GUN. MODEL 103/38.)

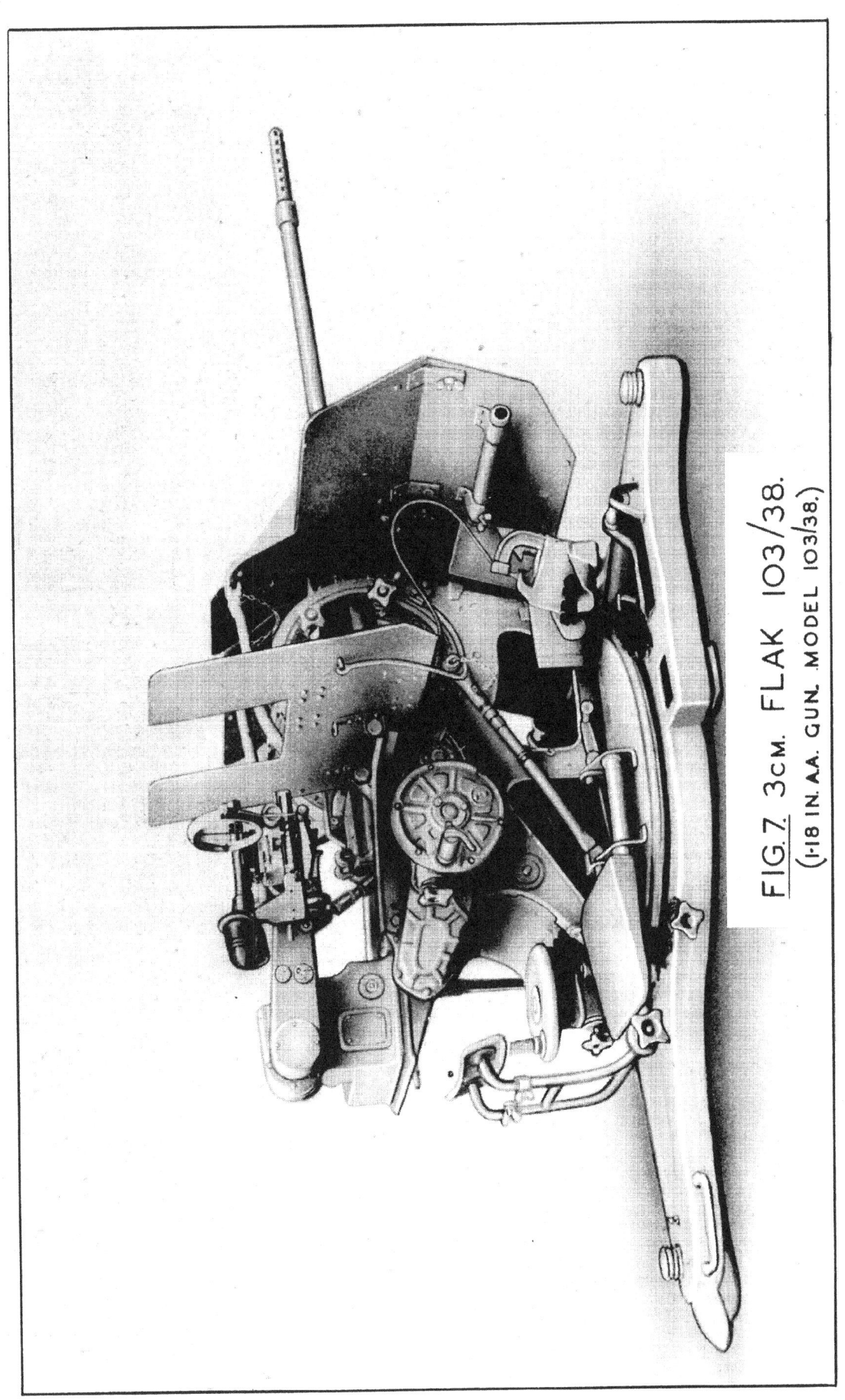

FIG.7 3CM. FLAK 103/38.
(1·18 IN. A.A. GUN. MODEL 103/38.)

The gun is a fully automatic gas operated weapon with rigid locked support, flap breech and belt feed. The gun casing is stationary, the gun barrel with breech locking mechanism moving backwards and forwards. The belt feed is actuated by the barrel recoil. The empty belt links of the disintegrating belt fall laterally out of the gun. The empty cases are ejected downwards. The two section breech is supported in the locked position in the breech locking mechanism, which is rigidly connected to the barrel. The rear rifled section of the latter has a gas vent to enable the charge gas to escape and operate the gas piston, which slides the breech locking slide valve against the breech mechanism, and thus draws out the breech locking leaves from the breech locking mechanism, locked to the barrel. After unlocking, only the breech retracts, as the barrel recoil has been braked by the buffer, and the recuperator spring is then moving the barrel forward. The breech continues to go backwards until it strikes the breech buffers and the breech closing spring then moves the breech forward to pick up and load the next round, providing that the trigger is pressed. If the trigger is not pressed, the breech is prevented from going forward by the trigger bolt; the latter is withdrawn when the trigger is pressed thereby allowing the breech to go forward. The breech, on reaching the closed position, is automatically locked and the striker moved to fire the round. The gun is fitted with a mechanical cocking and uncocking mechanism and can be set at safety by hand.

The equipment has one serious fault, in that the gun is distinctly muzzle heavy. The elevation equilibrators are of the spring type.

The mounting is designed so that the gun layer can operate both elevation and traversing gears, in addition to firing the gun by a foot pedal operated mechanism.

The sights are the suspension "cart wheel" sight No.103 for air and land targets and the telescopic sight 3 x 8° for direct laying on land targets.

2. **3 cm. Flakvierling. 103/38 (1.18 inch Quadruple A.A. Guns).** See Fig: 8

A quadruple gun equipment was produced for fixed mounting and for self-propelled mounting, in addition to a towed equipment.

If the photographs of the single and quadruple equipments are compared, it will be seen that the barrel casing as placed when used in single, is fitted on its side with the quadruple equipment.

3. Data: 3 cm. Flak. 103/38.

	Metric	British
(a.) Calibre	30 mm.	1.18 inch.
Muzzle Velocity:-		
M Cannon Shell	900 m/sec.	2953 f.s.
Incendiary Shell	900 m/sec.	2953 f.s.
Armoured Piercing Incendiary Shell	800 m/sec.	2625 f.s.
HE Shell	800 m/sec.	2625 f.s.
Rate of fire - theoretical	400 r.p.m. approx.	
" " " - practical	250 r.p.m. approx.	
Maximum Range.	5730 metres.	6250 yds.
Maximum Ceiling.	4700 metres.	15,420 feet.
Effective Ceiling:-		
M Cannon Shell.	1500 metres approx.	5000 feet.
A.P. Incendiary Shell	1600 metres approx.	5250 feet.
HE Shell	1600 metres approx.	5250 feet.
Time of Flight to Effective Ceiling:-		
M Cannon Shell	2.5 secs. approx.	
A.P. Incendiary Shell	3.2 seconds approx.	
H.E. Shell	3.2 seconds approx.	
Tracer Limit:-		
M Cannon Shell	1200 metres approx.	3950 feet.
A.P. Incendiary Shell	1600 metres approx.	5250 feet.
H.E. Shell	1600 metres approx.	5250 feet.

(b) **Gun**

Length of the gun complete with barrel (Rear edge of flap to leading edge of muzzle brake)	2318 mm.	91.26 ins.
Length of the barrel with muzzle brake.	1608 mm.	63.3 ins.
" " " " without " "	1338 mm.	52.67 ins.
Length of rifling.	1159.7 mm.	45.657 ins.
Number of grooves.		16.
Length of breech closing spring (free length)	1040 to 1100 mm.	41 to 43.3 ins.
Recoil power with muzzle brake	about 2000 kgs.	1.97 Tons.
Thrust power with muzzle brake	about 4000 kgs.	3.94 Tons.
Firing height in firing position	760 mm.	30 ins.
Firing height on special trailer No.51	1120 mm.	44 ins.

(c) **Mounting**

	Metric	British
Elevation	−10° + 80°	
Rate of Elevation per turn of handwheel single speed gear −	10°	
" " " with two speed gear − (fine and coarse setting)	4° and 12°	
Traverse	360°	
Rate of Traverse per turn of handwheel single speed gear −	20°	
" " " with two speed gear (fine and coarse setting)	10° and 30°	

(d) **Weights**

barrel (with muzzle brake)	24 kg.	53 lbs.
barrel (without muzzle brake)	20 kg	44 lbs.
equipment in firing position	619 kgs.	12¼ cwts.
equipment in travelling position	879 kgs.	17.3 cwts.
mounting	385 kgs	7.58 cwts.
gun	145 kgs.	3 cwts.
complete shield	80 kgs.	176 lbs.
casing muzzle brake	9 kgs.	20 lbs.
trailer No. 51 (without mud guards)	260 kgs.	5 cwts.
empty belt magazine	16 kgs.	35¼ lbs.
belt magazine with 30 shells	46 kgs.	101½ lbs.
belt magazine with 40 shells	56 kgs.	123½ lbs.
belt link deflector	5 kgs.	11 lbs.
belt link	.122 kg.	.27 lbs.

(e) **Space requirements**

Diameter of arc of sweep in firing position, with the barrel at:−

elevation of 0°	4640 mm.	182.67 ins.
" of 80°	1900 mm.	75 ins.

Firing Position:−

Length	2120 mm.	83.5 ins.
Breadth	1720 mm.	67.7 ins.
Height	2690 mm.	106 ins.

Travelling Position:−

Length	3000 mm.	118 ins.
Breadth	1820 mm.	72 ins.
Height	2980 mm.	117.3 ins.

Belt Magazine:−

Length	430 mm.	17 ins.
Breadth	410 mm.	16.14 ins.
Height	385 mm.	15.15 ins.

FIG. 9. 3·7 CM. FLAK 18.
(1·18 IN. A.A. GUN. MODEL 18.)

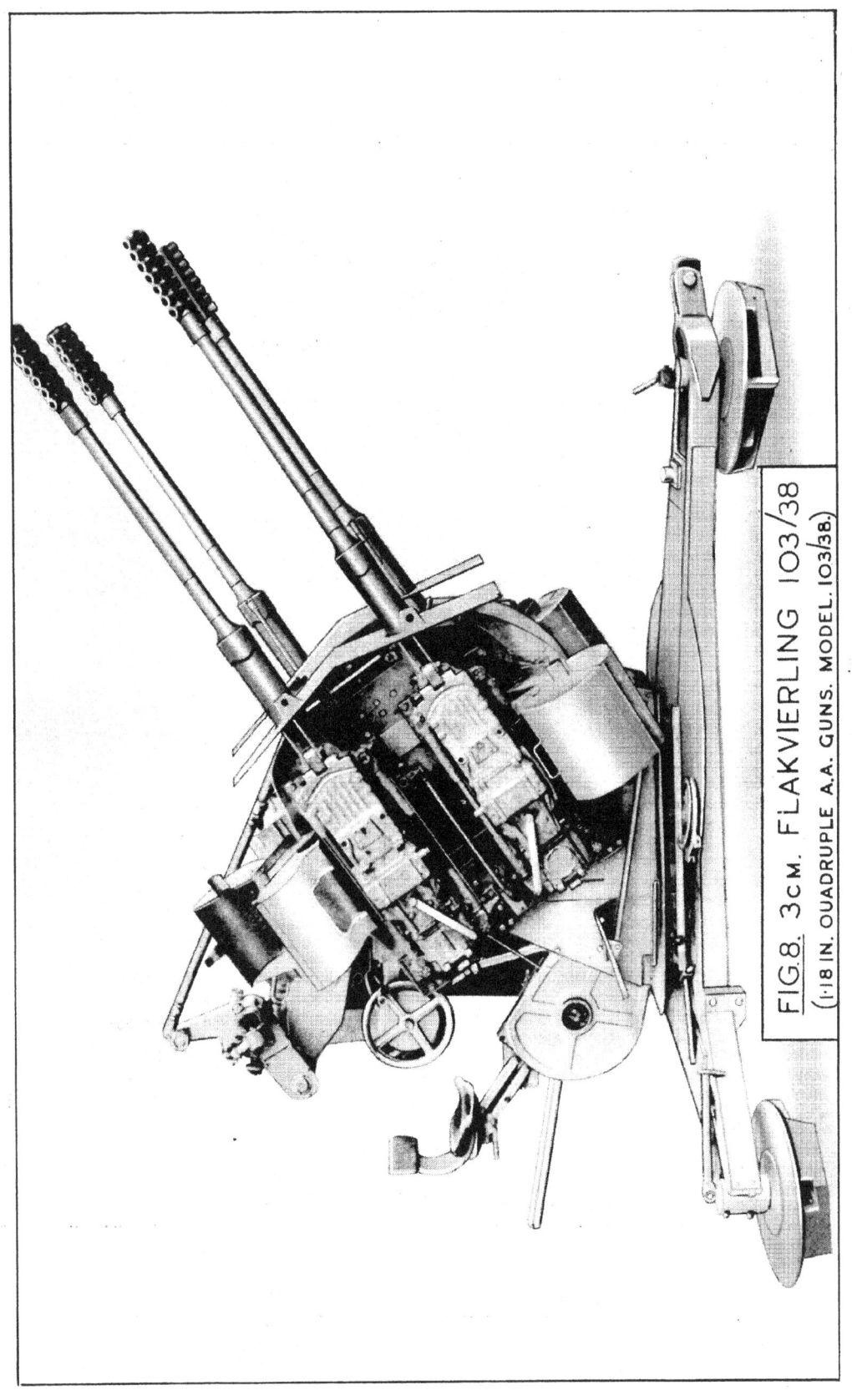

FIG.8. 3cm. FLAKVIERLING 103/38
(1·18 IN. QUADRUPLE A.A. GUNS. MODEL. 103/38.)

F. **3.7 cm. Flak. 18. (1.46 ins A.A. Gun Model 18). See Fig: 9.**

1. This weapon was developed in the early 1930's by Rheinmetall Borsig and was a gun recoil operated weapon, firing a projectile with a banded cartridge case similar in design to the 2 cm. Solothurn ammunition. The gun with a cyclic rate of fire of 150 r.p.m. was mounted on a cruciform platform and transported on two single-axle trailers.

The sight as employed, designed by Zeiss, was a mechanical computor sight, similar in principle to the Flakvisier 35 used with the 2 cm. Flak. 30. It was designated Flakvisier 33 and was mounted on the left front of the cradle side plate.

This equipment was in service by 1935, but after extensive trials under operational conditions it was decided that it was not sufficiently manoeuverable for a 3.7 cm. equipment and a new carriage was designed for transport on a two-wheel carriage. The new equipment was designated Flak. 36.

2. Data: 3.7 cm. Flak. 18

(a) Calibre   1.457 in. (37 mm.)
Length of Ordnance   142.5 in. (3626 mm.)
Rifling R.H. increasing
Rifling length   71.4 in. (1826 mm.)
No. of grooves   20
Traverse   360°
Elevation   -8° to 85°
Recoil Max.   7 in. (178 mm.)
Wt. of equipment complete   8013 lbs. (3634 Kg)
Type of carriage: Mobile, S.P. Static and Railway versions.
Type of sight. Flakvisier 33.
Rate of Fire-theoretical   160 r.p.m.
" " " -practical   80 r.p.m.
Ceiling max.   15,750 ft. (4,800 m.)

(b) Ammunition

	M.V.	Wt. of projectile
H.E. tracer	2690 ft/sec. (820 m.s.)	1 lb. 6½ oz.
A.P. "	2525 ft/sec. (770 m.s.)	1 lb. 8¼ oz.

(c) Fuze

Percussion S.D.

G. **3.7 cm. Flak.36 (1.46 ins. A.A. Gun Model 36). See Fig: 10 & 11.**

1. This equipment, being fitted with the Flak.18 gun, gave the same ballistic performance. The sight, still working on the same principle as for the Flak. 18, was modified for mounting on the new carriage and was redesignated Flakvisier 36.

The Flak.36 was in service at the outbreak of the war and was the standard 3.7 cm. Flak weapon.

Late in 1940, the gun barrel was modified by a slight shortening of the chamber. The shortening of the chamber was accounted for by the introduction of a new type of ammunition with a single-banded projectile, as against the earlier two-banded type. This modification did not occasion any change in nomenclature of the equipment, but such equipments had V (verkürzt) stamped on the rear of the barrel to indicate that the chamber had been modified. The modification became standard and the two-banded ammunition became obsolete.

In the same way as the mechanical computed sight on the 2 cm. Flak. 30 was dropped in favour of a tachymetric sight, the same development took place with the 3.7 cm. equipment. Instead of an electric tachymetric sight as for the Flakvisier 38, the one developed for the 3.7 cm. was entirely clockwork. The new sight was developed by Zeiss

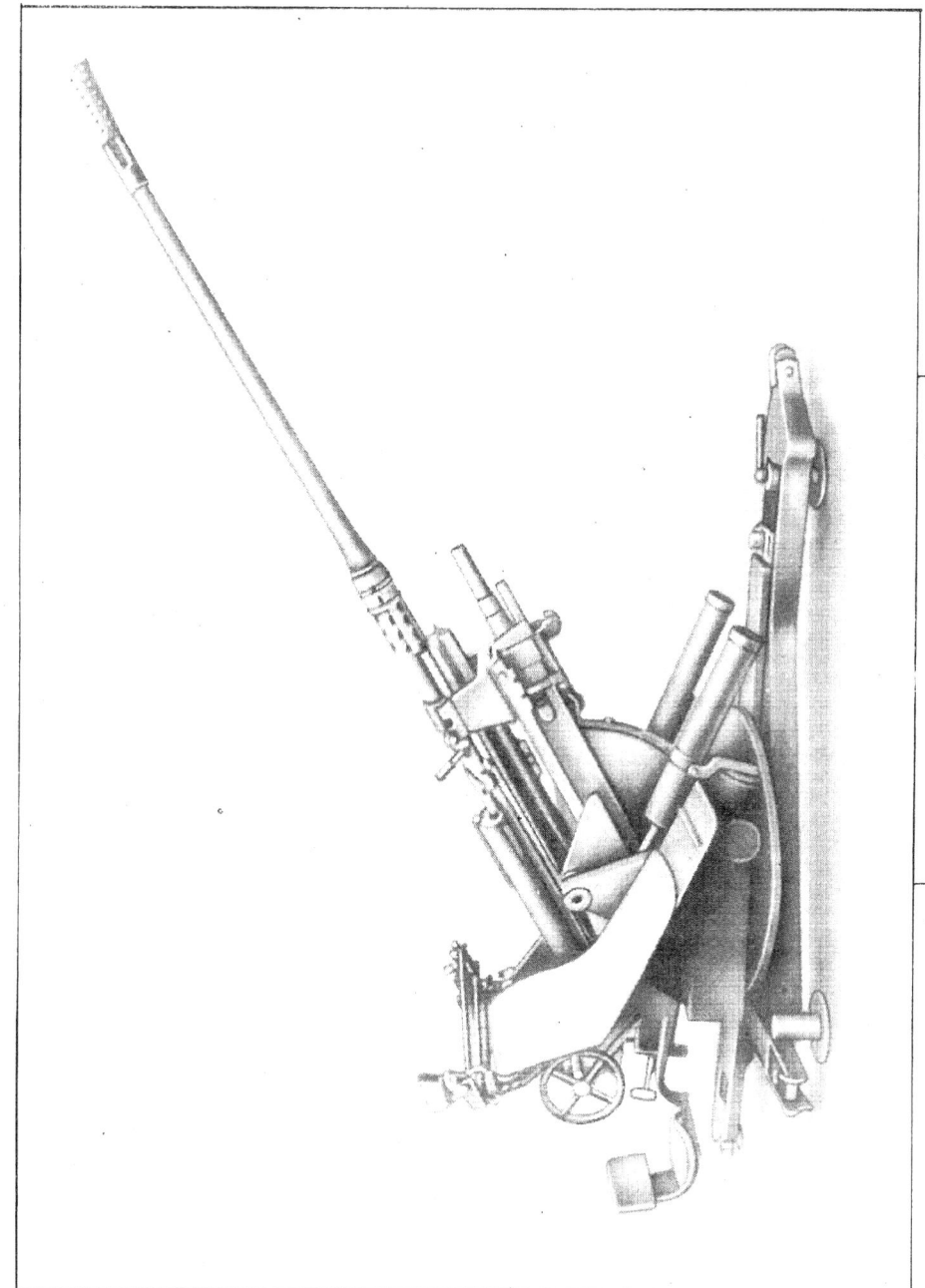

FIG.10. 3.7cm. FLAK 36.
(1.46 IN. AA GUN. MODEL 36.)

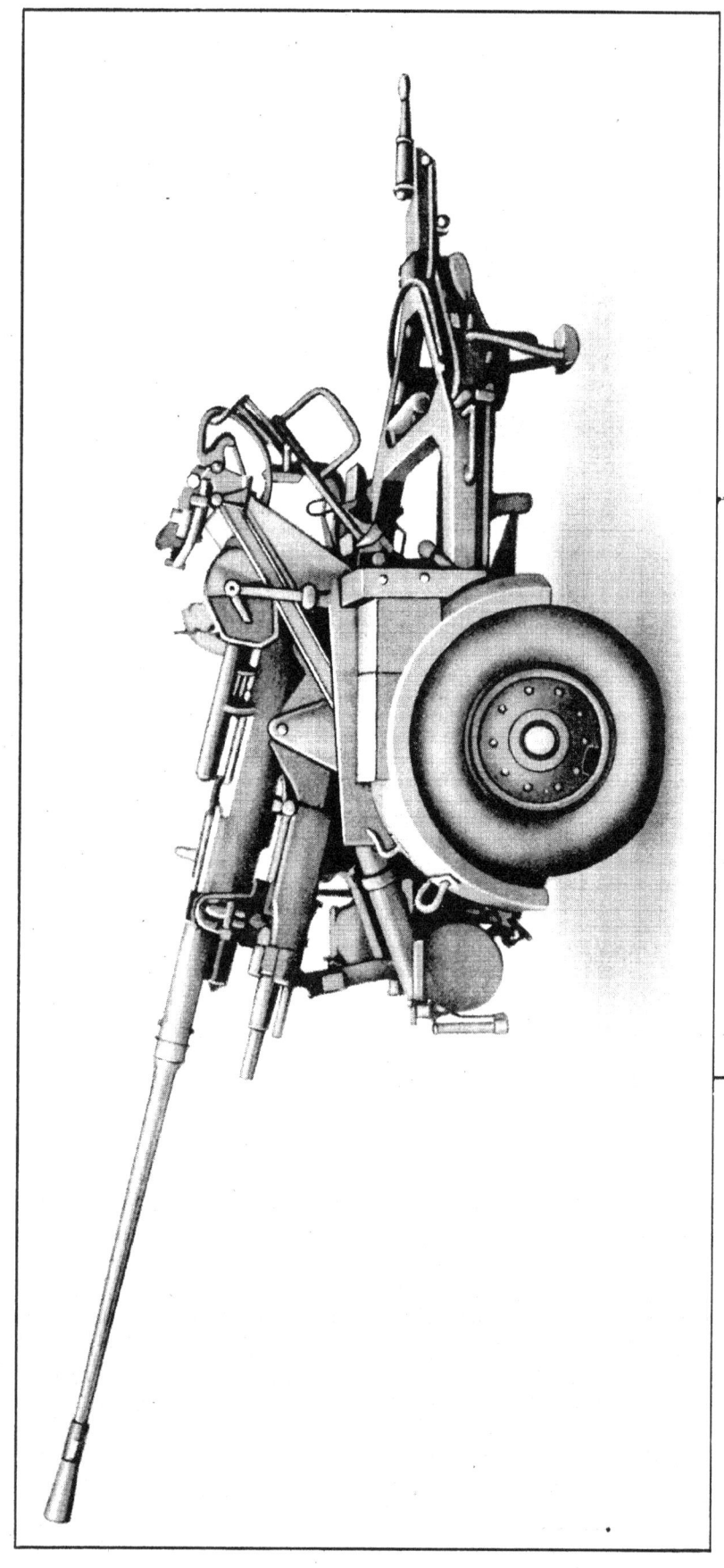

FIG. 11. 3·7CM. FLAK 36.
(1·46 IN. A.A. GUN. MODEL 36.)

and was called the Uhrwerks-visier. It was of compact design and mounted on the right plate of the carriage. Rates of elevation and traverse were fed back into the computer base and were modified by a constant speed motor, regulated according to range, before displacing the graticules according to the required deflection for aim-off. It was intended that this clockwork sight should replace the Flakvisier 36 on the Flak. 36, but the modifications necessary were rather extensive and equipments with the new sighting arrangements were redesignated Flak. 37.

2. **3.7 cm. Flak. 37.** (1.46 inch A.A. Gun Model 37).

The new sight was designated the Flakvisier 37. Only a limited number of converted Flak. 36 equipments were completed, as the clockwork sight was also employed with a later model of the 3.7 cm. A.A. gun, and this absorbed most of the available models produced.

3. Data: 3.7 cm. Flak. 36 (and 37)

(a)
Calibre	1.46 in. (37 mm.)
Length of Ordnance	142.5 in. (3626 mm.)
Rifling R.H. increasing	
Rifling length	71.4 in. (1826 mm.)
No. of grooves	20
Traverse	360°
Elevation	-8° to 85°
Recoil max.	7 in. (178 mm.)
Overall length of equipment	18 ft. 3.3 in. (5570 mm.)
Overall height	7 ft. (2130 mm.)
Overall width	7 ft. 11 in. (2420 mm.)
Wt. of equipment complete	5292 lbs. (2400 Kg.)
Type of carriage	Mobile, S.P., Static & Railway.
Type of sight	- Flakvisier 36 (on Flak 36)
" " "	- Flakvisier 37 (on Flak 37)
Rate of fire-cyclic	160 r.p.m.
" " " -practical	80 r.p.m.
Ceiling	15,750 ft. (4800 m.)

(b) Ammunition

	M.V.	Wt. of Projectile
H.E. Tracer	2,690 ft/sec (820 m.s.)	1 lb. $6\frac{1}{2}$ oz.
A.P. Tracer	2,525 ft/sec (770 m.s.)	1 lb. $8\frac{1}{2}$ oz.

(c) Fuze

Percussion S.D.

Note:- Flak. 37 similar to Flak. 36 except:-

(i) Sight bracket modified to take Flakvisier 37.

(ii) Layers seat is displaced for employment of Flakvisier 37.

H. **3.7 cm. Flak.43.** (1.46 ins. A.A. Gun Model 43.). See Fig: 12.

1. This new model was produced by the Rheinmetall Borsig firm and was of completely new design. A gas-operated weapon, the equipment also gave an increased rate of fire, quick traversing, easy working and reliability; in fact this weapon was a great improvement.

The breech mechanism was improved, but the barrel was ballistically that of the earlier models, consequently the range was still limited. The gun was fitted with a ring trunnion of entirely new design, which enabled the ammunition to be fed through the centre of the trunnion. This eliminated a change of centre of gravity of the elevating parts due

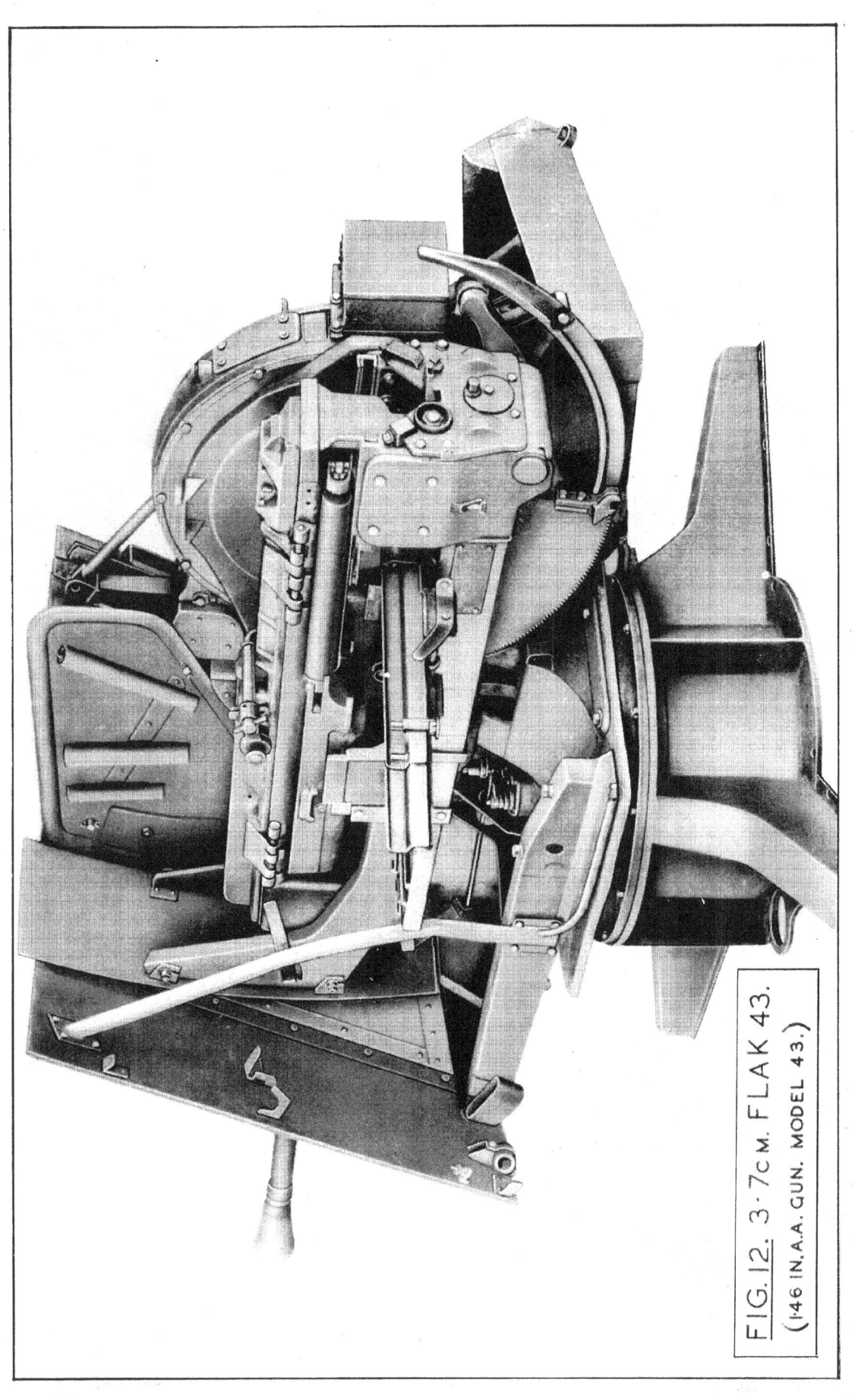

FIG. 12. 3·7 CM. FLAK 43.
(1·46 IN. A.A. GUN. MODEL 43.)

to a changing amount of ammunition in the feed. The superstructure was mounted on a standard type of triangular platform. The same range of ammunition was used as for the Flak. 36. The equipment was transported on a single-axle carriage.

The sight employed was the Zeiss Uhrweksvisier, which was similar to the model used with the Flak 37; but it was designated Flakvisier 43, when used with this equipment.

There were many interesting features in this equipment, such as a clockwork type of spring equilibrator and an ingenious arrangement of effecting graduated recoil.

2. **3.7 cm. Flakzwilling. 43. (1.46 ins. Twin A.A. Guns model 43). See Fig: 13 & 14.**

This twin equipment is quite an ingenious design and consists of two single barrels mounted in the same vertical plane. The guns are fitted with the same type of ring trunnion as used with the single equipment and use a double type of clockwork spring equilibrator. The same type of sight is also used, as is also a similar type platform, but the latter is of larger dimensions.

3. **Data: 3.7 cm. Flak. 43.**

    (a) Calibre   1.457 in. (37 mm.)
         Length of Ordnance   129.9 in. (3300 mm.)
         Rifling R.H. increasing
         Rifling Length   71.4 in. (1826 mm.)
         No. of grooves   20
         Traverse   360°
         Elevation   -7°30' to 90°
         Recoil Normal   5 in. (127 mm.)
         Overall length   11 ft. 6 in. (3493 mm.)
            "   height   5 ft. 4 in. (1619 mm.)
            "   width   5 ft. 10 in. (1778 mm.)
         Wt. of equipment complete   2688 lbs. (1219 Kg.)
         Type of carriage- Mobile, S.P., Static
         Type of sight - Flakvisier 43 - clockwork computer sight.
           "   "   " - Schwebedornvisier - open type sight.
         Rate of fire - Theoretical   250 r.p.m.
           "   "   " - Practical   150 - 180 r.p.m.
         Ceiling   15,750 ft. (4800 m.)

(b) Ammunition	M.V.	Wt. of Projectile
H.E. tracer	2757 ft/sec. (840 m.s.)	1 lb. 6½ oz.
A.P. "	2525 ft/sec. (770 m.s.)	1 lb. 8½ oz.

    (c) **Fuze**

Percussion S.D.

4. **Data: 3.7 cm. Flakzwilling. 43.**

The data for the 2 gun model is the same as that shown above, except that the rate of fire is as follows:-

         Rate of Fire - Theoretical   500 r.p.m.
           "   "   " - Practical   150 r.p.m.

J. **4 cm. Flak 28 (1.56 inch A.A. Gun Bofors Model 1936). See Fig: 15.**

A limited number of this well known light A.A. Bofors type equipment were being used by the Germans. Most of them were probably captured weapons.

FIG. 13. 3·7 CM. FLAKZWILLING 43.
(1·46 IN. TWIN A.A. GUNS. MODEL 43.)

FIG.14. 3·7cM. FLAKZWILLING 43.
(1·46 IN. TWIN A.A. GUNS. MODEL 43.)

FIRING POSITION

TRAVELLING POSITION

4 cm. Light Anti-Aircraft Gun.   Flak 28 Bofors

FIG. 15

CHAPTER III

THE DEVELOPMENT OF GERMAN MEDIUM ANTI-AIRCRAFT ARTILLERY

A. General

During the middle 1930's, the Germans realised that a medium A.A. gun was required to bridge the gap between the maximum effective height at which the 37 mm, and the minimum height at which the 88 mm, could efficiently engage low flying aircraft.

A 47 mm A.A. gun Model 1936 of Skoda design was given a trial by the Germans, but it was considered that the equipment was unable to meet the requirements of a medium A.A. gun adequately.

During 1936, the firm of Rheinmetall Borsig were ordered to develop a 5 cm equipment. In 1939, Krupp were also ordered to develop a similar gun in competition with Rheinmetall Borsig. The stages in the development can be traced from the following table:-

	Rheinmetall Prototype I Model 1936	Krupp Prototype II Model 1939	Rheinmetall Production Model 5cm Flak 41
Calibre	5cm	5cm	5cm
Muzzle Velocity	860m/s.(2820f.s.)	860m/s.(2820f.s.)	840m/s.(2755f.s.)
Cyclic Rate of Fire	100 r.p.m.	120 r.p.m.	150 r.p.m.
Length of Gun	5200mm (17 ft.)	4240mm (14 ft.)	4686mm.(15ft.4in.)
Weight of Gun	650 kg. (13 cwt.)	550 kg.(10¾cwt.)	550 kg.(10¾cwt.)
Weight of Gun and Carriage in draft	4300 kg.(4.23 tons)	5200kg.(5.1 ton)	5750kg.(5.65tons)
Weight of Gun and Carriage in action	2500 kg.(2.46 tons)	2875kg.(2.83tons)	3100kg.(3.1 tons)
Rates of Traverse per turn of the handwheel	3.5°/9°	4°/8°	2°/8°
Rates of Elevation per turn of the handwheel	1°/2.5°/3.5°/8°	1°/2°/4°/8°	1°/2°/4°/8°
Gun Detachment	7	7	7
Type of Carriage	Cruciform	3 point support with 2 arms	3 point support with 2 arms

B 5cm. Flak. 41 (1.97 inch A.A. Gun Model 1941) See Figs. 16, 17 and 18

1. Production of this equipment, which was introduced into service in November, 1940, was on a limited scale; the main object was the trial of a medium A.A. gun under field conditions. The equipment was not a success and several modifications of a minor degree were made in an effort to improve its mobility, stability and reliability.

2. Data: 5cm. Flak. 41

    (a) Calibre   1.97 in.   (50mm)
            Length of ordnance   184.5 in.   (4686.3mm)
            Rifling R.H. increasing
            Rifling length   117.28 in.   (2978.9mm)
            No. of grooves   20
            Traverse   360°
            Elevation   -10° to + 90°

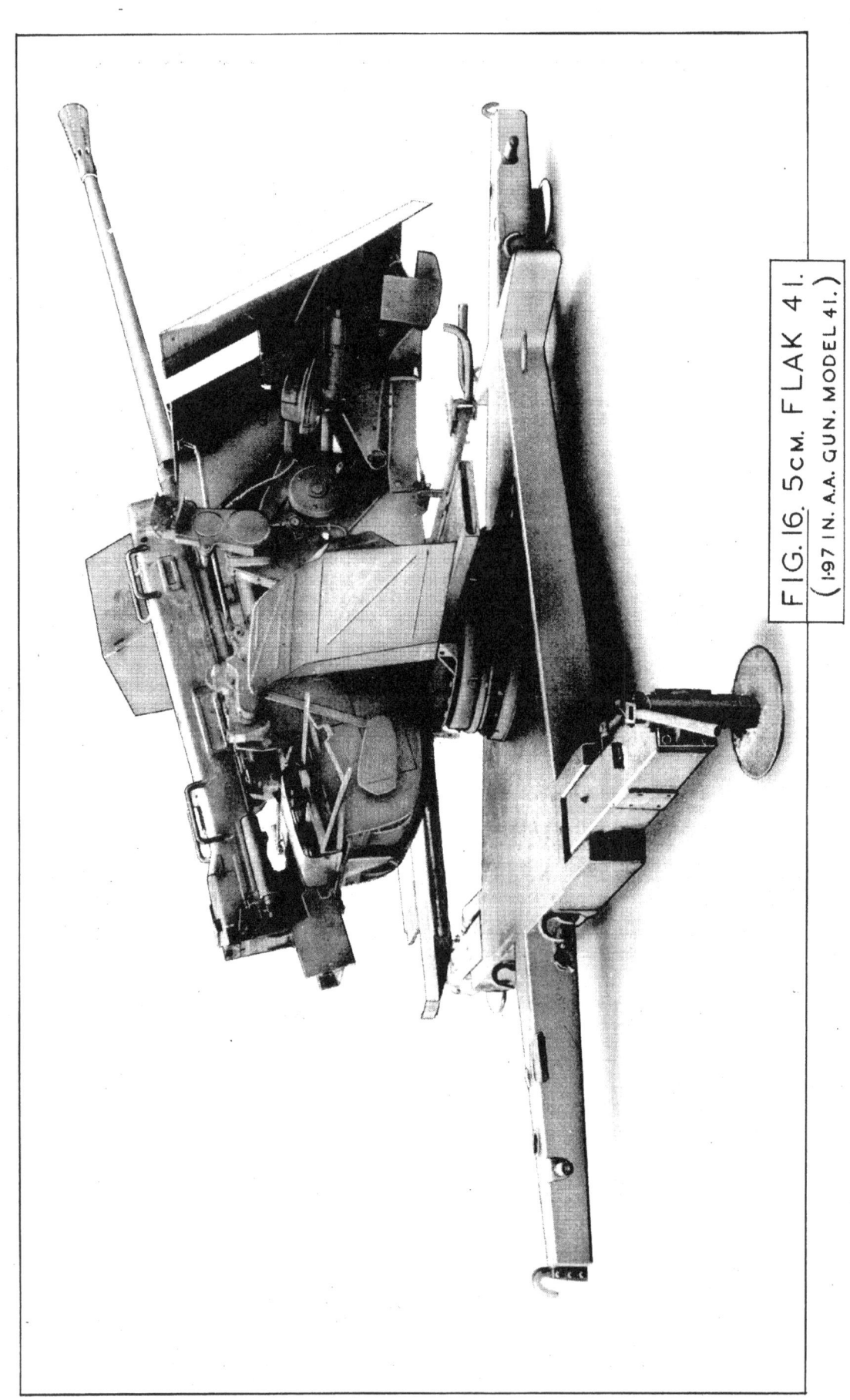

FIG. 16. 5cm. FLAK 41.
(1·97 IN. A.A. GUN. MODEL 41.)

FIG. 17. 5cm. FLAK. 41.
(1·97 IN. A.A. GUN. MODEL.)

FIG. 18. 5cm. FLAK 41.
(1·97 IN. A.A. GUN. MODEL.)

Data (contd.)

   (a) contd.

Recoil Normal	7 in.	(178mm.)
" Max.	8.2 in.	(208mm.)
Overall length	28 ft. 1 in.	(8555mm.)
" height	7 ft. 1 in.	(2160mm.)
" width	7 ft. 9 in.	(2360mm.)
Wt. of equipment complete	12128 lbs.	(5500 kg.)
Type of carriage	- Mobile, S.P., and Static versions.	
Type of sight	- Flakvisier 41 - Tachymetric.	
Rate of fire (practical)		130 r.p.m.
Ceiling-max.	18375 ft.	(5600 m.)
" -effective	10000 ft.	(3050 m.)

   (b) Ammunition

	M.V.	Wt. of projectile
H.E. tracer	2755 ft/secs (840 m.s.)	4 lbs $13\frac{1}{2}$ oz.
H.E./Incendiary/ tracer	2755 ft/secs (840 m.s.)	4 lbs $13\frac{1}{2}$ oz.
A.P.C.B.C.		4 lbs $14\frac{1}{2}$ oz.

   (c) Fuze

      H.E. - Percussion S.D. Two fuze settings - short $5\frac{1}{2}$ - 8 secs.
                                                                     - long 14 - 18 secs.

      A.P.C.B.C. - Base fuze, tracer burning time 2 secs (approx. 1400 m.)

C. **5 cm. Flak 214.** (1.97 inch A.A. Gun Model 214)

The ever increasing Allied air attacks, and the comparative failure of the 5 cm Flak. 41, caused the Germans to look around for a weapon which could be suitably improvised to make good the existing gap, until the projected new 5.5 cm Flak equipment could be put into service.

During the early years of the war, the Germans had produced a very good 5 cm anti-tank gun known as the 5 cm Pak. 38. The German Air Force subsequently decided to utilize this weapon as the armament for some of their aircraft, among which was their J.U.88. To do this work efficiently, it was considered essential to fit an automatic feed. This development work was given to the Mauser firm, who produced a circular type of feed. Incidently this project, utilizing an anti-tank gun as the basis for an aircraft cannon, runs parallel to the action taken by the British Air Force, by which an automatic feed was fitted to the 6 pdr Anti-Tank gun and the equipment used as the armament for the "Mosquito".

To get back to the German search for a "stop gap" medium A.A. gun, it was finally decided to utilize the 5 cm Pak. 38 aircraft cannon with automatic feed, and convert it into a Flak weapon by mounting it on the same carriage (slightly modified), which had been developed for the new 5.5 cm Flak weapon. The equipment was to be known as the 5 cm Flak 214.

Only a limited number (50 to be exact) were being produced during the latter stages of the war; these were to undergo field trials.

The rate of fire of the equipment was reputed to be approximately 140 r.p.m.

D. **5.5 cm. Flak Gerät 58** (2.1 in. A.A. Gun Development 58). See Figs. 19, 20 and 21.

   1. General

During the war, the Germans were faced with low and medium level air attacks on an ever-increasing scale. These were made at heights up to about 4,000 feet, below which the German heavy A.A. was relatively ineffective. Experience had shown the Germans that their 20 and 37 mm. light A.A. was not sufficient protection. It was also realised that to bring down a heavy bomber several hits by 2 cm or 3.7 cm shells were required, but it was estimated that one 5.5 cm shell would be sufficient to accomplish destruction. High priority was given, and great efforts made, to devise schemes for defeating this method of attack. Among these was a new medium A.A. gun known as the "Gerät 58". Development of the equipment had almost been completed at the time of the surrender.

Prior to the development of the 5.5 cm "Gerät 58", much experimental work had been carried out from 1936 on a 5 cm equipment. Both Krupp and Rheinmetall were ordered to develop a satisfactory equipment. The 5 cm Flak. 41, the final gun evolved by Rheinmetall Borsig, was introduced into service in November 1940, and has been dealt with in a preceding section. Experience in the field had shown that the 5 cm Flak. 41 was totally unsuited to perform the task of a medium A.A. gun efficiently. The main criticisms were as follows:-

(a) The stability of the mounting was unsatisfactory.

(b) Levelling of the gun, by pivotting the pedestal in the mounting, involved great complications and a considerable addition to weight.

(c) The trunnion height was too great for good stability in transport and ease of concealment in action.

(d) Rates of traverse and elevation were too slow.

(e) Fire control by an on-carriage sight could only be regarded as an emergency expedient.

Certain of these criticisms followed from the development of the tactical idea behind medium A.A., rather than from the failure of the gun to fulfil its specification. This new medium A.A. theory, which the Germans had developed, is worth while stating in full since it forms the seed from which the "Gerät 58" sprang.

"The employment of a medium A.A. gun can only be justified in positions where it is vital to destroy every attacking aircraft. The above conditions will only occur relatively infrequently, but they are liable to occur both in the furthest rear areas (such as the defence of the Möhne dam) and in the forefront of battle (such as the defence of the Remagen bridge). In each case, one single aircraft in escaping destruction can cause a catastrophy. An expensive equipment can therefore be justified, so long as it is 100% successful.

The solution to this problem is the employment of extremely accurate and massed fire from several guns. This can be achieved by controlling four to six guns from one predictor, the guns being equipped with displacement correctors. The guns must be provided with power-operated traverse and elevation, remotely controlled from the predictor. The whole equipment, despite its complication, must be highly mobile."

2. To meet these requirements the proposed fire control equipment consisted of the following:-

(a) A small Radar

(b) A predictor with separate tracker and computer

(c) A fire unit of four to six guns controlled by one predictor

(d) A displacement corrector for each gun to correct for the displacement of the gun from the datum instrument (tracker or Radar).

(e) Electro-hydraulic remote power control of guns

(f) Flakvisier 41 as an on-carriage fire control equipment.

3. Brief Description of Weapon

   (a) The Gun

   The gun is gas-operated and fires at the end of the run forward. The gas vent in the barrel is in the forward barrel support. The gun casing is rigidly connected to the barrel. The ammunition feed is from the side (left or right) by means of clips of four rounds. The feed mechanism is rigid with the cradle. Spent cartridge cases are ejected downwards from the gun and then carried forward on a chute clear of the lower carriage. The equilibrator balancing gear consists of a flat spiral (clock) spring and is mounted at the rear of the equipment. It can be assembled without special tools, and is of similar type to that used with the 5 cm Flak. 41. The recocking gear is operated by the traversing handwheel. The tension on the run-out operating spring is increased with elevation, to maintain a constant rate of fire.

   (b) The Carriage

   The saddle consists of two side plates with small trunnion bearings. Position for both layers is on the right of the gun. There is one man sighting, the second layer lays for line with a "follow the pointer" dial. There is clutch overload safety in the laying gears. The carriage is levelled and supported on three jack arms, which can also be operated when the gun is on its trailers.

   (c) Remote Control

   There is provision in the laying gears for remote control. The two hydraulic motors and the resetters are built into the carriage, but the remainder of the equipment including the displacement corrector is mounted as a unit at the front of the loader's platform.

   (d) The Twin Mounting

   Owing to the small width of the gun and the ejection of the spent cases downwards, the inter-axial distances between the two barrels is only 333 mm. The total weight of the tipping parts is only 100 kg greater than the prototype single gun and hence the same carriage could be used.

   (e) Production

   Pressed steel plates are largely used in the construction to simplify production. In addition, the employment of alloy steel has been cut down to the barest minimum at the cost of a slight increase in weight.

4. Performance and Dimensions

   (a) Ballistic performance

	Metric		British
Calibre	5.5	cm	2.17 ins
Muzzle velocity	1050	m/s	3445 f.s.
Weight of shell	2.03	kg	4.416 lbs
H.E. content of shell	0.485	kg	1.07 lbs
Muzzle energy	104	mt	102.35 tons
Chamber pressure (practical)	2600	kg sq.cm	16.5 tons sq.ins
" " (max designed)	3500	kg sq.cm	22.2 tons sq ins
Length of complete round	687	mm	27.05 ins
Weight of complete round	4.8	kg	10.58 lbs
Position of C of G of round from base	275	mm	10.83 ins
Weight of cartridge case	1.9	kg	4.19 lbs
Weight of propellant harge	1.1	kg	2.42 lbs

(a) Ballistic performance (contd.)

	Metric	British
Time of flight to 3000 m	4.2 secs	4.2 secs
Shot travel	3800 mm	149.6 ins
Rate of fire	140 r.p.m.	140 r.p.m.
Recoil force on trunnions - normal	2200 k.g.	2.16 tons
Recoil force on trunnions - maximum	3600 k.g.	3.54 tons

(b) Dimensions

(i) Gun:

	Metric	British
Length of complete gun	6150 mm	20' 1.2"
Length of barrel	4211 mm	13' 9.75"
Recoil - maximum	280 mm	11.02 ins

(ii) Carriage:

	Metric	British
Height of trunnions in action	1150 mm	45.27 ins
Height of trunnions in draught	1630 mm	64.17 ins
Length in action	8150 mm	26' 8.85"
Width in action	3400 mm	11' 1.85"
Height in action including shield	1690 mm	66.53 ins
Height in action gun elevated to 90°	6750 mm	22' 1.75"
Length in draught	10510 mm	34' 5.75"
Width " "	2360 mm	7' 8.9"
Height in draught, gun at 0° elevation	2170 mm	7' 1.43"
Height in draught, gun at 90° elevation	7230 mm	23' 8.64"
Wheel base	4920 mm	16' 1.7"
Ground clearance	530 mm	20.86 ins
Length on static mounting	7100 mm	23' 3.5"
Width " " "	3400 mm	11' 1.85"
Height on static mounting, gun at 0° elevation	1690 mm	66.53 ins
Height on static mounting, gun at 90° elevation	6750 mm	22' 1.75"
Extent of elevation (in action or draught)	-10° to + 90°	-10° to + 90°
Extnet of traverse (in action or draught)	Unlimited	Unlimited

(iii) Rates of laying by hand:

Elevation   1.5° and 6° per turn of handwheel
Traverse   2° and 8°   "   "   "   "

(iv) Rates of laying by power or remote control:

Elevation   40° per sec
Traverse   40° per sec
Extent of cross-levelling 7°

(v) Trailer, Type 204:

	Metric	British
Track width	1985 mm	6' 6"
Wheel diameter	1015 mm	40"
Width of tyres	250 mm	9.84 ins
Tyres	9.75 - 20 Extra	
Maximum load	4500 kg	4.43 tons

(c) **Weights**

Tipping parts	1255 kg	1.23 tons
Saddle	775 kg	.75 tons
Shield	300 kg	.3 tons
Carriage	510 kg	.5 tons
Supporting arms	150 kg	.15 tons
Equipment in action	2990 kg	2.95 tons
Two trailers type 204	2500 kg	2.46 tons
Equipment in draught	5490 kg	5.4 tons

(d) **Weight of additional components**

Weight of additional components for power-laying and remote control:

Displacement corrector (stur 44 or 56)	65 kg	143.3 lbs
Input driver to displacement corrector	85 kg	187.4 lbs
2 Selsyn transmitters	12 kg	26.5 lbs
Slip ring	40 kg	88.2 lbs
Cable junction boxes and sockets	10 kg	22.04 lbs
Switch gear	10 kg	22.04 lbs
2 Hydraulic motors	50 kg	110.2 lbs
Hydraulic pump with electric motor	250 kg	5 cwts
Wiring and electric conduit	20 kg	44.1 lbs
Additional gearing	70 kg	154.3 lbs
	612 kg	1349.2

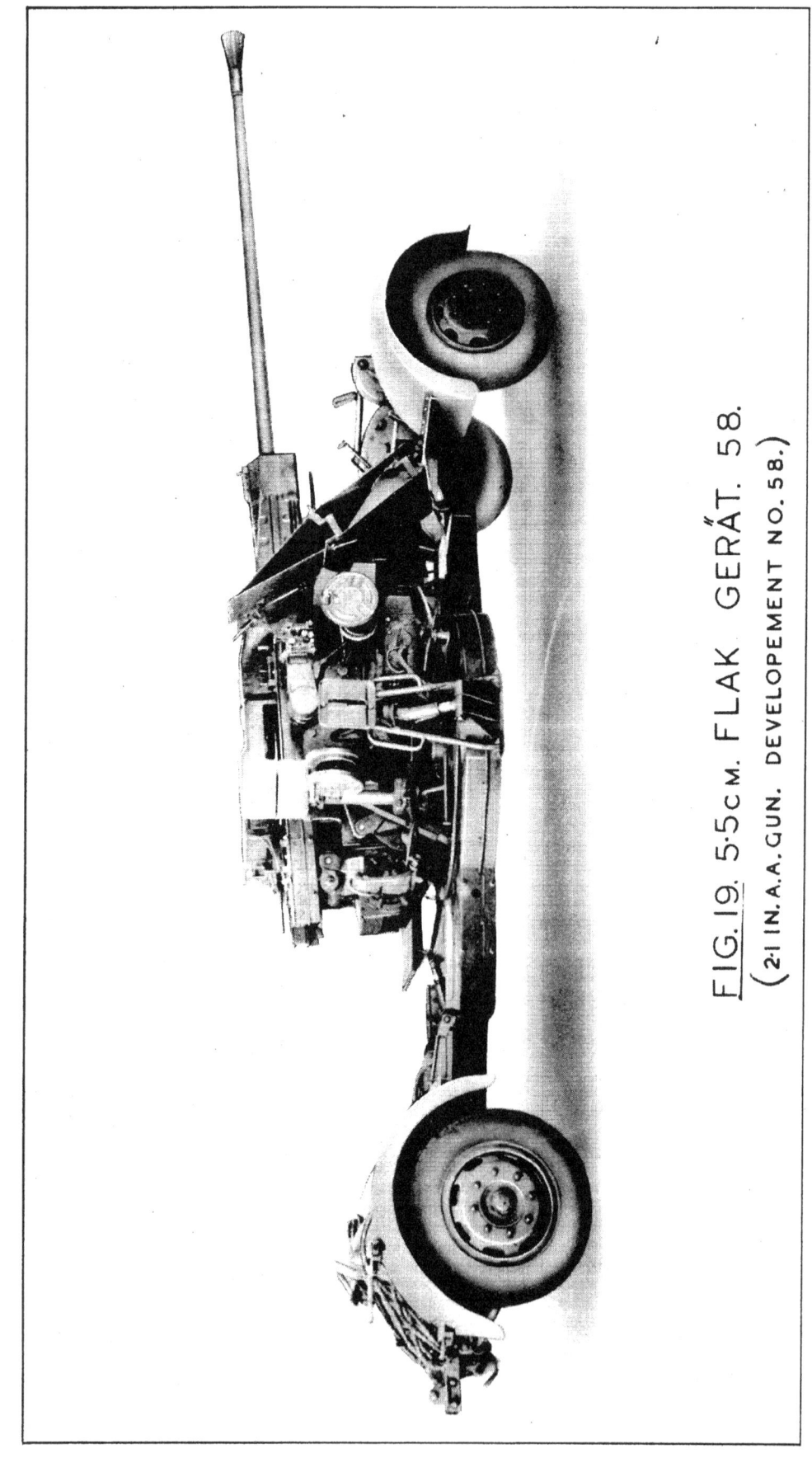

FIG. 19. 5·5 cm. FLAK GERÄT. 58.
(2·1 IN. A.A. GUN. DEVELOPEMENT NO. 58.)

FIG. 20. 5.5 cm. FLAK GERÄT. 58.
(2.1 in. AA GUN. DEVELOPEMENT Nº 58.)

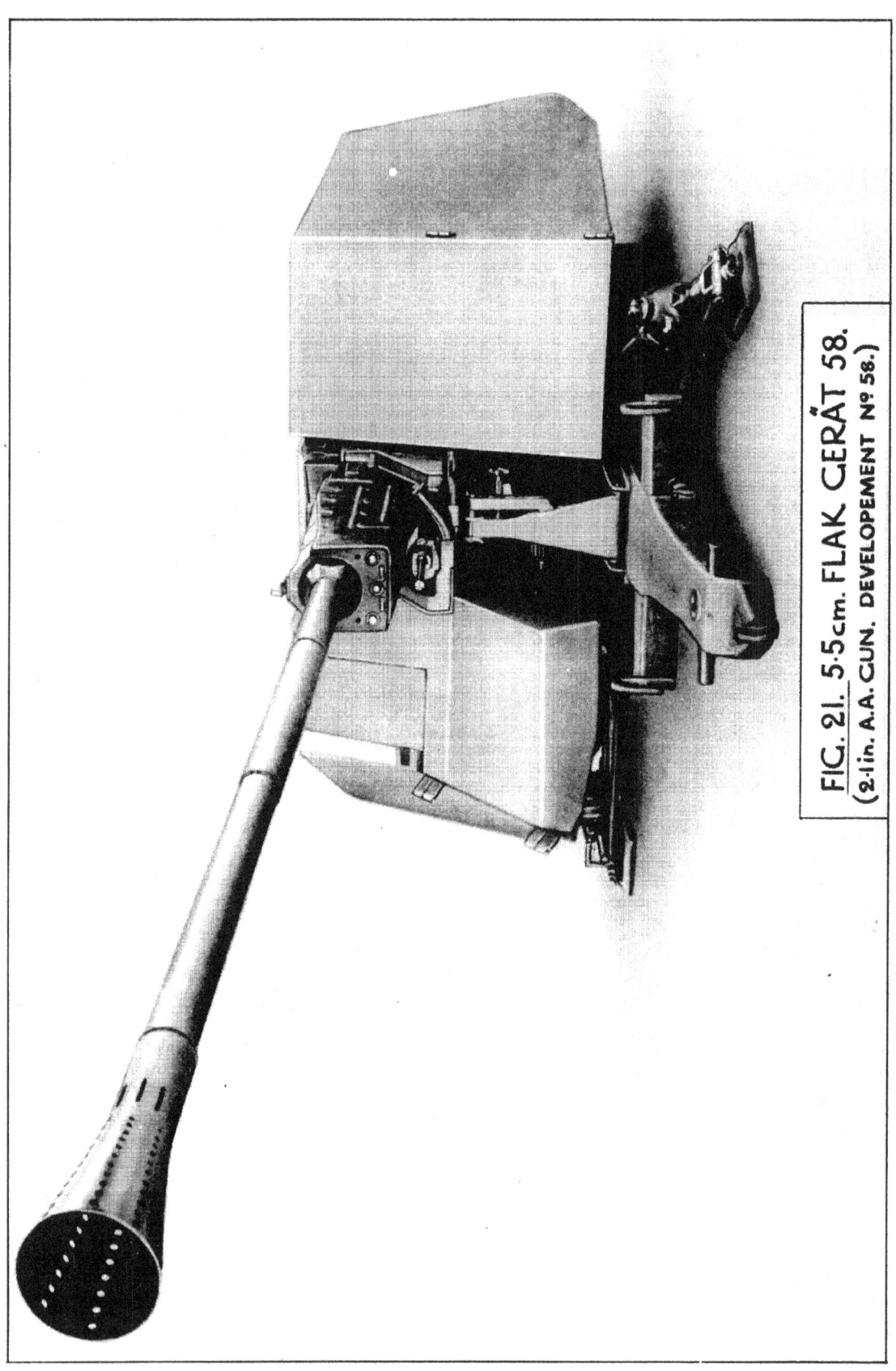

FIG. 21. 5·5cm. FLAK GERÄT 58.
(2·1in. A.A. GUN. DEVELOPEMENT Nº 58.)

CHAPTER IV

THE DEVELOPMENT OF GERMAN HEAVY ANTI-AIRCRAFT ARTILLERY

A. **General**

1. The development by the Germans of heavy A.A. guns is of particular interest since, under the influence of unremitting air attacks from 1942 onwards, a large proportion of their ordnance research facilities was devoted to the development of A.A. equipment.

The two German firms concerned with the design of heavy A.A. guns and ammunition were Krupp and Rheinmetall-Borsig. After the rise to power of the Nazi Party, Rheinmetall-Borsig became part of the Reichswerk Hermann Goering. As a result, in competitive tenders and trials, Rheinmetall always received the benefit of any doubt. Of the two firms, Krupp were more conservative and produced designs which were very simple, robust and well-suited to stand up to service conditions. These features ensured a ready market for Krupp guns all over the world, but involved very slow and meticulous development compared with Rheinmetall. The latter appeared to be able to devote many more designers to each project and in their designs they seemed to be willing to sacrifice simplicity to give the maximum performance and the shortest design time. As a result of these features, their guns were usually accepted for production, but proved extremely difficult to produce and to maintain in service.

It was the usual practice for the Ministry of Supply (HWA), after consultation with the War Office, to work out the specification for the new gun in very general terms. It was then the almost invariable rule, with A.A. guns, to issue the same specification to both Krupp and Rheinmetall.

If there were two distinct lines of approach to the design, either both firms would be told to produce a gun based on each or, if time was short, one firm would be directed along one line and the other along the alternative. During the development sometimes, many projects were discussed between the H.W.A. and each firm, as a result of which models were constructed.

Each firm would then produce its final model and prove it; after which, the models would be subjected to comparative trials by the H.W.A.. Depending on these trials, the prototype model would be selected or the project dropped.

The parent firm of the selected prototype model would then be instructed to produce a Trial Series of guns (about 20), which were employed in full scale field trials. As the result of the experiences in the field trials, and the production of the Trial Series, the final production design was decided upon. Contracts were then issued for the full scale production.

2. In order to place the development, which was carried out after 1918, in its proper sequence, the following table of German heavy A.A. guns in use at the end of the 1914-1918 war is of value.

The Versailles Treaty and the activities of the Disarmament Commission had a very adverse effect on all gun design in Germany, since the design and production of guns below 17 cm., by Krupp, and above 17 cm., by Rheinmetall-Borsig, was forbidden. In addition only a very small number of these guns, which were allowed, could be made in each year.

Various subterfuges were instigated by individual firms to defeat the regulations; for example, Krupp came to an arrangement whereby Bofors of Sweden acquired the foreign rights of Krupp guns, whilst Krupp sent three designers to Bofors.

	Length of barrel (Calibres)	Wt. of shell (Kg.)	M.V. (M/s)	Max. Range (metres)	Max. Height (metres)	Wt. in Action (Kg.)	Wt. in Draft (Kg.)
7.7 cm. light Flak M. 1911	27	6.85	465	7800	4250	950	7000
7.7 cm. Pedestal Flak on wheels	35	6.85	510	8500	4750	2500	6800
8 cm. Flak mtd on trailer	45	8.0	715	10100	6450	2610	6800
8.8 cm. Flak mtd on trailer	45	9.6	785	10800	6850	3000	7300
10.5 cm. Flak " " "	45	17.4	720	13900	7350	4000	9000
10.5 cm. Static Flak	45	17.4	720	13900	7350	5520	-

By 1925, a new policy had been adopted, on which it was intended to develop a new range of guns of 7.5 cm. calibre and upwards. As a result, Krupp (Koch and Kienzle) and Rheinmetall were ordered to produce designs for a 7.5 cm. heavy A.A. gun. Trials were carried out with both prototype guns up to 1930, but neither gave complete satisfaction and no 7.5 cm. A.A. gun was introduced for general service. A.A. guns of this calibre, built by Krupp and Rheinmetall for overseas sale, and which were in production at the beginning of the war or captured during the war, were taken over by the Navy and used for coastal A.A. work.

3. In 1931, the Krupp A.A. gun designer, who had been attached for work with Bofors, returned to Essen bringing the designs of an 8.8 cm. A.A. gun with him. A prototype was built by the beginning of 1932, and, because of the intensive research carried out with Bofors, the gun was an immediate success. It was put into production straight away and introduced in 1933 as the 8.8 cm. Flak 18. Thus started the new range of modern German heavy A.A. Artillery, which, as a matter of interest, came under the control of the German Air Ministry.

B **8.8 cm. Flak 18, 36 and 37.** (3.46 in A.A. gun models 18, 36 and 37).
See Figs: 22, 23 and 24

1. The 8.8 cm. gun, in its various models, has been the main German H.A.A. gun throughout the war. The Flak 18, 36 and 37 have the same ballistic performance and differ only slightly from each other.

The Flak 18 is of loose barrel construction and differs from the later models, which are of the multi-section type.

As the result of large scale experience in exercises and in the mass production of the equipment, several improvements were decided upon in 1936 and put into production in 1937. These improvements included a new cruciform platform and new limbers, both designed by the firm of Linders. The changes were intended to improve mobility and stability in action and to simplify mass production of the equipment. Concurrently with this development, a new three section barrel was introduced and the whole equipment was then called the 8.8 cm. Flak 36; nevertheless Flak 18 barrels were often used on Flak 36 carriages and vice-versa.

When the Übertragung 37 transmission system was introduced in 1939, the Flak 36 was modified to take it; the new design being called the 8.8 cm. Flak 37. This new transmission 37 is a regular selsyn system, recognised externally by its "follow the pointer" dials. With the earlier transmission system 30, which links the Flak 18 and 36 to their fire control instruments, the receiver dials have three concentric circles of bulbs, and three mechanical pointers pivotted centrally. The appropriate bulbs light up in accordance with the data transmitted from the predictor (fire control instrument) and coincidence is obtained by covering the lights with the appropriate pointer.

The 8.8 cm. Flak equipments were modified at different times during the war and fitted with shields and telescopic sights, so that the equipments could be used in the anti-tank role. Some were modified to such an extent that they could no longer be used in their original A.A. role.

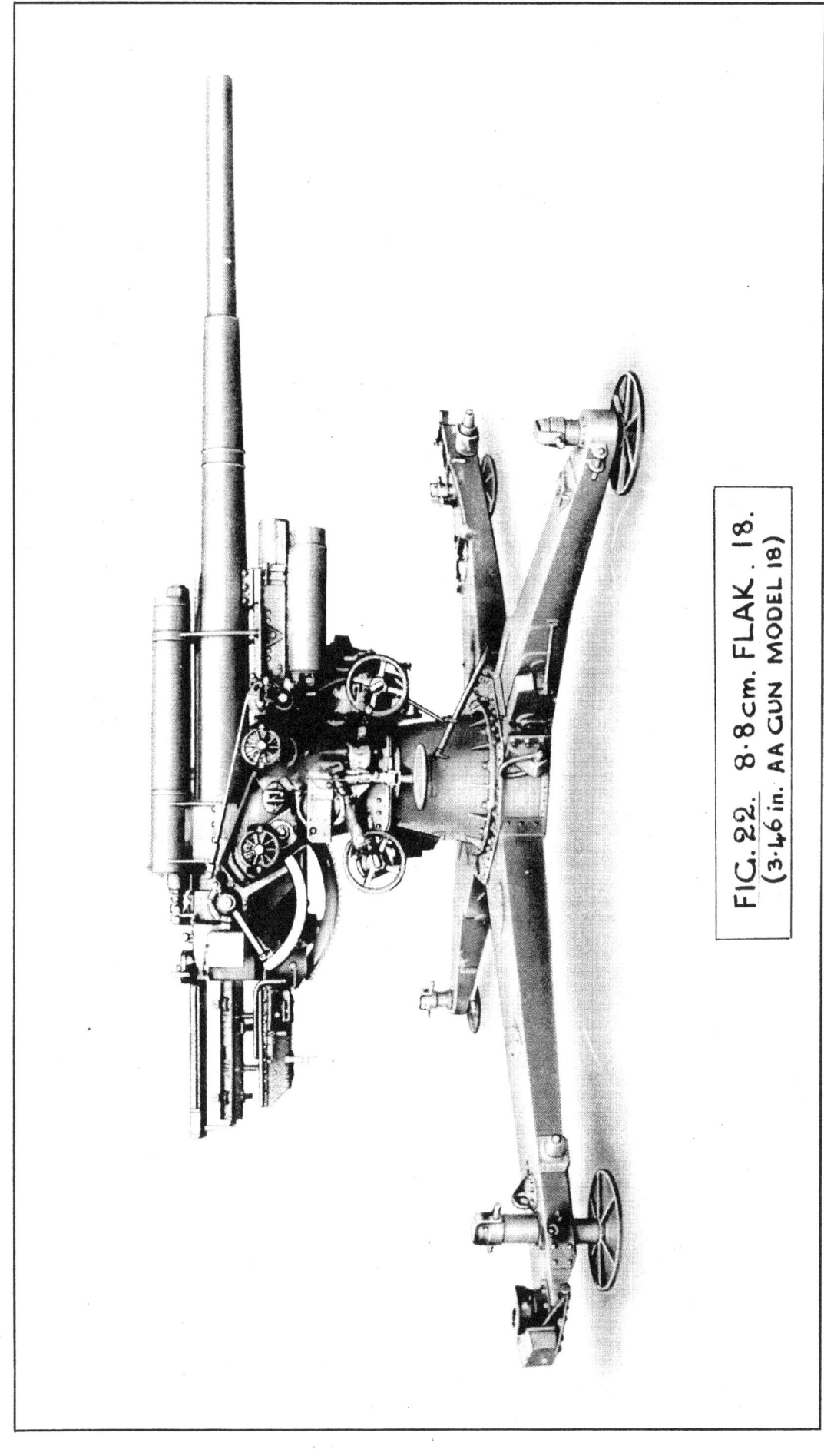

FIG. 22. 8·8 cm. FLAK. 18.
(3·46 in. AA GUN MODEL 18)

FIG. 23. 8·8 cm. FLAK. 36.
(3·46 in. AA GUN MODEL 36.)

FIG. 24. 8·8cm. FLAK.36.
(3·46 in. AA GUN MODEL 36.)

2. __Data: 8.8 cm. Flak 18, 36 and 37.__

    (a) Calibre   3.465 in.   (88 mm)
        Length of ordnance   194 in.   (4930 mm)
        Rifling R.H. increasing.
           " length   162 7/16 in.   (4124 mm)
        No. of grooves   32
        Traverse   2 x 360°
        Elevation   -3° to 85°
        Recoil at 0°   41.34 in.   (1050 mm)
          " at 25°   33.46 in   (850 mm)
          " at 85°   27.75 in.   (700 mm)
          " Max   42.5 in.   (1080 mm)

Transmission System	Flak 18 and 36	Flak 37
	Übertragungsgerät 30 (lamp receiver data type)	Übertragungsgerät 37 (Selsyn Data type)

        Firing System   Percussion
        Rate of fire   15 - 20 rpm
        Ceiling-Max.   34,770 ft.   (10,600 m)
          " -Effective   26,250 ft.   (8,000 m)
        Carriage:- Static, mobile and railway versions.
               Mobile - Cruciform platform, transported on two
                  2-wheeled trailers.
        Overall length   25 ft   (7620 mm)
          " height   7 ft 11 in.   (2418 mm)
          " width   7 ft 7 in.   (2305 mm)
        Wt. of equipment complete   15,129 lbs.   (6861 Kg)

Fuze Setter	Flak 18 and 36	Flak 37
	Zünderstellmaschine 18 (lamp receiver data type)	Zünderstellmaschine 19 or 37 (Selsyn data types)

    (b) __Ammunition__

Type of projectile	M.V.	Weight of projectile
H.E. Time	2690 f/s (820 m.s.)	20 lb 1 oz.
H.E. percussion	2690 f/s (820 m.s.)	20 lb 5½ ozs.
A.P.C.B.C.	2600 f/s (795 m.s.)	21 lb ½ oz.

C   __8.8 cm. Flak 37/41.__ (3.46 in A.A. gun model 37/41).

1. In the spring of 1942, it became clear to the German Air Ministry that, although the new 8.8 cm. Flak 41 (dealt with in the next section) was in full production and would eventually replace the Flak 18, 36 and 37, the latter guns, aided by the 10.5 Flak, would have to bear the brunt of the attacks for the next two years. It was therefore decided to try and improve the performance of the 18-37 series. Originally, it was proposed to place the Flak 41 gun on the earlier types of carriages, but the Flak 41 barrels were not numerous enough and the carriages would not stand up to the increased stresses of the Flak 41 barrel performance. After a number of experimental modifications, it was shown that a muzzle brake would have to be used. The most suitable one was found to be that produced by using an additional length of barrel with holes bored in each side and two flange plates screwed on to the outside. This brake gave an efficiency of 45 %. The good results obtained showed that it would be possible to increase the length of the barrel to 74 calibres and achieve the same performance as the Flak 41. The only additional modification necessary, in this case, was the use of new and more powerful springs in the equilibrators. For efficient use in action, it was considered necessary to provide the gun with a new fuze setter and rammer, eventually adopting the same types as were used with the Flak 41.

    The modification to the barrel involved boring out the chamber which, though possible with the loose barrels of the Flak 18, was not possible with the Flak 36 sectional barrel. The solution adopted, in this case, was the production of a new loose barrel to fit the Flak 36 jacket.

    The equipments resulting from this series of modifications were known as the 8.8 cm. Flak. 37/41, but as there was considerable trouble with the extraction of cartridge cases (a fault which was never really absent from the 8.8 cm. Flak 41), it is believed that the design was never cleared for full scale production.

2. Data: 8.8 cm. Flak 37/41

	Metric	British
(a) Calibre	88 mm	3.465 ins.
Length of Ordnance (Including Breech Ring) (Add 5 ins. for loading mechanism)	7027 mm	23 ft. 5/8"
Length of Ordnance in calibres	80	
Length of chamber	881 mm	2' 10"
Length of Rifling	5850 mm	19' 2½"
Length of unsupported barrel	3619 mm	11' 10½"
Length of Breech Ring	540 mm	1' 9¼"
Rifling: P.P.S. R.H. increasing		
Grooves - number	32	
" - width	5.2 mm	.2047 ins.
" - depth	1.05 mm	.0413 ins.
Traverse	360°	
Elevation	- 3° + 85°	
Transmission System	Übertragungsgerät 37. (Selsyn data type)	
Firing System	Electrical or mechanical Firing Mechanism.	
Strengthened equilibrators (Springs)		
Horizontal type Fuze Setter 37/41		
Rate of Fire	16 - 20 r.p.m.	
Maximum Ceiling	15000 m.	49,200 ft.
Carriage:	As for 8.8 cm. Flak 37	
Roller Loading Gear		
Weight of complete equipment	7111 kg	7 tons

(b) Ammunition

Type of projectile	M.V.	Weight of projectile
H.E.	1000 m/s. (3280 f.s.)	20 lbs. 11 ozs.
A.P.C.B.C.	980 m/s. (3214 f.s.)	22 lbs. 8 ozs.

D. 8.8 cm Flak 41. (3.46 inch A.A. Gun Model 41). See Figs. 25, 26, 27 and 28.

1. During 1938/39, the Germans decided that an 88 mm gun with a much higher performance than the Flak 36 (37) was required in view of the increased performance of aircraft. It would require a much higher muzzle velocity than that previously used. This was considered possible owing to the development of Gudol propellant and sintered iron driving bands. It was considered that this new weapon, in addition to being extremely mobile, would have to be capable of really effective anti-tank fire, in the light of experience in Spain. Because of the weight factor, it was not intended to employ any power-operated mechanism, and, as a result, the weight of the round and the effort required for the traverse and elevating gears were very critical. In the autumn of 1939, a contract was issued to Rheinmetall for the development of a new 8.8 cm. A.A. gun (Gerät 37). Brief details of the specification, which included the requirements listed above, were as follows:-

Muzzle Velocity at least	1000 m/s	(3280 ft/sec)
Shell Weight	9.4 kg.	(20.7 lbs.)
Weight in Action (Maximum)	8000 kg.	(about 8 tons)
Rate of Fire (approx.)	25 rounds per minute	

Owing to trouble caused by the confusion of 8.8 cm. Flak 37 with Gerät 37, the name of the latter was changed to 8.8 cm. Flak 41 in the summer of 1941.

For some unknown reason, Krupp was not asked to design a gun to the new specification until the early spring of 1941.

The first Rheinmetall prototype equipment was ready for trials in the summer of 1941. By the winter of that year it was clear that, though all the teething troubles had not yet been eliminated, no suitable alternative equipment would be available for some years. The Rheinmetall Flak 41 was therefore adopted for production in the spring of 1942 and the guns began to reach the troops in the spring of 1943. The future of the Krupp gun was considered concurrently with the decision to put the Rheinmetall gun into production. Since the Rheinmetall design had not given complete satisfaction, mainly due to constant trouble with jammed cartridge cases necessitating the use of brass cases only, it was decided to continue with the development of the Krupp design. An alteration in the performance from 9.4 kg. and 1000 m/s to a shell weight of 10 kg. and 1020 m/s, which had been tentatively considered since the summer of 1941, was adopted at the same time and the name changed to Gerät 42.

2. The development of Gerät 42, especially of the barrel and ammunition, became more and more interrelated with that of the new 8.8 cm. tank and anti-tank guns, the KWK.42 and the Pak.42. The latter finally emerged as the 8.8 cm KWK (Tank Gun) 43 and the 8.8 cm. Pak (Anti-Tank Gun)43. The project for the A.A. gun was reviewed in the winter of 1942 and it was decided to continue development for three reasons; the greater muzzle energy compared with the Flak 41, the absence of trouble with the ejection of steel cartridge cases, which was still giving trouble with the Flak 41, and the possibility that, if the Flak 42 could be introduced into service, all the 8.8 cm. A.A., Tank and Anti-Tank guns would fire the same ammunition. At this date it was anticipated that, if no other alterations were called for, the prototype gun would be ready by the spring of 1943. Already however, G L Flak has suggested that an increase in muzzle velocity would be desirable, and the following tentative suggestion was considered:-

Shell weight 9.4 kg (20.7 lbs).   Length of round 1220 mm (48 ins)
Weight of round 23 kg (51.6 lbs)   Length of barrel 80 cals. (23'1")
Muzzle Velocity 1100 m/s (3610 f.s.) Weight of barrel 1920 kg. (38 cwts)

In February 1943, owing to the greater importance of other design work and the shortage of design staffs, the whole project of Gerät 42 was dropped. So the Rheinmetall production model 8.8 cm. Flak 41 went ahead unchallenged in the 8.8 cm Flak series for the rest of the war.

3. Compared with the previous models 18, 36 and 37, the Flak 41 was a much superior model. It had a turntable in place of a pedestal, giving it a much lower silhouette; the muzzle velocity had been increased by about 600 f.s. A "power-operated" roller loading mechanism was fitted. The "power" was obtained by fitting an auxiliary hydro-pneumatic "recuperator" gear; the piston was drawn to the rear during recoil and held withdrawn until released by a catch, when the round was placed in the breech opening. On release, the rod was taken forward by the increased air pressure reasserting itself in the "recuperator", and teeth on the rod rotated the gear to operate the rubber rollers. The spinning rollers gripped the round and impelled it into the chamber.

4. Data: 8.8 cm. Flak 41.

  (a) Calibre   3.465 ins.   (88 mm)
       Length of ordnance   257¾ ins.   (6548 mm)
       Rifling R.H. increasing
       " length   213 ins.   (5411 mm)
       No. of grooves   32
       Traverse   360°
       Elevation   -3° to +90°
       Recoil at 0°   47 ins.   (1200 mm)
       " at 90°   35¼ ins.   (900 mm)
       Transmission System   Übertragungagerät 37. (Selsyn data type)
       Firing System   Electrical
       Fuze Setter   Zünderstellmaschine 41. (Selsyn data type)
       Rate of fire   15 r.p.m.
       Ceiling max.   49200 ft.   (15000 m)
       Carriage: Mobile - Cruciform platform transported on two
                           2-wheeled trailers.
       Overall length   31 ft. 8 ins.   (9658 mm)

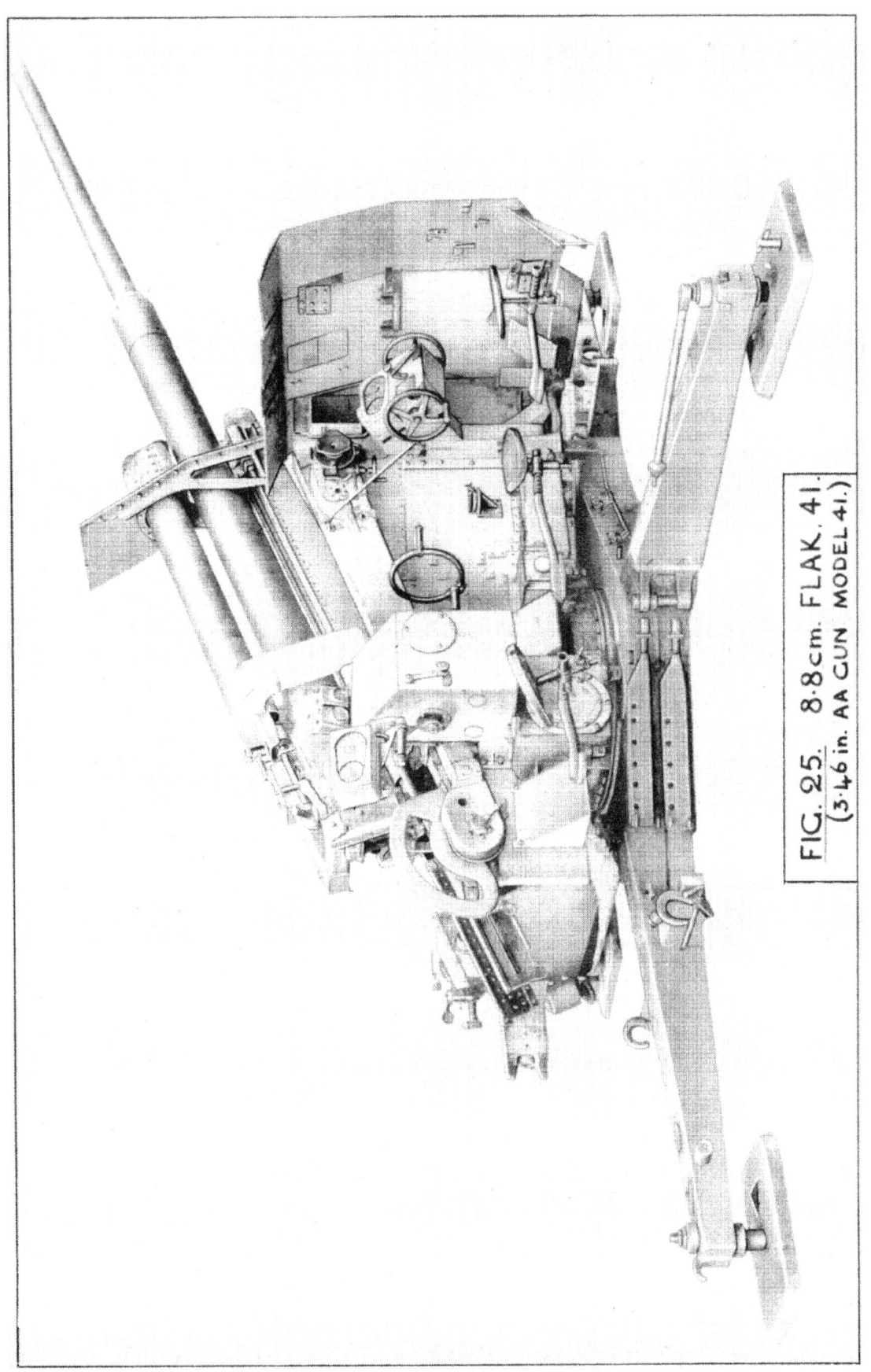

FIG. 25. 8·8cm. FLAK. 41.
(3·46 in. AA GUN MODEL 41.)

FIG. 26. 8·8 cm. FLAK. 41.
(3·46 in. AA GUN MODEL 41.)

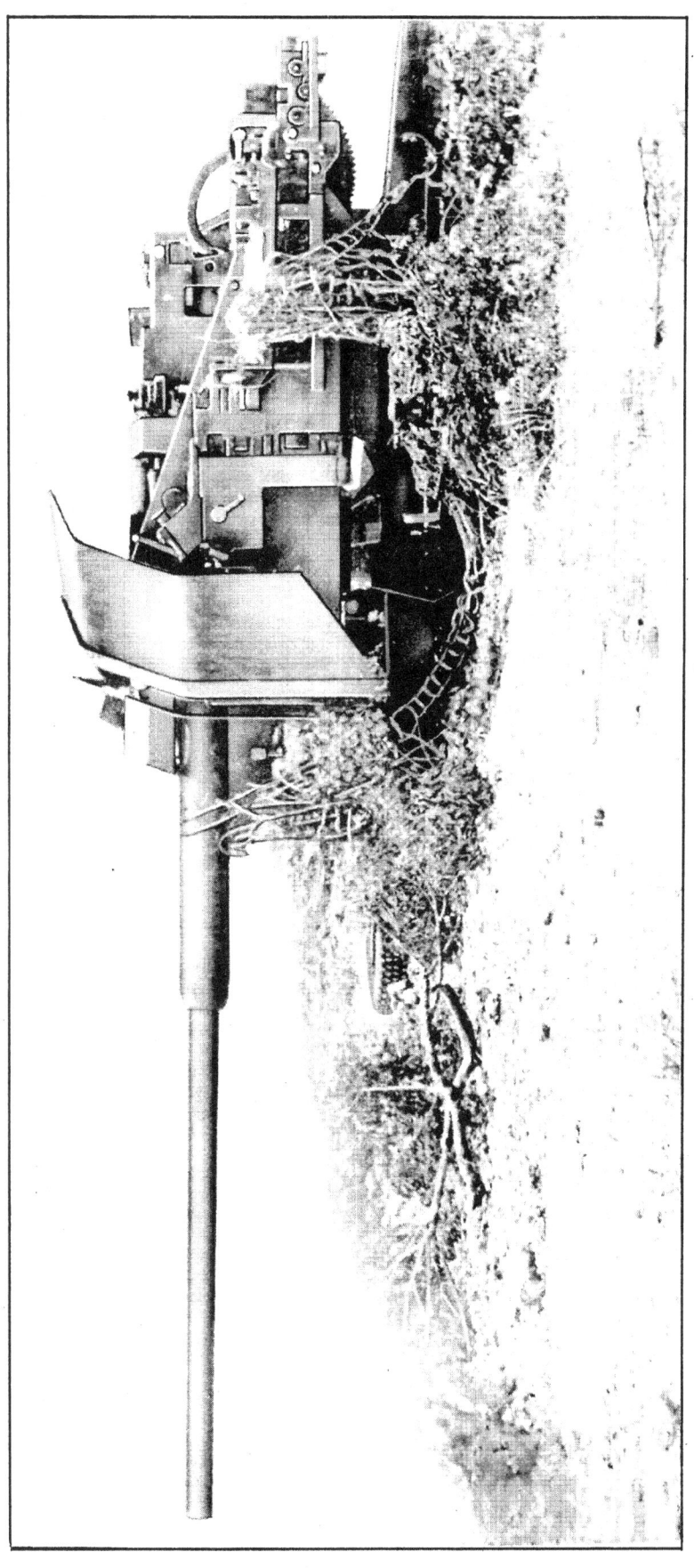

FIG. 27. 8·8cm. FLAK. 41.
(3·46 in. AA GUN MODEL 41.)

FIG. 28. 8·8cm. FLAK. 41.
(3·46 in. AA GUN MODEL 41.)

Overall height	7 ft. 9 ins.	(2360 mm)
" width	7 ft. 10½ ins.	(2400 mm)
Wt. of equipment complete	24784 lbs.	(11240 kg)

(b) *Ammunition*

Type of projectile	M.V.	Weight of projectile
H.E. Time	3280 f/s (1000 m.s.)	20 lbs. 11 ozs.
H.E. Percussion	3280 f/s (1000 m.s.)	20 lbs. 11 ozs.
A.P.C.B.C.	3214 f/s (980 m.s.)	22 lbs. 8 ozs.

(c) <u>Barrel Construction</u> (Extraction from German Document)

(i) In five parts:-	(ii) In four parts:-	(iii) In three parts:-
Jacket	Jacket	Jacket
Sleeve	Sleeve	Forward section inner tube
Forward section inner tube	Forward section inner tube	Rear section inner tube
Central section inner tube	Rear section inner tube	Barrel Nos. 0286 onwards.
Chamber section inner tube	Barrel Nos. 0153 to 0285	
Barrel Nos. 0001 to 0152		

Type (iii) has been adapted as standard on account of production difficulties.

Guns fitted with type (i) barrel will only fire ammunition with brass cartridge cases. Yellow band on forward section of tube and M in yellow on left side of breech ring.

E. <u>10.5 cm. Flak 38.</u> (<u>4.13 inch A.A. Gun Model 38</u>). See Figs. 29

1. To consider the development of this weapon, we must go back to 1933. Although the 8.8 cm. Flak 18 could deal perfectly satisfactorily with targets up to heights of 6,000 m. (19,000 feet), it was apparent that the tactical ceiling for long-range bombers would soon be well above this height. While the development of the gun had been rapid, the development of aircraft had been even more rapid, and the heavy A.A. gun problem had by no means been solved. At that date, the Germans did not consider an A.A. gun with a muzzle velocity above 800 to 900 m/s to be a practical proposition, owing to rapid barrel wear and to the difficulties experienced with copper driving bands at very high velocities. A further factor affecting the decision on a new gun was that it did not need to be tactically mobile, since it was intended to use the 8.8 cm Flak 18 as a mobile equipment and the new and heavier weapon in a static role, i.e. the two guns in supplementary roles. The third and final factor in the situation was that, in the opinion of the German authorities at that date, the most fruitful method of increasing the effectiveness of the A.A. gun lay in the use of larger calibres and heavier shell. All these three factors combined to form a policy of heavier and heavier A.A. guns; a policy followed by the HWA (Ministry of Supply) until 1942.

As a result of these considerations, specifications for the design of a new 10.5 cm. A.A. gun (Gerät 38) were issued to Rheinmetall and Krupp at the end of 1933. The gun was to be equipped with power laying, loading and ramming; it was to have a high rate of fire. Stability in action and high road speed were emphasised at the expense of tactical mobility and possible speed into action. Krupp and Rheinmetall were each ordered to produce two prototypes; the intention being to produce a further four of each type to form an experimental battery for field trials. In each case, one of the two prototype guns and two of the later four guns were to be equipped with power control, consisting of an electric motor connected to a Pittler variable speed hydraulic drive, the speed and direction being controlled by a handwheel. Emergency hand-laying was also provided. The other three guns, in each case, were to be provided with a fully electric remote control, designed by S.A.M., which gave the following alternatives:- remote control from the predictor, hand power control or hand laying.

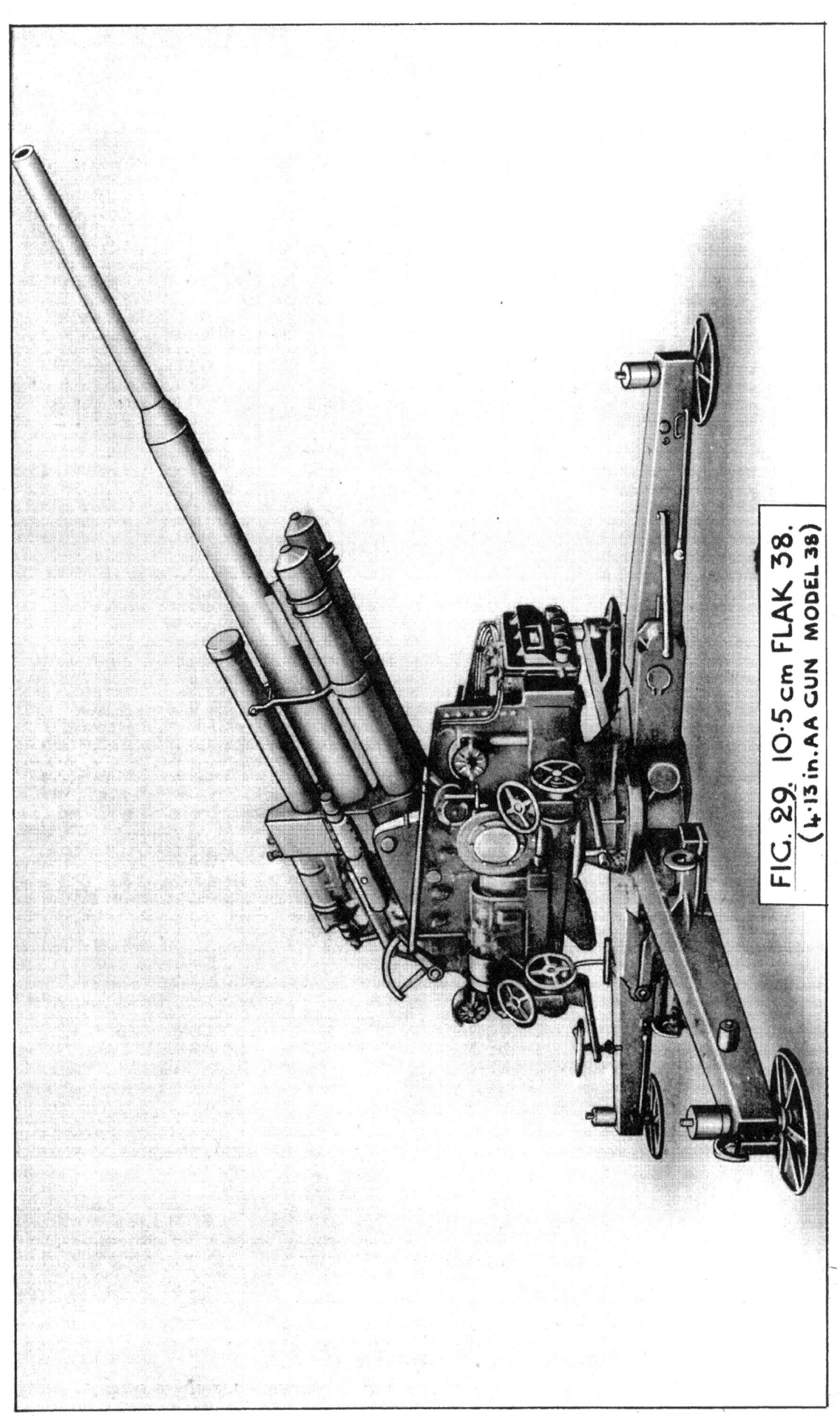

FIG. 29. 10·5 cm FLAK 38.
(4·13 in. AA GUN MODEL 38)

All four prototype equipments were finished by the summer of 1935 and comparative trials and various improvements were carried out up to the end of the year. In addition to the normal cruciform carriage, both the Krupp and the Rheinmetall guns fired experimentally from two types of railway mountings.

The two experimental batteries were finished in 1936 and field trials were carried out until the autumn, by which time sufficient experience had been gained with both designs of gun and both types of power control. In October 1936, it was decided to adopt the Rheinmetall gun, with hydraulic power control, for full scale production as the 10.5 cm. Flak 38.

2. <u>10.5 cm. Flak 39. (4.13 inch A.A. Gun Model 39)</u>. See Figs. 30, 31 and 32

In 1939, various improvements were made in the design, the new model being given the name of 10.5 cm. Flak 39. These improvements included the change over of the electric equipment from DC to AC (in order to be able to use the local supply in static emplacements), the employment of the new five piece multi-sectional barrel and the modification of the gun to use the UTG 37 transmission system (i.e. the "follow the pointer" system on the receiver dials, instead of the older system with the lighting bulbs to indicate firing data).

During the time in which the 10.5 cm. Flak 38 was being developed by both firms, the HWA was considering some new projects, in order that the superiority in performance, which was regained by the 10.5 cm. Flak 38, could be retained.

An unusual feature in the construction of the traversing rack of this equipment was the substitution for steel (normally used) by a material, which appears to be made up of laminations of fibre bonded together with some form of resinous material and compressed at very high pressure. It is extremely light in weight. The material is quite hard and appears to stand up well to the stresses applied during traverse.

The "ramming" mechanism consists principally of four rotating rubber rollers, which grip the round and impel it into the chamber. The principle is the same as that employed with the 8.8 cm. Flak 41, but the power is electric, or, in the event of this failing, obtained by spinning a top. This is effected by pulling by hand on a wire hawser coiled around a rotatable barrel, or spinning top.

3. Data: <u>10.5 cm. Flak 38 and 39</u>

(a) Calibre 4.13 in (105 mm)
Length of Ordnance 261.5 in (6,648 mm)
Rifling R.H. increasing
" length 217.7 in (5,531 mm)
No. of grooves 36
Traverse 360°
Elevation -3° to +85°
Recoil at 0° 35.4 in (900 mm)
" " 85° 32.7 in (830 mm)
" " Max. 35.8 in (910 mm)
Transmission System:-
Flak 38-Übertragungsgerät 30. (lamp receiver data type)
Flak 39-Übertragungsgerät 37. (Selsyn data type)
Firing System Electrical
Fuze Setter Zünderstellmaschine 38 (Selsyn data type)
Rate of fire 10 - 15 r.p.m.
Ceiling (Max.) 42,000 ft (12,800 m)
Carriage - Static, mobile, and rail versions.
    Mobile - Cruciform mounting transported on two
        2-wheeled trailers.
Overall length 33 ft 10 in. (10,310 mm)
" height 9 ft 8 in. (2,900 mm)
" width 8 ft 4½ in. (2,450 mm)
Wt. of equipment complete 32,193 lbs. (14,600 kg)

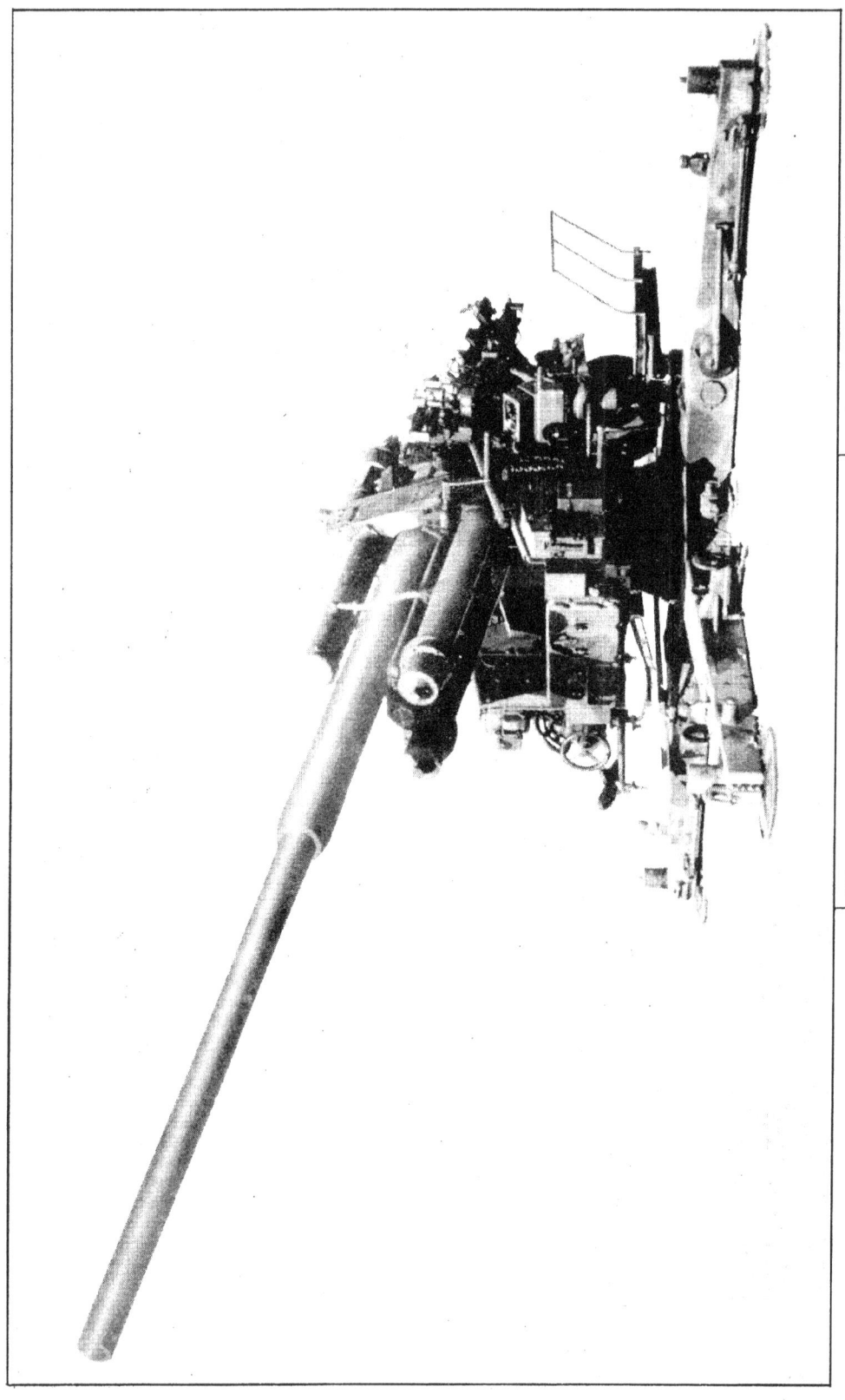

FIG. 30. 10·5 cm. FLAK 39.
(4·13 in. AA GUN MODEL 39.)

FIG. 31. 10.5 cm. FLAK 39.
(4.13 in. AA GUN MODEL 39)

FIG. 32. 10.5cm. FLAK 39.
(4.13 in. AA GUN MODEL 39.)

(b) **Ammunition**

Type of Projectile	M.V.	Weight of Projectile
H.E. Time	2886 f/s (880 m.s.)	33 lb 5 oz.
H.E. Grooved	2886 f/s (880 m.s.)	33 lb 5 oz.
A.P.C.B.C.	2823 f/s (860 m.s.)	34 lb 5 oz.

F. <u>12.8 cm. Flak 40.</u> (5.04 inch A.A. Gun Model 40). See Fig. 33, 34 and 35

1. The continued increase in the performance of aircraft hastened a decision on two new projects under consideration and, in line with the general policy of medium velocity and increasingly heavy calibre, two new specifications were issued, early in 1936, for 12.8 cm. and 15 cm. mobile A.A. guns.

The specifications for these were briefly:-

	12.8 cm.	15 cm.
M.V. (approx.)	900-950 m/s (2950-3120 f.s.)	850-900 m/s (2800-2950 f.s.)
Weight of Shell (approx.)	25 to 30 kg (55 to 66 lbs)	35 to 40 kg (77 to 88 lbs)
Laying	Power assisted	
Loading	Power loading and ramming	
Method of transport	2 loads	3 or 4 loads

In the early summer of 1936, a contract was issued to Rheinmetall for the design of a 12.8 cm. A.A. gun to these new specifications; the new gun being given the code name "Gerät 40" or "equipment 40." (This was the standard method of naming guns, whilst in development, during and shortly before the war). Krupp did not receive a contract for the new 12.8 cm. gun.

Gerät 40 was ready for trials by the autumn of 1937. The Rheinmetall design created a very good impression with Wa Prüf 10 and it was decided to put it into limited production as the 12.8 cm. Flak 40. As originally issued, the equipment was mounted on a cruciform carriage similar to that of the 10.5 cm. Flak 38. It was transported in two loads, the piece on a transporter and the carriage on two single-axled limbers or trailers. Experience with the pilot series of guns showed that the transport of a heavy A.A. gun in two loads was most undesirable. In the autumn of 1938, a large number of firms were therefore ordered to produce designs for a method of transporting in one load. Wa Prüf 10's own idea, which was worked out in detail by the trailer firm of Meiller, was finally adopted for production. In this, the gun was carried on two twin-axled articulated bogies, which clamped on to the front and rear of the gun platform. Since the Flak 40 did not reach full mass production until 1942, few of the old type of carriages were produced. Since the production of mobile guns above 10.5 cm. calibre was cancelled in that year, few of the new mobile mountings were issued.

Concurrently with the design of the gun, Rheinmetall were ordered to design a railway mounting. Trials were carried out with a prototype, when a gun from the pilot series was available and the design was finally adopted. Large numbers were built during the war.

With the introduction of the 12.8 cm. Flak 40, the problem of a home defence heavy A.A. gun was solved satisfactorily, at any rate for the time being. This was not true of the heavy A.A. gun for field use, for the following reasons. The 12.8 cm. Flak 40 was very heavy and therefore not really mobile in a tactical sense. This was true especially of the earlier version carried in two loads. On the other hand, the performance of the 8.8 cm Flak 36 (37) and the 10.5 cm. Flak 38 (39) was not up to that demanded by aircraft performance in 1938, particularly in regard to the time of flight to the target and the effective ceiling. These deficiencies in performance at this period led to the development of the 8.8 cm. Flak 41 for field use.

During this period of development, projects for 15 cm. A.A. guns were being considered and the advent was seen of Flak Towers which were to be used for the 15 cm. weapons. By the end of 1940, the decision had been

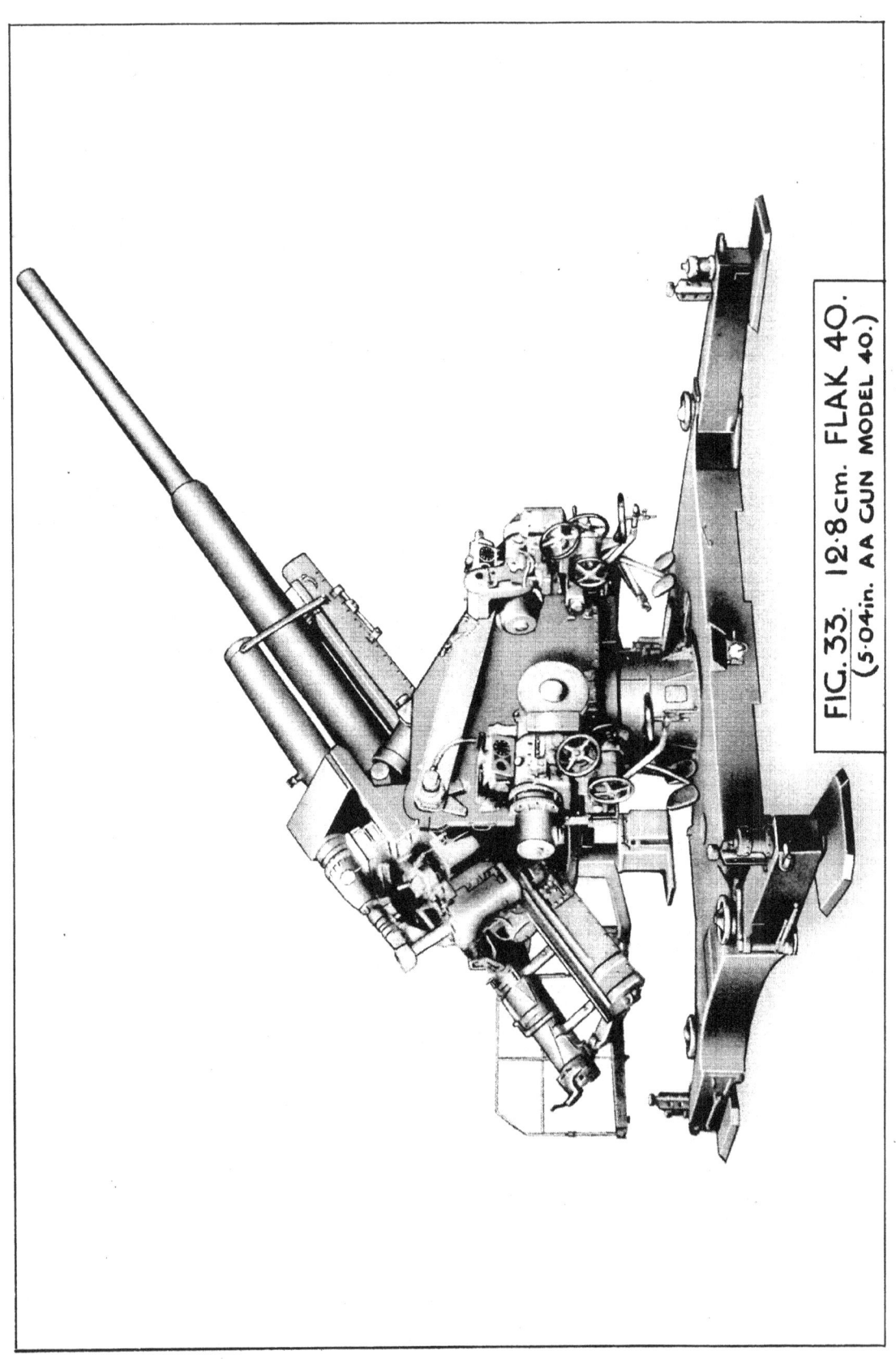

FIG. 33. 12·8 cm. FLAK 40.
(5·04 in. AA GUN MODEL 40.)

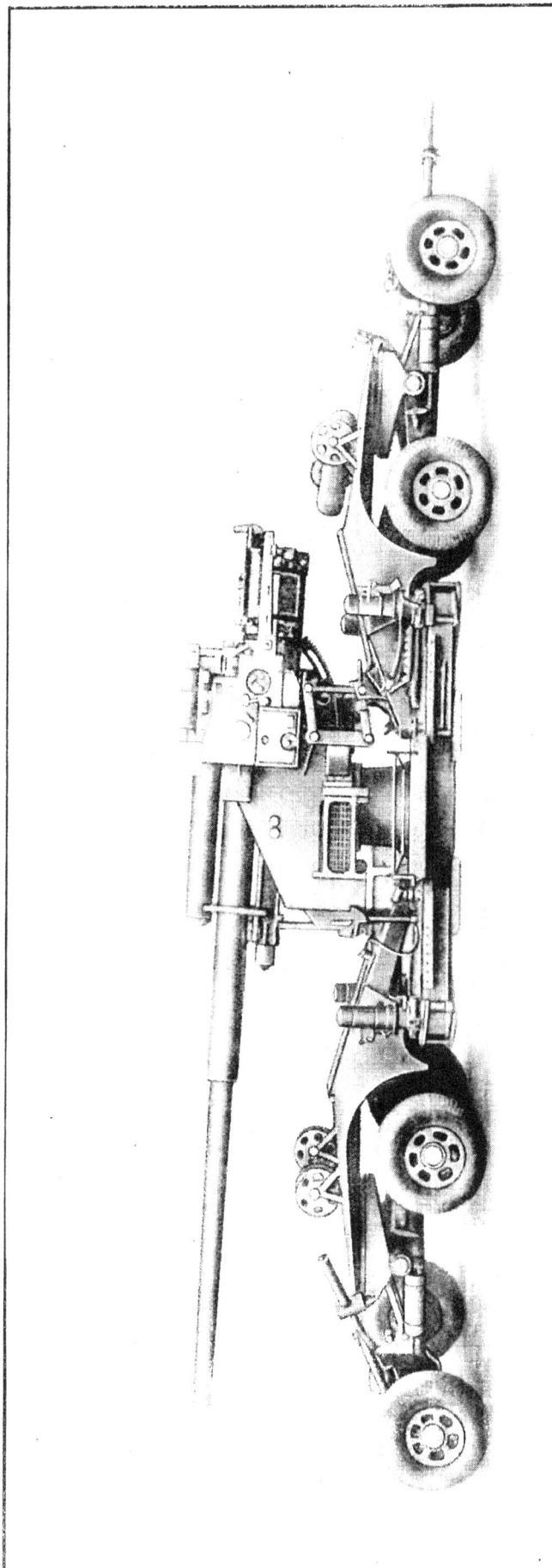

FIG. 34. 12.8cm. FLAK 40.
(5.04 in. AA GUN MODEL 40.)

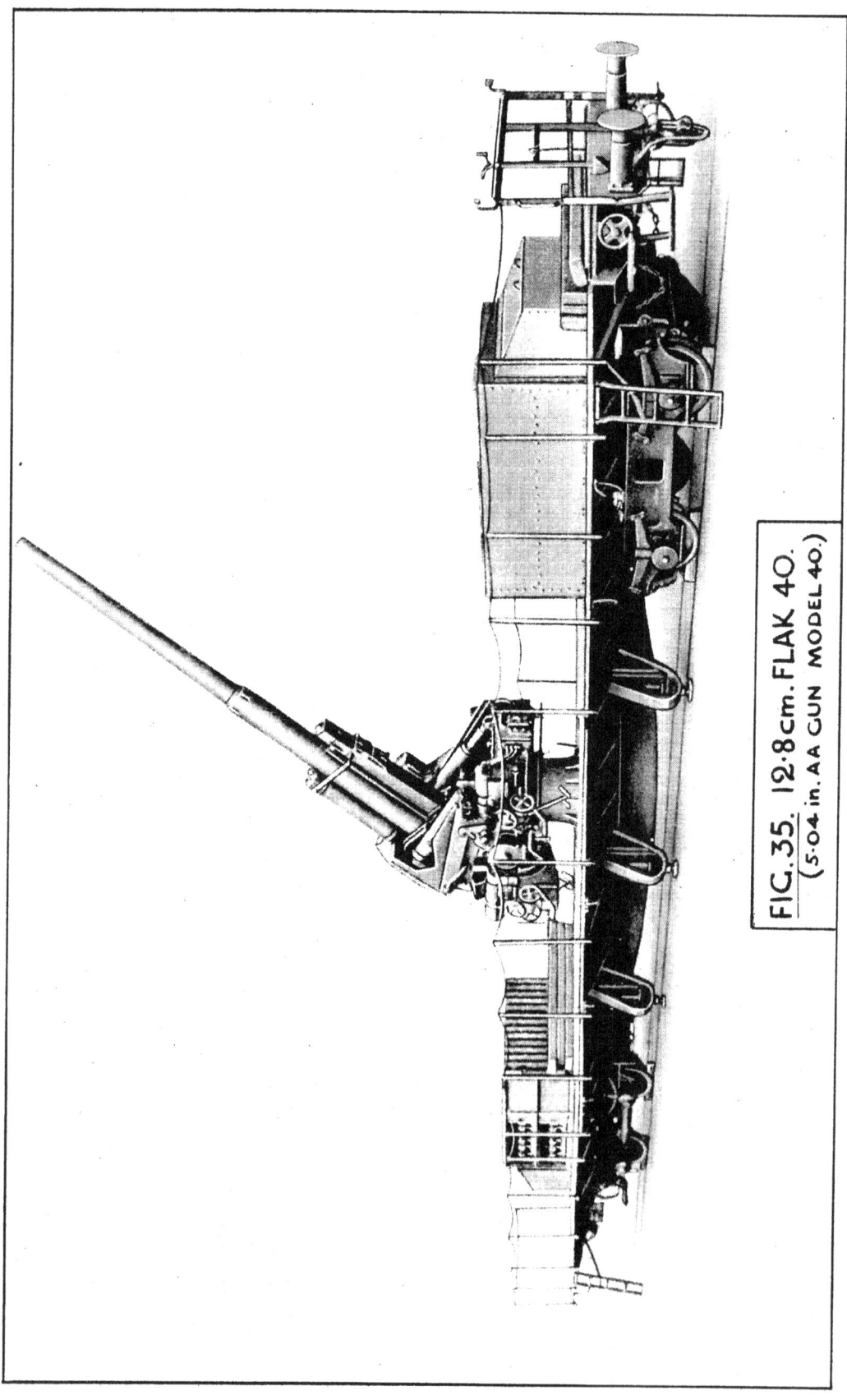

FIG. 35. 12·8 cm. FLAK 40.
(5·04 in. AA GUN MODEL 40.)

taken to build some Flak Towers as a means of A.A. defence of major cities, or at any rate for the defence of Berlin. Since the 15 cm A.A. guns would not be ready under any circumstances before the end of 1943, some stop-gap expedient had to be found for the intervening years. The standard 12.8 cm. Flak 40 would not have utilised the full potentialities of the Flak Tower, so it was decided to build a 12.8 cm. twin, using the piece, cradle and loading mechanism of the 12.8 cm. Flak 40. As the latter was of Rheinmetall design, the contract for the new equipment was given to them as "Gerät 44", the name being later changed to 12.8 cm. Flakzwilling 40.

2. <u>12.8 cm. Flakzwilling 40.(5.04 Twin A.A. gun Model 40).</u> See Figs. 36 and 37.

Since the design employed the complete piece, cradle and loading mechanism of the Flak 40 (one equipment normally and the other reversed as in a mirror image), the only parts, which had to be specially designed, were the saddle, pedestal and laying gears. The equipment was put straight into production without any trials. Eight were available for installation on the towers by the spring of 1942.

3. In the autumn of 1943, it was decided to increase the effective ceiling of the Flak 40. The barrel was lengthened and the chamber increased, the modified gun being known as the <u>12.8 cm. Flak 45</u>. It fired a new streamlined shell, slightly heavier than that of the old Flak 40. The modifications to the carriage of the 12.8 cm. Flak 40 consisted of fitting the new barrel with its muzzle brake and also alterations to the fuze setter and loading mechanism. A prototype of the new gun was produced just before the end of the war.

4. <u>Data: 12.8 cm. Flak 40.</u>

   (a) Calibre   5.04 ins   (128 mm)

       Length of ordnance   308.5 ins   (7835 mm)

       Rifling   R.H. increasing

       "   length   255 ins   (6478 mm)

       No. of grooves   40

       Traverse   360°

       Elevation   -3° to + 88°

       Recoil at 0°   51.27 ins   (1300 mm)

       "   at 85°   39.37 ins   (1000 mm)

       Transmission System   Übertragungsgerät 37. (Selsyn data type)

       Firing System   Electrical

       Fuze Setter   Zünderstellmaschine 40 (Selsyn data type)

       Rate of fire   12 r.p.m.

       Ceiling   48,500 ft   (14800 m)

       Carriage: Static, Mobile, and Railway versions

              Mobile - Transported on two 4-wheeled trailers.

       Overall length   49 ft 2 ins   (15000 mm)

       "   height   13 ft   (3965 mm)

       Wt. of equipment complete (mobile) 59,535 lbs (27000 Kg)

   (b) <u>Ammunition</u>

Type of Projectile	M.V.	Weight of projectile
H.E.	2886 f/s (880 m.s.)	57 lbs 5 ozs.
A.P.C.	2820 f/s (860 m.s.)	58 lbs 2 ozs.
A.P.C.B.C.	2820 f/s (860 m.s.)	62 lbs 8 ozs.

5. <u>Data: 12.8 cm. Flakzwilling 40</u>

   (a) Calibre   5.04 in   (128 mm)

       Length of ordnance   308.5 in   (7835 mm)

       Rifling   R.H. increasing

       "   length   255 in   (6478 mm)

       No. of grooves   40

       Traverse   360°

       Elevation   0° to 88°

       Recoil at 0°   51.27 in   (1300 mm)

       "   at 85°   39.37 in   (1000 mm)

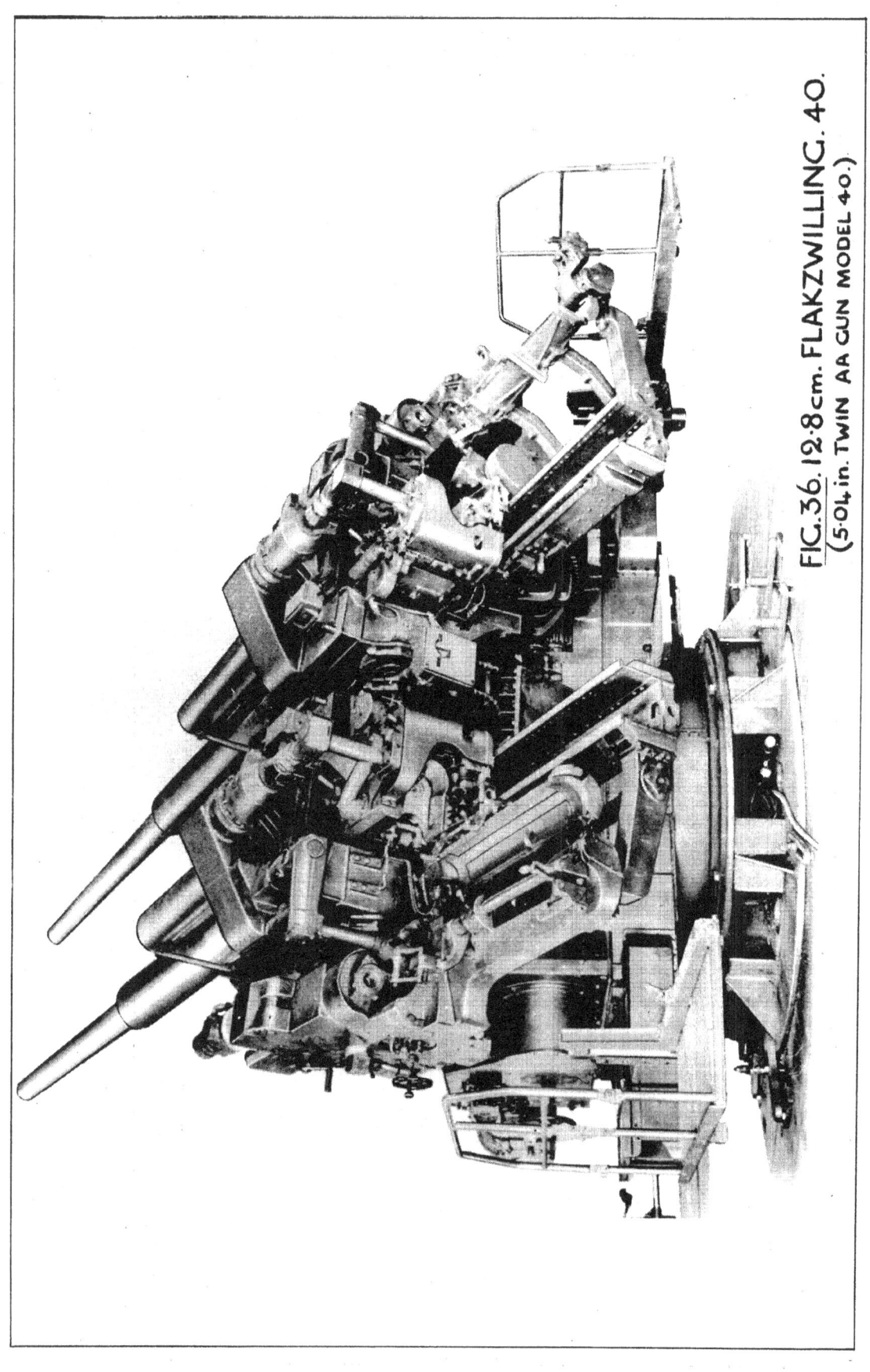

FIG. 36. 12·8 cm. FLAKZWILLING. 40.
(5·04 in. TWIN AA GUN MODEL 40.)

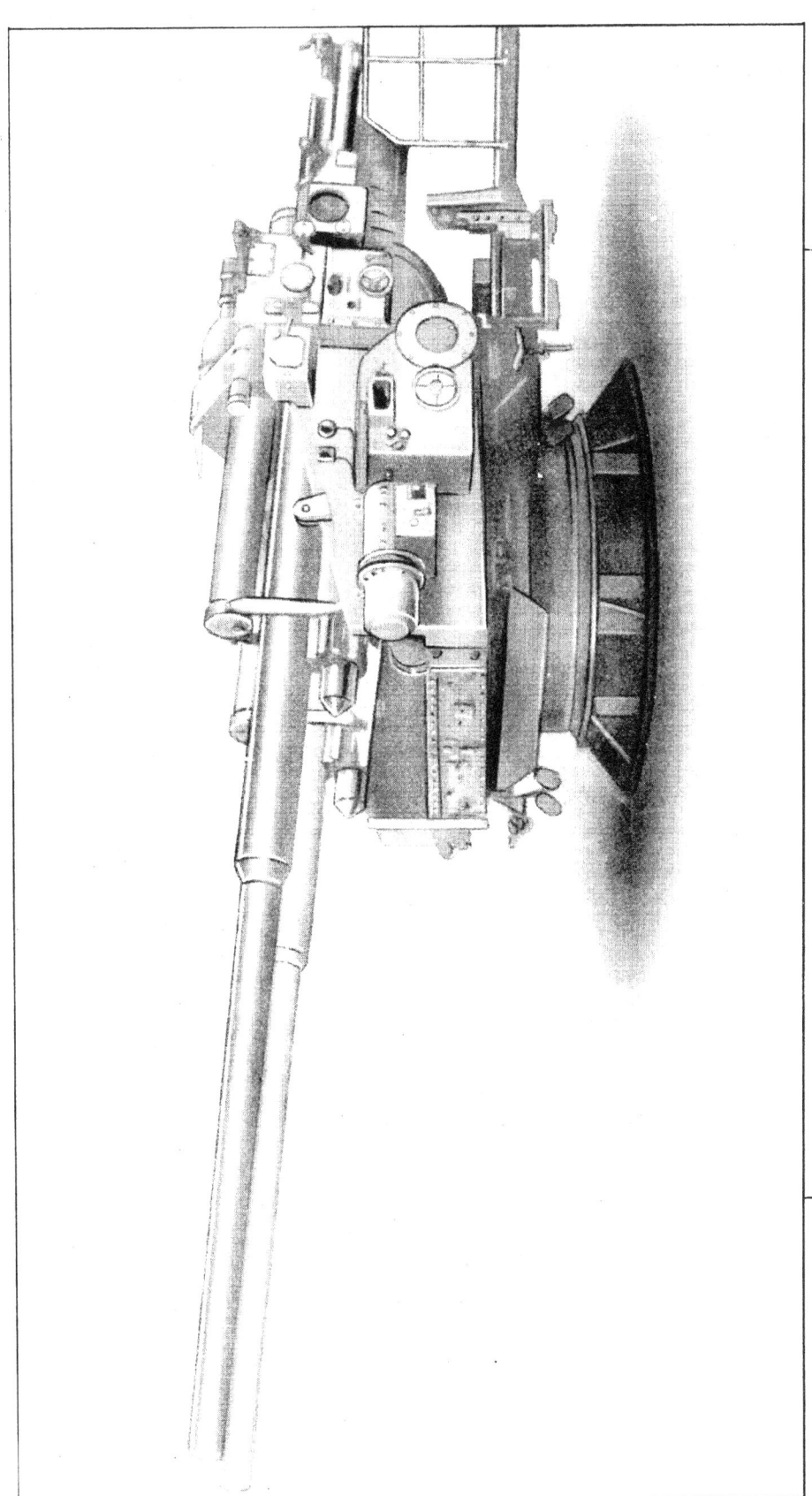

FIG. 37. 12·8 cm. FLAKZWILLING. 40.
(5·04 in TWIN AA GUN MODEL 40.)

Transmission System   Übertragungsgerät 37. (Selsyn data type.)
Firing System   Electrical
Fuze Setter: left barrel - Zünderstellmaschine 40. (Selsyn data type)
            right barrel - Zünderstellmaschine 41. (Selsyn data type)
Rate of Fire   20 - 25 r.p.m.
Ceiling   48,500 ft   (14,800 m)
Carriage - Static version only
Overall length   29 ft 11 in   (9120 mm)
"   height   9 ft 8¾ in   (2950 mm)
"   width   16 ft 6¾ in   (5045 mm)
Wt. of equipment complete   59,535 lbs   (27000 Kg)

(b) Ammunition

Type of Projectile	M.V.	Weight of projectile
H.E.	2886 f/s (880 m.s.)	57 lbs 5 ozs.
A.P.C.	2820 f/s (860 m.s.)	58 lbs 2 ozs.
A.P.C.B.C.	2820 f/s (860 m.s.)	62 lbs 8 ozs.

G.   **15 cm. A.A. Gun Development - Gerät 50 and Gerät 55**.   See fig:- 38

1. It will be remembered that a specification for a 15 cm. A.A. gun was issued early in 1936, about the same time as that for the 12.8 cm. Gerät 40 development. The contract for the 12.8 cm was issued to Rheinmetall, whilst that for the 15 cm. went to Krupp, the project being known as the "Gerät 50". In the autumn of 1936, Rheinmetall also received a contract for the design of a 15 cm. A.A. gun (Gerät 55) to the new specification. Krupp, whose 15 cm. design was progressing very slowly, received no contract for a 12.8 cm. gun however.

2.   **15 cm. Gerät 50 and Gerät 55 specifications.**

Muzzle Velocity (approx.)   850 to 900 m/s   (2800 to 2950 f.s.)
Weight of Shell (approx.)   35 to 40 kg.   (77 to 88 lbs)
Laying   Power assisted
Loading   Power loading and ramming
Method of Transport   3 or 4 loads

The Rheinmetall version Gerät 55 was finished in the early summer of 1938 and the Krupp Gerät 50 in September of that year. The Rheinmetall design formed the logical trend of development from the 10.5 cm. and the 12.8 cm. Flak 40. It was practically identical with the latter, except for the addition of an electrically driven lift, which raised the ammunition from the ground to the loading tray.

The Krupp design on the other hand progressed very, very slowly. This was partly due to two departures from current practice which were incorporated. In an attempt to increase the barrel life of a high velocity gun, the Krupp ballisticians had developed a system using conical rifling in conjunction with a shell having a driving band at the shoulder and a skirt shaped driving band at the base. This design, though not so necessary for this gun, was later developed for other guns. The second novelty was in the loading mechanism. The Krupp designers did not consider that ammunition of this type (each round being a two man load) could be fed to the gun, whilst firing under battle conditions. A magazine, which carried ten rounds (including one on each of two loading trays), was therefore built on to the rear of the cradle. The magazine was loaded by hand with the gun elevated to 80 degrees, the operation taking about 30 - 40 seconds with a well trained detachment. All ten rounds could then be fired semi-automatically in under 60 seconds.

3. The transport for the two equipments was entirely different. Rheinmetall's Gerät 55 was similar to the early design of the 12.8 cm. Flak 40, except that the carriage was carried in two loads (pedestal and platform). Krupp's Gerät 50, on the other hand, was carried in four loads:- barrel, cradle and upper carriage, lower carriage and platform. Needless to say, both equipments could be assembled for their transports without a crane. In addition, a special railway truck mounting was designed by Krupp to be suitable for either gun. A prototype was built and both guns tried out on it with complete success in 1940.

FIG. 38. 15cm. FLAK GERÄT 55.
(5·9 in. AA GUN DEVELOPEMENT Nº 55.)

4. In November 1938, although the two 15 cm. guns had only been finished a short time, sufficient experience had been obtained from them (and other projects) to show that they both suffered from two serious disadvantages:-

    (a) First and foremost, the slant range for a time of flight of 25 seconds was considerably worse than that from the 12.8 cm. Flak 40. To overcome this, it was decided to improve the performance of the two 15 cm. equipments, at least up to that of the 12.8 cm., by the use of a better shell and by increasing the muzzle velocity, using a slightly longer barrel and more powerful propellant.

    (b) The second disadvantage (transport in several loads) was similar to the trouble experienced with the 12.8 cm. Flak 40. At first, it was decided to transport the equipment in two loads (barrel and carriage). After the Meiller "limber-trailer" solution for the 12.8 cm. gun had been produced in the spring of 1939, it was decided to concentrate on the redesign of both guns, so as to be mobile in one load using two six-wheeled Meiller limbers. The total weight, in draught, of either gun was estimated at 30 tons.

5. The redesign of both equipments, to incorporate these two improvements, continued throughout 1939. By the middle of 1939, it was clear that, even with the increased M.V., the range for a time of flight of 25 seconds, would not materially exceed that of the 12.8 cm. Flak 40. In addition the modified guns would not be ready for some considerable time. It was this consideration, which led to the adoption of the 12.8 cm. Flak 40. By January 1940, it had become perfectly clear that no amount of modification could produce a satisfactory design; consequently work on the Gerät 50 and 55 was dropped to make way for a new specification.

6. The position at the end of 1939 was as follows:-

Field Army Equipment	- 8.8 cm. Flak 36(37) standard and in full production.
	8.8 cm. Flak 41 being developed for use in this role and eventually to replace the Flak 36(37)
Home Defence Heavy Equipment	- 8.8 cm. Flak 36(37) standard and in full production.
	10.5 cm. Flak 38(39) standard and in full production.
	12.8 cm. Flak 40 about to go into production, possibly to replace both the 8.8 and 10.5 cm. guns.
Home Defence Super-Heavy Equipment	- 15 cm. Gerät 50 and 55 abandoned.

H. **15 cm. Gerät 60 and Gerät 65.** See figs:- 39 and 40.

1. The development of the Gerät 50 and 55 had only been abandoned to make way for a new design. In January 1940, G.L.Flak issued a new specification for a 15 cm. A.A. gun. Contracts for a gun to this specification were given to Krupp and Rheinmetall as Gerät 60 and Gerät 65 respectively. In each case, the new design formed a development of its predecessor, except that it was to be transported in one load on two Meiller limbers or transporters. In addition, the muzzle energy was increased, as far as the new method of transport and the use of a muzzle brake would allow (i.e. from 40 kg and 870 m/s to 42 kg (92.4 lbs) shell weight and 960 m/sec (3150 f.s.) velocity), to give a higher ceiling and shorter time of flight.

These new guns were being designed to obtain a definitely high performance and it appeared to G.L.Flak that all possible eventualities had been catered for. However, by the beginning of 1941, it was realised

that the introduction of jet and rocket motors for aircraft was a
possibility of the near future. These would enable aircraft to fly at
higher speeds and at greater altitudes than had been thought possible,
when the new 15 cm. gun specification had been issued.

2. G.L.Flak considered the new problem for some time, and then,
apparently unable to come to any decision on the subject, passed it to
Krupp, Rheinmetall and Skoda in the summer of 1941 with a request for
concrete suggestions as soon as possible. The German Navy had also become
interested in a similar problem with a view to the defence of their
harbour installations. The equipment required by the Navy, however, had
the additional complication that it should be suitable for use in a dual
role for coast defence. As a result of these requirements, two separate
projects were being developed by each Service (Air Force and Navy), each
in two alternative calibres.

The projects were:-

	AIR FORCE		NAVY	
Calibre:	21 cm.	24 cm.	20.3 cm	24 cm.
Weight of shell:	123 kg (270.6 lbs)	198 kg(435.6 lbs)	110 kg(242 lbs)	177 kg(389 lbs)
Muzzle Velocity:	1040 m/s(3412 f.s.)	1000 m/s(3281 f.s.)	1000 m/s(3281 f.s.)	965 m/s(3165 f.s.)
Slant Range for 25 secs flight:	18000 m(59050 ft)	18000 m(59050 ft)	16700 m(54790 ft)	16800 m(55100 ft)
Radius of blast:	29 m (95 ft)	35 m (115 ft)	29 m (95 ft)	35 m (115 ft)
Rate of Fire:	10 r.p.m.	8 r.p.m.	2 x 10 r.p.m.	2 x 8 r.p.m.
Type of Mounting:	Single pedestal mounting in concrete pit with armoured cupola. Ammunition supply partly by hand.		Twin turret on concrete emplacement with power ammunition supply.	

3. In response to a demand from the Armament Ministry, the Air Force
and the Navy agreed to work out a common specification for a super-heavy
A.A. gun and then to develop only one project. Conferences on this
subject continued until the summer of 1942. Eventually, a compromise was
reached, based on the 24 cm. ballistics of the Air Force and the carriage
design of the Navy. Contracts for the design of a gun, to the new
specifications, were issued to Krupp and Rheinmetall as Gerät 80 and 85
respectively. The latter firm do not appear to have attacked the problem
with their usual energy, since the only designs, which were worked out in
detail, were those of Krupp. In the autumn of 1942, further work on the
two projects was suspended, in order to await the results of the trials with
the 15 cm. Gerats 60 F and 65 F. Finally, the two contracts were cancelled
in the autumn of 1943, when all super-heavy A.A. development was abandoned.

4. Meanwhile, the development of Gerät 60 and 65 was being pushed forward
as fast as possible. The design of the laying and fire control equipment
for the two guns was basically similar and formed a considerable step
forward. In addition to remote control from a predictor, the guns were
to be equipped with a course and speed sight for A.A. and C.D. use,
developed by Hagenuk of Kiel. The sight, known as the Kom-Vis 41, had
range, course and speed fed into it and, from these, computed traverse
and elevation lead and fuze setting. The former two values were allowed
for by deflecting the line of the sight itself. The fuze setting was fed
by the standard electrical transmission system to the fuze setter. As a
result of the experience gained with the 10.5 cm. and 12.8 cm. equipments
and the previous 15 cm. projects, a new electro-hydraulic remote control
was designed by S.A.H.

By the beginning of 1942, an experimental barrel for the Gerät 65 was
ready for firing trials. The barrel was of the multi-sectional five piece
design, and, in the firing trials which took place in the spring of 1942,
it gave constant trouble due to jammed cartridge cases, when using steel
as opposed to brass cases. After investigation, this trouble was traced
to the very high elastic expansion of the five piece barrel in the region
of the chamber. The brass case, but not the steel, could follow this
expansion without exceeding the elastic limit. The problem was tackled
from two different aspects; the provision of rolled steel cartridge
cases, built up from sheet which had a better performance than draw steel
cases, and the design of new monoblock barrels for both guns.

In the summer of 1942, it was anticipated that the two prototype
guns would be ready for trials by the autumn of 1943. However, there had

already been suggestions that the specification might be altered, since the firms were ordered, in February 1942, to produce designs for alternative static and transportable mountings. In October 1942, the design and production of mobile mountings for all A.A. guns over 10.5 cm. calibre was cancelled, so as to devote the capacity, thus released, for the improvement in output of static heavy A.A. guns. At the same time, the firms were asked what improvements it would be possible to make in the performance of Gerät 60 and 65, as a result of this change in policy.

5. In December 1942, it was decided that, although both guns would have to be almost completely redesigned, the advantages gained were sufficient to justify an increase in the performance from shell weight of 42 kg and velocity of 950 m/s to 42 kg (92.4 lbs) and 1200 m/s (3935 f.s.). The designation of the two designs were altered to Gerät 60.F and Gerät 65.F (F = FEST = STATIC), to indicate this change in the specification. It was anticipated, at the time the new specifications were issued, that the two prototype guns of each type would be ready by June 1944, an experimental battery by the end of 1944 and a pilot series of 20 guns by the spring of 1945.

6. The first experimental barrel of Gerät 65 was finished in August 1943 and firing trials were started in September. In the middle of September, however, the Air Ministry issued an order, cancelling the design and development of all A.A. guns over 12.8 cm. The capacity, thus released, was to be used to speed up the development of controlled A.A. rockets and fighter aircraft. Great efforts were made by the gun branch of G.L.Flak, and by the firms themselves, to have this decision reversed. Finally it was confirmed in October with only one reservation. The development of experimental barrels and ammunition was to be continued, in order to provide valuable data on very high muzzle velocities. By the end of the war, though this experimental firing had not been finished, it was clear that the conical rifling and special driving band of the Gerät 60.F would give an increase of life over the Gerät 65.F.

C.2/3/7/48.

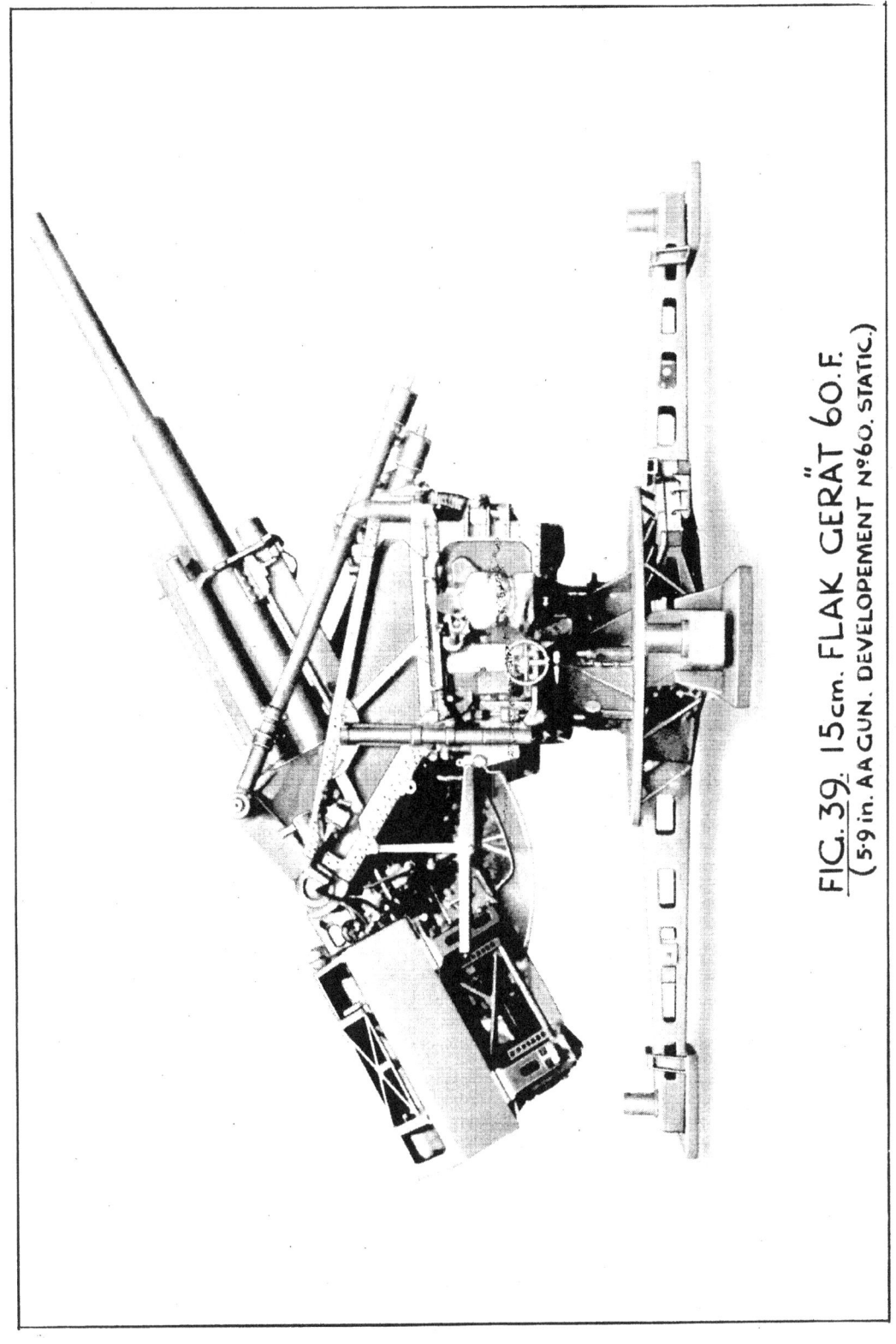

FIG. 39. 15cm. FLAK GERÄT 60.F.
(5·9 in. AA GUN. DEVELOPEMENT Nº 60. STATIC.)

FIG. 40. 15cm. FLAK GERÄT 60.F.
(5·9 in. AA GUN DEVELOPEMENT Nº 60. STATIC.)

CHAPTER V

THE DEVELOPMENT OF GERMAN COAST DEFENCE ARTILLERY

A. General

1. Introduction

The old adage that "History repeats itself" was never more true than of Coast Defence Artillery. During World War I, every conceivable type of gun was deployed along the coasts of the belligerent countries. Some of these were really a farce with their slow and crude methods of loading and gun laying. In 1940, twenty-six years later, Germany was doing the same thing again. With the fall of France and the occupation of the coast line from NARVIK to BIARRITZ, they had to utilize every type of gun for which there was ammunition. Any gun was considered better than no gun, no matter how old the weapon and irrespective of its proper role.

A large variety of guns were used by the Germans, therefore, as C.D. Artillery; it is not proposed to give a long catalogue of these equipments. As a considerable proportion were captured weapons, they are of little interest in this record.

As stated in the introduction to this part of the volume, the German coastal defences came under Naval control, and it is difficult to determine which were actually the standard artillery weapons. From the variety of types used, the following are considered to have been the standard C.D. weapons:-

(a) 3.7 cm. S.K. C/30. in Einheitslafette C/34.
(1.65 in. Q.F. CD/AA Gun on dual-purpose mounting C/34).

(b) 10.5 cm. S.K. C/32 n.L. in 8.8 cm. M.P.L. C/30. D.
(4.14 in. Q.F. CD/AA Gun, modified, on 8.8 cm mounting C/30. D).

(c) 15 cm. S.K. L/40.
(5.9 in. Q.F. C.D. Gun, Model L/40).

(d) 24 cm. S.K. L/35 and L340.
(9.4 in. Q.F. C.D. Gun, Models L/35 and L/40).

(e) 28 cm. S.K. L/40, L/45 and L/50.
(11 in. Q.F. C.D. Gun, Models L/40, L/45 and L/50).

(f) 30.5 cm. S.K. L/50.
(12 in. Q.F. C.D. Gun, Model L/50).

(g) 38 cm. S.K. C/34. ("Seigfreid").
(15 in. Q.F. C.D. Gun, Model C/34).

(h) 40.6 cm. S.K. C/34. ("Adolf").
(16 in. Q.F. C.D. Gun, Model C/34).

However, the vast majority of the C.D. guns proper were those originally designed for mounting on board ship. Some of these equipments had been dismantled and installed as C.D. weapons ashore, without any but very minor modifications. In fact, even the magazine arrangements and assembly, as on board ship, had been reconstructed ashore, where the need for such strict safety precautions did not arise. The standardisation of Naval and C.D. weapons is obviously not a satisfactory arrangement, as the conditions are so different. It would appear, however, that the German Naval Authorities simply thought that what was good enough for their ships was good enough in a C.D. role!

A limited number of German field guns were provided with special platforms, which enabled them to be used more efficiently in the dual role. They are described in the chapters, dealing with their respective primary role. (Two such weapons are the 15 cm. K. 39, provided with a separate turntable and radially rigged platform, and the 15 cm. K. 18, which has a plate platform and turntable slung under the carriage).

Other heavy artillery weapons (used primarily in the field role) were fitted with firing platforms, which made them suitable for a mobile C.D. role. These were the 15 cm. S.K. C/28, 21 cm. K. 38, 24 cm. K. 3 and also the A.A. and heavy A.Tk equipments with cruciform type platforms. The 8.8 cm. 10.5 cm. and 12.8 cm. A.A. guns were also used as mobile CD/AA guns.

2. Weapon Trends and Designs

   (a) Long Range guns

      The Germans realized that with the control of the sea in the hands of the Allies, they were subject to attack by naval forces, standing off at long range from their coastal defences. This led to the development of ultra-long range weapons in the heavier calibres. The increased range was obtained by the normal methods of increased charge and length of barrel, allied to modification of projectiles.

   (b) Sliding Breech Blocks

      The horizontal sliding breech block entailing the use of cartridge cases was standard practice even with the largest calibres of German guns.

   (c) Loose Gun Barrel Liners

      Loose liners were used with some of the largest calibre weapons and in some cases even entailed the demolition of a portion of the protective structure to enable the liner to be changed.

   (d) Removal of Foul Air from Turrets and Guns

      Smoke and fumes were removed from guns and turrets by clapper valves and suction ducts.

   (e) Rates of Fire

      Were relatively slow in comparison with Allied coast-defence weapons.

   (f) Mountings

      Design features of mountings were quite normal compared with the equipments of the Allies. In some features, such as speed of traverse and elevation, the German equipments were considered inferior. In their races, the Germans appeared to prefer ball bearings to those of the roller type. Balls are more simple to produce and, of course, the Germans have long held a high reputation for the production of ball bearings.

3. Protection

   (a) Two general types of turrets, housing one, two or three guns, were used, viz:-

      (i) The compact vertical type, as removed en bloc from ship, having three or four floors extending below ground level.
      (ii) The long flat shallow type extended on one floor, built especially for the coast defence role.

      The turret mounted weapon, without constructed earthwork or concrete protection (casemate) above gun level, invariably had 360° (all round) traverse.

The coast defence weapon, with or without turret, which has earthwork or concrete protection above the gun level has its maximum traverse limited by the size or arc of the front opening, through which the gun fires. The modern overhead protection is constructed to allow for the normal maximum elevation of the gun.

The platform below the naval type of turret normally consisted of gun, machinery, spacer, powder, and shell platforms. The ammunition hoists were power operated, but emergency hand hoists were also provided.

(b) It would appear that the German policy was to give armour protection to every gun whenever possible, even if the armour was only of a lightweight type. The amount of armour protection depended, not upon the weight of attack that could be brought against the weapon, but on its size. Therefore heavy guns had heavy armour, and the lighter the gun the lighter the armour. The heaviest armour was with the naval turrets. In most cases, the coast defence guns were only provided with light fragment proof armour. Lack of steel eventually forced the Germans to depend upon casemate construction for protection. Armour of frontal shields in casemates was generally too light, being in fact much too weak in comparison with the strength provided by the casemate.

Four types of armour protections were used, viz:-

(i) The Cupola (dome shape)
(ii) The Box shield
(iii) The Hood
(iv) The Frontal Shield

(c) (i) <u>The Cupola Turret</u>

This dome shaped turret was undoubtedly the most efficient form of armour protection and proved its worth under heavy bombardment.

(ii) <u>The Box shield Turret</u>

This type was undoubtedly more roomy than (i), but its high silhouette and vertically faced armour plate made it much more vulnerable to armour-piercing projectiles.

(iii) <u>The Hood</u>

This light weight armour protection was really an improvisation, fitted as an addition to the frontal shield to provide overhead cover against fragments.

(iv) <u>The Frontal Shield</u>

Sometimes called an "apron" shield, this did not provide overhead cover. In most cases, it was in the form of a curve having swept back wings. In quite a number of equipments, it was a simple flat shield inclined back from the vertical. (A very inefficient form of protection even when the weapon is mounted in a casemate).

4. <u>Ammunition</u>

The demand for ultra long range usually ended successfully, but at the expense of projectile weight. This production of lighter weight shell decreased the lethality or hitting power of the projectile and was therefore of doubtful value. The types of projectiles used by the Germans were essentially the same as those used by the Allied Powers.

Many kinds of propellant have been developed during the last two decades but, despite this, those used by the Germans during the last war were very similar to those used by the Allies. This is not so remarkable as it may seem at first sight, because all powers were striving to produce propellants, which were flashless, smokeless, and cool.

Developments seemed to have progressed along similar lines.

Fuzes and primers, generally speaking, were of quite normal type. The Germans appeared to prefer electric firing rather more than the other Powers.

5. **Fire Control Instruments and Methods**

   (a) **General**

   It is considered by the experts that German methods and instruments were quite appreciably inferior to those used by the Allies. One outstanding lesson of the recent war was that lines of communication between guns and fire control instruments must be adequately protected against bombardment. Several examples were found of guns undamaged under their concrete protection, but with their communications to the fire control instrument stations destroyed.

   (b) **Fire Direction Systems**

   (i) **Long Base Optical Cross Observation**

   A series of directors were sited at fixed surveyed positions, transmitting target bearings to the Battery Plotting Room. Angular deviations from target to fall of shot were also transmitted. The Battery Plotting Room converted the target plot into range and bearing for the guns, this being transmitted by a Selsyn system to receiver dials on the guns. Corrections for meteor etc. were embodied in the target data to the guns. Target future position was computed with time of flight as a function of future range.

   (ii) **Oriented Single Director and Stereoscopic Range Finder**

   Bearing and range were converted to gun firing data with embodied corrections and transmitted as under (i) above.

   (c) **Calculator Instruments**

   (i) **Graphical Range Rate Calculator**

   The present battery pivot range from either (b) (i) or (ii) was fed into the G.R.R.C. This instrument measured the range rate and so evaluated "future" battery pivot range.

   Facilities for the application of "spotting" and meteor correction to range were incorporated.

   (ii) **Fall of Shot Correction Calculator**

   The F.S.C.C. evolved spotting corrections to range and bearing when fed with target bearings and fall of shot observations from two displaced Observation Posts (Directors). It could also be used to calculate travel corrections, when target location and its course and speed were set.

   (iii) **T.V. Rechentish C.39**

   An instrument used to calculate range and bearing corrections for wind and abnormal ballistic conditions.

   (d) **Gun Instruments**

   (i) The Seipa-Empfänger (Bearing Receiver)

   (ii) The Epa-Empfänger (Range Receiver)

   These receivers on the gun received the battery pivot future bearing and range by a selsyn type of transmission and were used for indirect laying.

The Bearing Receiver computed the bearing displacement correction and applied it to the gearing between the gun traversing gear and the mechanical pointer matching the bearing selsyn input pointer. Therefore "follow the pointer" methods were used to lay the gun for line (direction).

The Range Receiver corrected the input data for the displacement of the gun from the battery pivot, corrected range being shown on a two-speed dial, whence it could be set on the gun.

The receivers catered for displacements up to 600 metres and a maximum range of 72,000 metres (650 yards displacement and 78,750 yards range).

Average permissible error in bearing was of the order of 6 minutes, with a maximum of 15 minutes at very short ranges with large displacements.

Errors in range displacement correction should not exceed 15 metres in more than 10% of readings in static tests and, in no case, should the error be greater than 45 metres. This rule applied for displacement settings of 40, 200, 300 and 400 metres.

6. **Range Finders**

   (a) **General**

   These were of the stereoscopic type. There appeared to be two standard sizes in use, the 10.5 metre base (34.44 feet effective base) and the 4 metre base equipment (13.1 feet effective base); 6 metre base equipments were also used (20 feet approx.)

   It is believed that there were only a very limited number of the long base equipments; these were normally mounted in a turret. The 4 metre base equipment, in quite common use, was mounted in a variety of ways.

   (b) **10.5 metre base Range-finder**

   The 10.5 metre equipment was quite an elaborate affair. It was transported in two parts consisting of:-

   (i) The rangefinder tube, which is approximately 37 feet long and two feet in diameter, weighs 12 tons.

   The range finder tube contains four instruments:-

   A stereoscopic rangefinder of 10.5 m base.
   A stereoscopic spotting telescope of 11 m base.
   A stereoscopic laying telescope of 6 m base.
   A stereoscopic training telescope of 6 m base.

   The granuated range scale has a range of 3000 metres to 100,000 metres (109,350 yards).

   (ii) The rangefinder turret, which is approximately 10 feet square and 8 feet 6 inches high, weighs 38 tons.

   The sides of the turret consist of steel plate approximately 6 cm (2.36 inches) thick. The thickness of the centre of the top plate is about 15 cm. (5.9 inches) and it tapers radially to a minimum of 6 cm (2.36 inches).

   The range finder is sunk to ground level to give increased protection; access to the turret is from beneath.

   (c) **4 metre base Rangefinder**

   This equipment is mounted on a three point support metal stand. The equipment is levelled by the operation of jack pads at the three points of support. The equipment can be used in a mobile role or it can be secured to a concrete base. A spotting telescope and binoculars for the elevation and traverse layers are fitted to the instrument.

Magnification	32
Range	1200 – 100,000 metres
	(1315 – 109,350 yards)
Overall length of rangefinder tube	14 feet
Diameter of rangefinder tube	7.8 inches
Height of the axis of the rangefinder tube	4 feet
Total weight	500 lbs.

7. **Searchlights**

Two sizes of searchlights were mounted in a coast defence role. These were a naval development and were used also in an anti-aircraft role.

150 cm. Model 43.K.	(59 inch)
Maximum range of Beam	13,000 metres
	(14,000 yards approx.)
200 cm. Model 43.K.	(78.75 inch)
Maximum Range of Beam	22,000 metres.
	(24,000 yards approx.)

8. **German Railway Guns used in a Coast Defence Role**

The use of railway equipments in a coast defence role was quite popular with all the major Powers and not less with Germany, who considered every gun a potential coast defence weapon. Those listed below are known to have been used primarily in the field role and are dealt with in the next chapter, others were dismounted from their railway undercarriages and mounted in various ways as fixed weapons with varying degrees of traverse. The latter are dealt with in this chapter as coast defence guns; the former comprise:-

15 cm. Kanone. (E).	5.9 ins. Gun on Railway Mounting.
17 cm. Kanone. (E).	6.7 ins. " " " "
20 cm. Kanone. (E).	8 ins. " " " "
24 cm. Theodor. Kanone. (E).	9.4 ins. Theodor Gun Rly. "
24 cm. Theodor Bruno. Kanone. (E).	9.4 ins. Theodor Bruno Gun " "
24 cm. kurze Bruno. Kanone. (E).	11 ins. short Bruno Gun " "
28 cm. lange Bruno. Kanone. (E).	11 ins. long Bruno Gun " "
28 cm. schwere Bruno. Kanone. (E).	11 ins. Heavy Bruno Gun on" "
38 cm. Siegfried. Kanone. (E).	15 ins. Siegfried Gun " "
40.6 cm. Kanone. (E).	16 ins. Gun on Railway Mounting.

It will be seen later that practically the whole of the railway gun series were in action in a coast defence role, firing from rails, the notable exceptions being the 21 cm. and 28 cm. very long range guns.

9. **Subcalibre Guns**

To enable firing practice with coastal guns to be carried out without expending full size ammunition from the larger weapons, it is customary to use a small calibre barrel, secured either above the large calibre barrel or fitted within it. This enables normal laying drill and fire control to be practiced without incurring costly expenditure of ammunition and wear of the main barrel.

The following subcalibre barrels were used in German Coastal Defences.

(a) **3.7 cm. Abkommrohr. K. (1.456 ins Sub-Calibre Gun Barrel).**

Used for practice firing with the 8.8 cm. S.K. C/35.

Muzzle Velocity	406 m.s.	(1330 f.s.)
Weight of Projectile	0.47 kg	(16½ ozs.)
Type of Projectile	3.7 cm. Abk.Ldg. Übgr.	(H.E. practice shell).
Maximum Range	4573 metres	(5,000 yards)
Length of Barrel (20 calibres)	740 mm.	(29.1 inches).

(b) <u>5 cm. Abkommrohr.K. (1.96 ins. Sub-Calibre Gun Barrel)</u>

Used for practice firing with the 15 cm. S.K. C/28.

Length of barrel (35 Calibres)   1750 mm.   (68.9 ins).

(c) <u>12.7 cm. Abkommrohr.K. (5 ins. Sub-Calibre Gun Barrel)</u>

Used for practice firing with the 38 cm. S.K. C/34.

Calibre	127 mm	(5 ins)
Length of barrel (35 calibres)	4445 mm	(175 ins)
Muzzle velocity	600 m.s.	(1968 f.s.)
Weight of projectile	28 kg	(61.6 lbs)
Maximum Range	14,000 metres	(15,300 yds)
Type of projectile	12.7 cm. Abk.Ldg.Übgr L/44 KZ (m Hb)	H.E. practice shell L/44 with noze fuze and ballistic cap.

3. <u>3.7 cm. S.K. C/30 in Einheitslafette C/34. (1.45 ins Q.F. Gun Model 30 on dual purpose mounting model 34.)</u>

1. This naval dual purpose gun was employed extensively in a static AA/CD role in areas occupied by coast artillery and in defence of port installations. As was usual with most equipments of naval origin, the gun and mounting had separate identities. It is known that the gun was also mounted on a twin pedestal mounting, similar in principle to the single mounting described here.

The barrel is a monobloc and is attached to the breech ring by a collar, which screws into the front of the latter. The breech mechanism consists of a semi-automatic vertical sliding breech block and percussion firing mechanism. Firing is done by a lanyard attached to the firing lever on the right side of the breech ring. A firing signal light is mounted on a bracket fixed to the cradle above the breech. This is controlled by a pedal mounted on the foot rest of the left hand layer.

The piece is carried in a cylindrical cradle, a cylindrical slide-way being formed on the outside of the barrel. The buffer and recuperator cylinders are carried on the cradle above the barrel, the trunnions being mounted on the cylindrical portion. The hydraulic buffer and recuperator rods are connected to lugs on the top of the breech ring.

The single elevating arc is bolted to the underside of the cradle. No equilibrator is provided, since the piece is balanced at the trunnions. The traverse layer is carried on a seat on the right and is provided with a double grip handwheel. The elevation layer is carried on a seat on the left of the gun. A switch controlling the firing light is mounted on the footrest. A double grip elevating handwheel is provided, in addition to a socket for a second handwheel, linking up with the traverse gear. The gun can thus be layed by one man in an emergency.

The sighting system is similar to that employed on the 3.7 cm. Flak 36, except that two sight heads are employed. The calculating portion of the sight is marked 3.7 cm. S.K. C/30 and appears identical to the Flakvisier 36.

2. <u>Data: 3.7 cm. S.K. C/30</u>

(a)
Calibre	37 mm. (1.45 ins)
Length of piece (including breech ring)	307.6 cm. (121 ins)
" " barrel	296.2 cm. (116.6 ins)
Calibre over lands at muzzle	37.5 mm. (1.48 in)
" " Grooves at muzzle	39.0 mm. (1.54 ins)
Width of lands	2.5 mm. (.098 in.)
Number of lands	16
Elevation	-10° to + 80°
Rate of elevation (per turn of handwheel)	4°
Rate of traverse (" " " ")	8°

2. **Data: 3.7 cm. S.K. C/30** (contd.)

Maximum recoil	33 cm. (13 in)
Weight of Standard projectile (H.E.)	0.745 kg. (1.64 lbs)
Muzzle Velocity	1000 m.s. (3280 f.s.)
Effective ceiling	2000 metres (6500 ft)
Maximum Range	6600 metres (7200 yds)

(b) Ammunition:-

The ammunition is Q.F.(fixed) with a 15 in. tapered brass or zinc plated case, having a plain rim, and with a C/13 nA primer.

Nomenclature	Type	Fuze Fitted	Propellant
3.7 cm. Br.Sprgr. Patr.40.L/4.1 Lk 37	HE/Incendiary (with tracer)	KZ 40 or	350g. R.P.38 N (320 x 2.8/0.8) or
3.7 cm. Sprgr. Patr.40.L/4.1 Lk 37	HE (with tracer)	E.K. Zdr. f. 3.7 cm. C/30	360 g. R.P.32 (325 x 3.3/0.8) (both with 5 g. gunpowder igniter.)

The shells are fitted with either three copper or two sintered iron driving bands. Either a red, yellow or white tracer can be fitted. The colour is indicated by the colour of the band above the driving band.

C. **7.5 cm. Pak 40.M. in L.M. 39/43.** (2.95 ins. A/Tk gun Model 40 on Naval Pedestal Mounting model 39/43)

1. This equipment consists of a slightly modified Pak 40 (L/46) piece, muzzle brake, cradle and recoil gear, carried on a naval type pedestal mounting. It is presumed that the "M" in the nomenclature stands for "Marine" (Navy). The equipment is intended as a naval gun or for use in a coast defence role.

There are two modifications to the 7.5 cm. Pak 40 piece, cradle and recoil gear. The first consists of a modification to the recoil gear, which reduces the maximum recoil to 70 cm. The second consists of moving the trunnions and elevating arc forward on the cradle, so that the former are at the point of balance. This eliminates the need for equilibrators.

The mounting is carried on a turntable with internal traversing rack. Mounted on this is a saddle, which carries the trunnion bearings, shield and a seat on the left for the layer. The shield consists of a 10 mm plate, which protects the front and part of the sides of the gun.

The layer for line and elevation sits on a seat, mounted on the saddle on the left of the gun. The elevating and traversing hand-wheels are only provided with one gear ratio. A foot pedal operated trigger is provided. The rocking bar sight is mounted on an extension of the left trunnion. It is provided with a socket for a telescopic sight. The range scale is graduated from 0 to 30 degrees.

2. **Data: 7.5 cm. Pak 40.M.**

(a)
Calibre	75 mm.	(2.95 in.)
Elevation	-10° to + 40°	
Maximum range	7680 m.	(8400 yds)
One turn of elevation hand-wheel	4°	
Traverse	360°	
One turn of traverse hand-wheel	5°	
Maximum recoil	70 cm	(27.6 ins)
Height of trunnions	125 cm.	(49.2 ins)
Weight of piece	660 kg.	(1455 lbs)
Weight of mounting	2020 kg.	(4450 lbs)
Total weight	2680 kg.	(5905 lbs)
Length of ordnance	3700 mm.	(145.67 ins)
Length of rifling	2461 mm.	(96.85 ins)
Rifling - R.H. increasing - No. of grooves	32	

2. <u>Data: 7.5 cm. Pak 40.M.</u> (contd.)

    Length of chamber   716 mm.   (28.19 ins)
    Chamber capacity   3500 cc.   213.6 cu.ins.

  (b) <u>Ammunition</u>

	M.V.	Weight of Projectile
H.E. - 7.5 cm. Sprgr. Patr. 34.	550 m.s. (1803 f.s.)	5.74 kg. (12.6 lbs)
A.P. - 7.5 cm. Pzgr.Patr. 39.	792 m.s. (2600 f.s.)	6.8 kg. (15 lbs.)

D. <u>8.8 cm. S.K. C/35 in Ubts. L.C/35. (3.46 ins. Q.F. Gun on Submarine Mounting Model 35.)</u>

1. This equipment is entirely naval in design, but has been used by the German artillery in a CD role. Only a few guns of this type were found mounted in a casemate and its use in this role was probably exceptional.

    The barrel is of multi-section construction, a large screwed locking collar being fitted at the joint between the front of the jacket and the barrel. The breech ring is provided with lugs on its underside for the attachment of recoil system piston rods. A vertical sliding breech block with percussion firing mechanism is fitted. Firing levers are mounted on either side of the gun for use of the layers.

    The cylindrical portion of the piece slides in a cylindrical housing in the cradle. The spring recuperator is carried in the cradle on the left below the barrel and the hydraulic buffer on the right. The piston rods are coupled to lugs on the underside of the breech ring.

    The piece is carried in a saddle mounted on a low pedestal. A single elevating arc is bolted to the bottom of the cradle. The traverse gear drives on to an internal rack inside the pedestal.

    Identical duplicate sets of controls for two layers are provided on each side of the gun. Two chest supports are fitted for the two layers on each side, one facing forward and one facing the gun. Traverse and elevation handwheels are placed conveniently for the two layers. The traverse gear can be disengaged by a gear lever, when the traverse of the gun is chest controlled by the layer facing the gun. A firing lever is mounted conveniently for both layers.

    A rocking bar sight is mounted on top of the cradle. A cross-head at the front carries brackets at each end for the sights. The sighting telescopes were missing. A handwheel and deflection scale, graduated 128 right and 160 left, controls the deflection of the sight brackets. The range drum is graduated with the following scales for the engagements of ground targets.

    (a) 3.7 cm. Abk Ldg.   MV   406 m.s. (1330 f.s.)
        (This charge is for   Wt. of Proj. 0.47 kg (16½ ozs.)
        sub-calibre attachment
        for practice firing)

    (b) Gefechts Ldg.   MV   700 m.s. (2295 f.s.)
        (Fighting Charge)   Wt. of Proj. 9 kg. (20 lb)

    (c) Leuchtgeschoss   MV   600 m.s. (1970 f.s.)
        (Star shell)   Wt. of Proj. 9.4 kg. (20.7 lbs)

2. <u>Data: 8.8 cm. S.K. C/35</u>

	Metric	British
Calibre	88 mm.	3.46 ins.
Length of piece	3990 mm.	157.1 ins.
Length of barrel	3735 mm.	146.8 ins.
Length of rifling (approx.)	3344 mm.	131.65 ins.
Length of chamber (approx.)	391 mm.	15.39 ins.
No. of grooves in rifling	32	
Depth of grooves	2.0 mm.	.078 ins.
Width of lands	3.0 mm.	.12 ins.
Traverse - (if not limited by a casemate)	360°	
Elevation	-4° + 30°	

FIG. 41. 10.5 cm. S.K. C/32 in 8.8 cm. MPL. C/30. D.
(4.4.in. Q.F. Gun, model 32, on modified 3.46 in. naval mounting.)

FIG. 42. 10·5 cm. S.K. C/32 in. 8·8 cm. MPL. C/30. D. (4·1 in. QF Gun mod. 32, on modified 3·4 in. naval mounting.)

FIG. 43. 10·5 cm. S.K. C/32 in. 8·8 cm. MPL. C/30. D.
(4·4 in. Q.F Gun model 32, on modified 3·46 in. naval mounting.)

2. **Data: 8.8 cm. S.K. C/35 (contd.)**

	Metric	British
Muzzle Velocity (Standard H.E. Proj.)	700 m.s.	2295 f.s.
Weight of Standard charge	1.7 kg	3.74 lbs
Maximum range	12,350 m.	13,500 yds.

E. **10.5 cm. S.K. C/32.nL. in 8.8 cm. M.P.L. C/30.D. (4.14 ins. Q.F. Gun Model 32 on modified 3.46 ins Naval Mounting Model 30.D.)**
See figs:- 41, 42 and 43.

1. This Naval dual purpose, coast defence and anti-aircraft, gun was introduced into service in 1932. It was subsequently mounted on a 8.8 cm. mounting and was an equipment with modernised barrel construction and loading arrangements.

   The weapon was power controlled, using Pittler Thoma power gear, and had a Zünderstellmaschine 37 (Machine Fuze Setter Model 37).

2. **Data: 10.5 cm. S.K. C/32. nL**

   (a)
Calibre	105 mm.	(4.14 ins.)
Length of barrel (incl. breech ring)	4740 mm.	(186.6 ins.)
Rear face of breech ring to trunnions	1250 mm.	(49.2 ins.)
Recoil at 0° elevation	420 mm.	(16.5 ins.)
Recoil at 79° "	480 mm.	(18.9 ins.)
Max. recoil	500 mm.	(19.7 ins.)
Max. buffer pull at 0°	18500 kg.	(18.2 tons)
" " " " 79°	20200 kg.	(19.87 tons)
Traverse (not fitted with electrical contact slip rings)	350°	
Elevation	- 3° to + 79°	
Trunnion height	1900 mm.	(74.8 ins.)
Height - Base of pedestal to top of turret - Model C	3063 mm.	(120.6 ins.)
" " " " Model B	3005 mm.	(118.3 ins.)

   (b) **Weights**

Barrel with breech	1706 kg.	(1.68 tons)
Cradle with recoil gear	620 kg.	(.6 tons)
Carriage (incl. power gear)	2470 kg.	(2.43 tons)
Turret shield - Model C.	9435 kg.	(9.3 tons)
" " - Model B.	8054 kg.	(7.92 tons)
Sights	330 kg.	(.32 tons)
Electrical equipment	300 kg	(.3 tons)
Fuze Setter	370 kg.	(.36 tons)
Total weights - Model C	15231 kg.	(15 tons)
" " - Model B	13850 kg.	(13.62 tons)

   (c)
Ammunition	Weight of Projectile	Muzzle Velocity	Max. Range
H.E. L/4.4	15.06 kg. (33.2 lbs.)	785 m.s. (2575 f.s.)	15350 m. (16800 yds)
Star Shell L/4.1	14.7 kg. (32.4 lbs.)	650 m.s. (2130 f.s.)	9500 m. (10400 yds)

F. **10.5 cm. S.K. L/60. (4.14 ins. Q.F. Gun L/60)**

1. This dual purpose AA/CD weapon, developed by Rheinmetall Borsig, was introduced into service about 1938. The equipment is based on, and very similar to, the celebrated standard 10.5 cm. A.A. Gun, Model 38.

   The barrel is of the multiple section type with barrel sleeve and jacket, together with removable breech ring, the whole being secured by three locking rings. The vertical sliding breech block opens under the control of a semi-automatic gear. The loading is power operated by a set of rubber rollers, which grip the round when it is placed at the breech opening and impel the round into the chamber. The loading rollers are rotated by an electrical motor on the bridge of the cradle. During the "run-out" of the gun after recoil, the roller brackets are automatically separated to allow sufficient space for the ejection of the cartridge case from the chamber.

The cradle is of the sleeve type and is provided with the necessary fittings for securing the recoil mechanism and trunnion brackets.

The saddle is set on an additional pair of trunnions on the mounting pivot within the pedestal mounting. To level the equipment, the pivot can be rocked in two directions at right angles to each other.

The equipment is fitted with three "follow the pointer" receiver dials, one each for line, elevation and fuze length. The data is transmitted from the control post to the receiver dials by means of a multi-core cable.

The sighting gear permits the engagement of air, sea and land targets.

A twin fuze setter is located on the left side of the saddle. This incorporates a flywheel drive. A safety arrangement prevents premature removal of the shell from the fuze setter.

2. Data: 10.5 cm. L/60 Gun

(a)
Calibre	105 mm.	(4.14 ins.)
Length of barrel	6840 mm.	(269.3 ins.)
Twist of rifling – constant	1 in 30	
No. of grooves	36	
Maximum horizontal range	17500 metres	(19,100 yds.)
Maximum vertical range	12500 metres	(41,000 ft.)
Muzzle velocity	900 m.s.	(3,000 f.s.)
Length of bore (approx.)	6300 mm.	(248 ins.)
Maximum elevation	80°	
Maximum depression	– 10°	
Traverse	360°	
Elevation – per turn of hand wheel	3°	
Traverse – " " " " "	3°	
Rate of fire	15 r.p.m.	
Pressure of charge in chamber	2850 kg. per cu. cm.	
Energy of Recoil	14.7 m.t.	

(b) Weights

Weight of barrel and breech	4635 kg.	(4.56 tons)
Cradle	1350 kg.	(1.33 tons)
Mounting with automatic fuze-setter	3420 kg.	(3.36 tons)
Fuze setter mechanism	350 kg.	(.35 tons)
Electrical components	355 kg.	(.351 tons)
Weight in action	11,750 kg.	(11.7 tons)
Weight of Shell (H.E.)	15.1 kg.	(33.2 lbs)
Weight of complete round	26.5 kg.	(58.3 lbs)
Weight of charge	5 kg.	(11 lbs)

(c) Ammunition

(i) 10.5 cm. Sprgr. L/4.4. KZ. Zt Z S/30. H.E. shell with nose time fuze. (Nose percussion fuzes also used).

(ii) AP and AP/HE projectiles are also used.

G. 15 cm. S.K. C/28 in Küst. M.P.L. C/36. (5.9 inch Q.F. Gun Model 28 on Coastal Mounting Model 36)

1. This equipment is of the orthodox coast defence type. The barrel is of normal design, consisting of a barrel, jacket and removeable breech ring. The latter is fitted with a vertical sliding breech block. This is unusual, in that the same type gun, mounted on a cruciform mobile carriage, is equipped with a horizontal sliding block.

The recoil system consisting of three cylinders is located above the barrel. The elevating and traversing gear is of the manual operated type. The mounting, which is of the pedestal type, is fitted with an all round shield with sliding gun port shield and hinged sight port cover. The armour plate thickness is 5 - 6½ cm. at the front and 1½ cm. at the sides and top.

Data receiver dials are fitted to the mounting.

2. **Data: 15 cm. S.K. C/28**

    (a) Calibre   149.1 mm.   (5.87 ins.)

        Length of piece (55 calibres)   8291 mm.   (326.4 ins.)
        Length of barrel   7815 mm.   (307.7 ins.)
        Length of jacket   3975 mm.   (156.5 ins.)
        Length of chamber   1233 mm.   (48.5 ins.)
        Length of rifling   6584 mm.   (259.2 ins.)

        Rifling - system - P.P.S. Increasing R.H. twist
                - twist - 1 in 50 to 1 in 30.
                - grooves - number   44
                         - depth   1.6 mm.   (.063 ins.)
                         - width   6.1 mm.   (.24 ins.)
        Lands   - width   5.0 mm.   (.197 ins.)
        Muzzle velocity (H.E.)   875 m.s.   (2870 f.s.)
        Range scale graduated to   23,500 metres (25,700 yards)
        Traverse - Turret type   360°
               - Casemate type - depends
                  upon local conditions.
        Elevation - Varies with type of
                  mounting - normally about   -5° to +35°

    (b) **Ammunition**

        15 cm. Sprgr. L/4.6 KZ. (m Hb) - 5.9 ins. H.E. shell with
                                                       nose fuze.

        15 cm. Sprgr. L/4.5 Bd Z. (m Hb) - 5.9 ins. H.E. shell with
                                                      base fuze.
                                                 (both with ballistic cap.)

        Weight of both projectiles - 45.3 kg. (99.6 lbs)

H. **15 cm. S.K. C/28. in Zwillingslafette. (5.9 ins. Q.F. Gun Model 28 on twin Naval Mounting.)** See fig:- 44

1. Equipments of this type were used in a coast defence role, having been withdrawn complete from naval vessels and installed ashore without any major alteration.

The guns were elevated by hydraulic pressure with alternative hand control. The guns could be elevated independently by hand-wheels on each side of the mounting, but a control wheel was used if it was desired to elevate them together.

Power traverse was used with a speed of about 8 degrees per second at the high rate and about 1½ degrees per second at the low rate.

Power operation was used for supplying the ammunition from the underground magazines, but both shell and cartridge were hand loaded. At least three models of H.E. shells were used, in addition to a shorter A.P. projectile; these were all of nearly the same weight (approx. 100 lbs).

To clear smoke and unburnt gases from the turret, a series of small holes were provided on each side, near the top at the rear, for the intake of fresh air. Two suction ducts, one over the breech end of each gun, drew away foul air and smoke.

The breech blocks of the guns were of the vertical sliding type.

The recoil system was a normal hydraulic buffer and hydro-pneumatic recuperator type.

The sighting gear, of normal German type, consisted of "follow the pointer" dials, range scale and elevation indicators, together with the usual sighting telescopes.

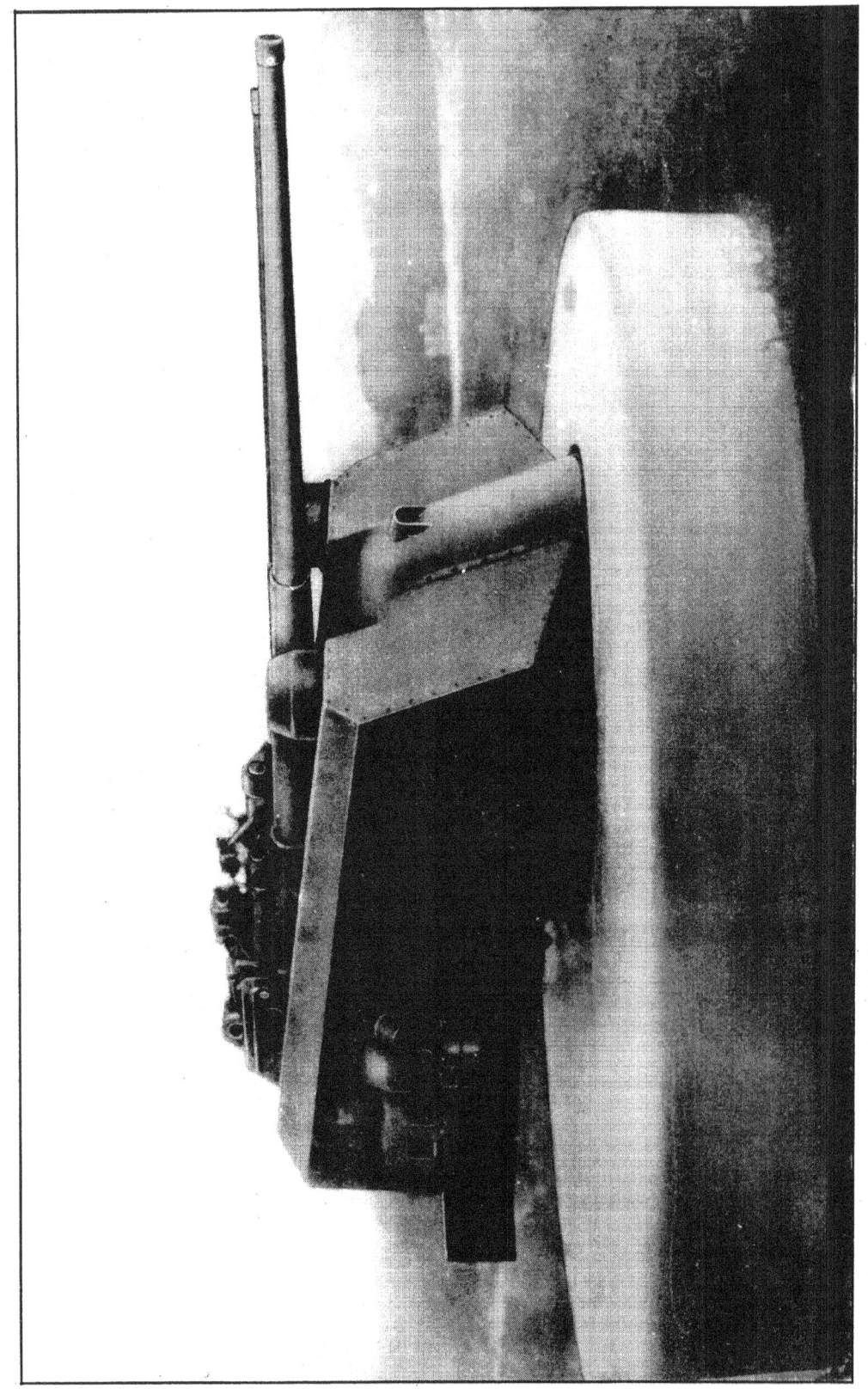

FIG. 44. 15 cm. S.K. C/28 in ZWILLINGS LAFETTE.
(5·9in. Q.F. Gun, Model 28, on twin naval mounting.)

2. **Data: 15 cm. S.K. C/28**

    (a) Calibre   149.1 mm.   (5.87 ins.)

            Length of bore   7815 mm.   (25.6 feet.)

            Length of rifling   6584 mm.   (21.6 feet.)

            Rifling – System – P.P.S. Increasing right hand twist.
                      – twist – 1 in 50 cals to 1 in 30 cals
                      – grooves   44

            Traverse   350°

            Elevation   – 7° + 40°

            Muzzle velocity (H.E.)   875 m.s.   (2870 f.s.)

            Range scale graduated to 23,500 metres   (25,700 yards)

    (b) **Turret Armour**

            Front   6 ins.

            Back   2 ins. approx.

            Top   2 ins. approx.

    (c) **Ammunition**

            15 cm. Sprgr. L/4.6.KZ (m Hb) – 5.9 ins. H.E. shell with nose fuze.

            15 cm. Sprgr. L/4.5.Bd Z (m.Hb) – 5.9 ins. H.E. shell with base fuze.

            15 cm. Sprgr. L/4.3.KZ (m Hb) – 5.9 ins. H.E. shell with nose fuze.

            15 cm. Pzgr. L/3.8.Bd Z (m Hb) – 5.9 ins. A.P. with base fuze.
               (all with ballistic cap)

            Weight of projectiles –   45.3 kg.   (99.6 lbs.)

            The weight of the propellant, contained in a wrapped (spiral) cartridge case, was approximately 14.1 kg.   (31 lbs.)

J. **15 cm. Tbts. K.C/36. (5.9 ins. Torpedo Boat Gun Model 36.)** See fig:- 45

1. This naval weapon was originally designed for mounting in torpedo boats, but was used extensively in a coast defence role.

    The gun piece consists of a monobloc barrel with half length jacket and removeable breech ring. The latter is fitted with a horizontal sliding breech block, opening to the right.

    The recoil system consists of two hydraulic buffers and one hydro-pneumatic recuperator and is fitted to the cradle and located above the barrel.

    The trunnions are fitted at the centre of gravity of the barrel and cradle; no equilibrators are fitted therefore.

    The elevating and traversing gears are manually operated and are of the arc and pinion and arc and rack types.

    Normal type "follow the pointer" dials are fitted to the mounting for receiving traverse and elevation data from the command post. This, as usual, is electrically transmitted by a multi-core cable.

    The pedestal of the mounting is unusually low. This, coupled with the fact that the gun and cradle are balanced at the centre of gravity, has an adverse effect on the amount of maximum elevation.

2. **Data: 15 cm. Tbts. K. C/36**

    (a) Calibre   149 mm.   (5.875 ins.)

            Length of Gun Body (47 calibres)   7013 mm.   (276.4 ins.)

            Length of barrel   6772 mm.   (266.6 ins.)

            Depth of breech opening   248 mm.   (9.77 ins.)

            Length of rifling   5551 mm.   (218.5 ins.)

FIG. 45. 15 cm. Tbts. K. C/36.
(5·9 in. Torpedo Boat Gun, Model 36.)

```
                Rifling - System - P.P.S. - increasing right hand twist.
                        - Twist  - 1 in 40 to 1 in 30
                        - Grooves - Number             44
                                  - Depth    1.7 mm.    (0.066 ins.)
                                  - Width    6.0 mm.    (0.239 ins.)
                Lands - Width                4.6 mm.    (0.180 ins.)
                Muzzle velocity              835 m.s.   (2740 f.s.)
                Weight of standard projectile 45.3 kg.  (99.6 lbs.)
                Maximum range                19,525 m.  (21,350 yards)
                Elevation                           - 4° + 40°
                Traverse - Dependent upon local conditions of mounting, (i.e.
                           whether turret or casemate).
```

(b) **Ammunition**

15 cm. Sprgr. L/4.6.KZ (m Hb) - 5.9 ins. H.E. shell with nose fuze.

15 cm. Sprgr. L/4.5.Bd Z. (m Hb) - 5.9 ins. H.E. shell with base fuze.
(both with ballistic cap)

K. **15 cm. S.K. L/40. (5.9 ins. Q.F. Gun Model L/40).** See fig:- 46

1. This equipment is used both by the German Army in fixed fortifications and by the Navy in coast defences. It is a somewhat antiquated design by Krupp. A very unusual point is that the ammunition is Q.F. fixed, the complete round being more than a two man load. The gun barrel is the same model as that used with the 15 cm. Railway equipment.

The piece is of typical early Krupp design, and consists of a built-up barrel and breech ring. The breech ring is screwed to the rear of the jacket. A horizontal sliding breech block is fitted, opening to the right. The percussion firing mechanism is operated by lanyard from the right of the block. The piece is carried in a cylindrical cradle, in which the jacket slides. The spring recuperator and hydraulic buffer are mounted on the right and left of the cylindrical portion of the cradle. An unusual detail (for German guns) is that the recoil system cylinders recoil, the piston rods being attached to the cradle at the front.

The saddle is mounted on a platform with an external traverse rack. The traverse handwheel is on the right and the elevating handwheel on the left. A single elevating arc is bolted to the underside of the cradle. No equilibrator is fitted. The trunnions are extended beyond the bearings to carry rocking bar sights.

A shield, enclosing the front, top and sides of the gun, is carried on brackets secured to the saddle. It gives full protection to the layers from the side. Slots are cut in the front plate for the barrel and the two sights. A mantlet shield is fitted to the front of the cradle.

2. **Data: 15 cm. S.K. L/40**

```
        (a) Calibre over lands          149 mm.      (5.87 ins.)
            Calibre over grooves        152 mm.      (5.98 ins.)
            Length of piece             6010 mm.     (236.6 ins.)
            Length of barrel            5585 mm.     (219.9 ins.)
            Length of rifling (approx.) 4715 mm.     (185.6 ins.)
            Rifling - no of grooves          44
            Width of lands              3.5 mm.      (0.137 ins.)
            Elevation                        - 10° to + 30°
            Traverse                         360°

        (b) Thickness of shield -

            Front                       105 mm.      (4.13 ins.)
            Sides                        55 mm.      (1.97 ins.)
            Top                          25 mm.      (0.98 ins.)
            Mantlet                      25 mm.      (0.98 ins.)
```

(c) **Ammunition**

H.E. and star shell are fired, the former being Q.F. fixed and the latter QF separate. A second QF separate H.E. round, fitted with two driving bands, is also fired.

(i) **H.E., Q.F. fixed**

Fuze:- Brass, nomenclature unknown, probably made in 1929. (It is a detonating fuze, an unusual practice for German ammunition.)

Weight of shell	45.5 kg.	(100 lbs)
Calibre over shoulder	147.5 mm.	(5.8 ins.)
Length overall	615 mm.	(24.2 ins.)
Length to shoulder	352 mm.	(13.8 ins.)
Width of copper driving band	30 mm.	(1.18 ins.)
Height of driving band above base	93 mm.	(3.66 ins.)

(Base is not streamlined)

(ii) **Star shell, Q.F. separate**

Fuzed, Lg Zdr S/38, (igniferous time fuze). The shell is not streamlined.

Calibre over shoulder	147.5 mm.	(5.8 ins.)
Length overall	570 mm.	(22.44 ins.)
Length unfuzed	543 mm.	(21.4 ins.)
Length to shoulder	475 mm.	(18.7 ins.)
Width of driving band	16 mm.	(.63 ins.)
Height of driving band above base	22 mm.	(.87 ins.)

(iii) **Cartridge Case**

The cartridge case for the Q.F. fixed round is longer than that for the Q.F. separate. Cases are fitted with three different types of percussion primer, C/12 nA, a brass primer with a 23 mm. screw gauge and a small brass primer with a 13 mm. screw gauge. Cases fitted with the two latter types of primer were made as far back as 1905. The Q.F. separate cases, fitted with C/12 nA primers, had the case design number 15 cm. C/95.

Dimensions of the Q.F. separate case are as follows:-

Length	575 mm.	(22.6 ins.)
Diameter over rim	176 mm.	(6.9 ins.)
Diameter under rim	160 mm.	(6.3 ins.)
Thickness of rim	6 mm.	(.236 ins.)
Diameter of mouth	156 mm.	(6.14 ins.)

(iv) **Propelling Charge**

For Star Shell:-

Hülsenkartusche f 15 cm.S.K.L/35(H) u L/40.(H)

Leuchtgeschossladung:- 7.10 kg. Lg P 40 Bu (550 x 5/2.3)
Igniter:- 50 gr grobk P.

For H.E. Q.F. separate:-

15 cm.S.K.L/40.(H)
10.4 kg.St.P. D M 9 - D 2

(v) **Ballistic performance:-**

Fixed H.E. range scale engraved:-

500 m (550 yds) to 13,000 m (14,200 yds).

FIG. 46. 15 cm. S.K. L/40.
(5·9 in. Q.F. Gun, Model L/40.)

Star shell range scale engraved:-

1,500 m (1,640 yds) to 7,000 m (7,660 yds).

The separate loading H.E. shell is fired to a maximum range of 21,870 yards with a muzzle velocity of 2,640 f.s.

L. **15 cm. Ubts u Tbts K.L/45. (5.9 ins. Submarine and Torpedo Boat Gun Model L/45)** See fig:- 47

1. This equipment is of modern German naval design. Though primarily designed as a ship mounted gun, it has also been encountered in fairly large numbers mounted in coast defence emplacements.

The piece consists of a barrel and breech ring carrying a horizontal sliding breech block, the two being connected by a collar, which screws into the front of the breech ring.

The breech ring is of rectangular cross section, attachments being provided at the top and bottom for the recoil gear. The breech mechanism is of conventional horizontal sliding wedge design and is operated by a lever mounted on the right side of the breech ring. The firing mechanism is operated by either of the two layers on the left of the gun, through a linkage which connects up with the right hand side of the breech ring.

The barrel is carried in a sleeve type cradle. Mounted side by side, above the barrel, are two spring recuperators, the "piston" rods being connected to the top of the breech ring. Mounted side by side, below the barrel, are two hydraulic buffers, the piston rods being connected to the bottom of the breech ring.

The trunnions are mounted directly on the cylindrical portion of the cradle. They are carried in a short saddle, mounted in a race on a pedestal fixed to the ground. The elevating arc is bolted at the rear of the cradle on the right side. A bracket is bolted to the right hand side of the saddle and extends to the rear to support the elevating pinion. No equilibrator is necessary, since the piece is balanced about the trunnions. The traversing rack is mounted on the outside of the pedestal. It is engaged by a traversing pinion, mounted on the front of the saddle.

There are two layers, both on the left of the gun. The layer for line is mounted on a seat facing forward. The layer for elevation is provided with a chest support facing inward toward the gun. Each is provided with a single handwheel and a gear change lever, there being two speed gears for both line and elevation.

The drive for the elevating gear is taken by a shaft running across the front of the saddle to a gearbox at the other end and then by a shaft running along the elevating pinion bracket to a gearbox, which provides the drive for the pinion. A socket for mounting a second elevation handwheel is provided on the right of the gun, just in front of the pinion gearbox.

The drive for the traversing gear is taken from the traversing handwheel, which is mounted on a shaft parallel to the gun, through two gearboxes and a short vertical shaft to a shaft running across the front of the saddle below the elevating shaft. A gearbox in the centre of this shaft provides the vertical drive down to the traversing pinion. A second traversing handwheel is mounted on the right hand end of the traversing gear cross shaft. A traverse indicator is mounted in front of the two layers on the left.

A rocking bar sight is mounted on the left trunnion. It carries a bracket at the front for the two telescopes for the layers. That for the elevation layer must presumably be cranked through 90°. The elevation arc for the sight is in rear of the two layers and is provided with an engraved range scale. The arc is engaged by a pinion driven by the range handwheel, which also drives the range drum. The latter has scales for elevation in degrees and range for ground targets and air targets at heights of 1, 2, 3 and 4 thousand metres. The rear of the bracket, on which the two telescopes are mounted, is led back to a deflection gear. This is operated by a handwheel and deflection scale drum graduated in degrees and 1/16 degree.

(German new degrees = 400 to circle, 1/16 degree = 1 German mil.).

2. Data: 15 cm. K. L/45

   (a) Dimensions

Length of piece	662 cm.	(260.6 ins.)
Length of barrel	624 cm.	(245.7 ins.)
Length of rifling	542 cm.	(213.4 ins.)
Calibre over grooves	152.5 mm.	(6.004 ins.)
Calibre over lands	149.5 mm.	(5.886 ins.)
Width of lands	4 mm.	(0.158 ins.)
Number of lands	48	
Elevation	$-4°$ to $+45°$	
Traverse	unlimited	

   (b) Ballistic Performance -

   (i) 15 cm.Lg L/3.5:- MV 500 ms (1640 f.s.)
   Max range 7500 m (8200 yards)

   (ii) 15 cm.Lg L/4.3:- Max range 10,600 m (11,600 yards)

   (iii) 15 cm. Sprgr. L/4.1.KZ.) MV 680 ms (2230 f.s.)
   15 cm. Sprgr. L/4.1 m Bd Z) Max range 1600 m
   15 cm. Sprgr. L/4.1.KZ u Dopp Z.) (17500 yards)

   Against air targets:-

(Height	1000 m	(3280 ft.)
(Max range	14300 m	(15650 yds.)
(Height	2000 m	(6560 ft.)
(Max range	14200 m	(15550 yds.)
(Height	3000 m	(9840 ft.)
(Max range	14000 m	(15300 yds.)
(Height	4000 m	(13120 ft.)
(Max range	13700 m	(15000 yds.)

   (iv) 15 cm. Hbgr 16:-

Charge I	MV	555 ms	(1820 f.s.)
Charge II	MV	657 ms	(2155 f.s.)

   (c) Ammunition

   The ammunition is QF separate. Six types of shell are fired:-

   (i) H.E. Star Shell - Two types.

   15 cm.Lg.L/3.5
   15 cm.Lg.L/4.3

   Details of the latter are as follows:-

   Shell is painted green with a red band below shoulder.

   Fuze Zt Z S/60 nA.

Calibre over shoulder	148.5 mm.	(5.48 ins.)
Length overall	650 mm.	(25.6 ins.)
Length unfuzed	580 mm.	(22.8 ins.)
Length to shoulder	500 mm.	(19.7 ins.)
Width of both driving bands	16 mm.	(.63 ins.)
Separation of driving bands	16 mm.	(.63 ins.)
Height of rear DB above base	37 mm.	(1.45 ins.)

   Base is not streamlined

(ii) H.E. nose fuzed –

   15 cm.Sprgr.L/4.1.KZ.

   Shell is painted yellow with a black band below the fuze. Either a steel nose fuze, the only marking being "m Sch" or a time fuze, Zt Z S/60 nA, are fitted in conjunction with a Zdlg "A" gaine.

Weight of shell	45.3 kg.	(100 lbs)
Calibre over shoulder	148.5 mm.	(5.84 ins.)
Length overall	620 mm.	(24.4 ins.)
Length unfuzed	555 mm.	(21.8 ins.)
Length to shoulder	350 mm.	(13.77 ins.)
Width of both driving bands	21 mm	(.83 ins.)
Separation of driving bands	10 mm.	(.39 ins.)
Height of rear DB above base	25 mm.	(.98 ins.)

   The base is not streamlined.

(iii) Common Pointed – Base Fuzed – Two Types

   15 cm.Sprgr.L/4.1. m.Bd Z.

   Shell is painted yellow with a black tip to the nose. Fuze is a Bd Z.C/36., in conjunction with a Zdlg "A" gaine.

Weight of shell	45.3 kg.	(100 lbs.)
Calibre over shoulder	148.5 mm.	(5.84 ins.)
Length overall	625 mm.	(24.6 ins.)
Length to shoulder	350 mm.	(13.8 ins.)
Width of both driving bands	20 mm.	(.79 ins.)
Separation of driving bands	16 mm.	(.63 ins.)
Height of DB above base	22 mm.	(.87 ins.)

   The base is not streamlined.

   No details of the other shell are available –
   15 cm.Sprgr.L/4.1 KZ u Dopp Z (HE nose and T and P fuze).

(iv) H.E. B.C. nose fuzed –
   15 cm.Hbgr.16

   Shell is painted green with the type of fuze fitted, stencilled in black on the ballistic cap. Fuzes fitted are the Hbgr Z 17/23 or Hbgr Z 17/23 umg or Dopp Z 16 m K or Dopp Z 16 n F.

Weight of shell	51.4 kg.	(114 lbs.)
Calibre over shoulder	148.6 mm.	(5.85 ins.)
Length overall	752 mm.	(29.6 ins.)

   Shell is fitted with 2 driving bands and the base is not streamlined.

(v) Cartridge Case –

   A solid drawn brass case, 15 cm. C/95, is used, fitted with a C/12 nA. primer. Dimensions are the same as those given for the 15 cm. S.K. L/40.

(vi) Propelling Charge –

   For the H.E. shells –

   Hülsenkartusche f 15 cm. Tbts K L/45 und 15 cm. Ubts u Tbts K L/45.

   Gefechtsladung:– 8.1 kg.RP 12. (550 x 8.75/4)
   Igniter:–   50 g grobk P.
   For the Star Shell –
   Hülsenkartusche f Leuchtgeschosse 15 cm Tots K und 15 cm Ubts u Tbts.K.L/45.
       7.5 kg. Tri R.P. (550 x 8/5)

FIG. 47. 15 cm. Ubts u Tbts. K. L/45.
(5·9 in Submarine & Torpedo Boat Gun, Model L/45.)

M. 17 cm. S.K. L/40. (6.8 inch Q.F. Gun Model L/40). See fig:- 48

1. This equipment mounts the same gun as is used on the railway mounting equipment. Many of these gun barrels were made as long ago as 1903.

In the purely coast defence role, the gun is mounted on a fixed pedestal in separate casemates. A curved front shield is normally fitted, with thickness of armour, 10 cm. (4.0 ins.) at the front and 4 cm. (1.5 ins.) at the top.

The gun piece is of the built up tube and jacket type. The open jaw breech ring is fitted with a horizontal sliding breech block, opening to the right. Two recoil slides are fitted to the jacket, one on either side.

The cradle is of the sleeve type. The recoil system consists of two spring recuperators and one hydraulic buffer and is located below the gun barrel.

Both elevating and traversing gears are operated manually.

The fire control equipment, fitted to some of the weapons, is of modern and efficient design, consisting of a Rechentisch C.39. (computing table), Rw Zielsäule (tracking instrument), Lg Zielsäule (range tracker) and 5 metre base range finder. Data transmission system and receiver dials were of modern design. A long base plotting board is maintained as reserve equipment.

2. Data: 17 cm. S.K. L/40

(a) Calibre   172.6 mm.   (6.8 ins.)
    Length of piece (40 calibres)   6900 mm.   (271.6 ins.)
    Length of rifling   4991.5 mm.   (196.5 ins.)
    Rifling - increasing right hand
                                twist 4° to 6°
    Chamber capacity   31.7 litres   (7 galls.)
    Elevation $-5^{o} + 45^{o}$
    Traverse - Arc of fire varies with local conditions.
    Weight of Standard projectile   62.8 kg.   (138 lbs.)
    No. of charges   one
    Muzzle velocity   875 m.s.   (2870 f.s.)
    Chamber pressure   3100 atmospheres (20.3 tons
                                                            sq. in.)
    Muzzle energy   2367 m.t.
    Maximum range   27,200 metres (30,620 yds.)

(b) Ammunition

    H.E. Shell:- 17 cm. Sprgr. L/4.7.KZ.(m Hb), Weight 138 lbs.

    Fuzes:- E K Zdr f Sprgr. or Dopp Z S/90.

    Primer:- C/12 nA or C/12 nA.St.

    Igniter:- 200 g (3086 grains) Black Powder.

    Propellant Charges:-

    C.32 Tubular   or   C.12 Tubular
    23.6 kg. (52 lbs)   20.5 kg. (45 lbs)

N. 20.3 cm. S.K. C/34 (8 inch. Q.F. Gun Model 34.)   See Fig.:- 49

1. The gun, of naval design, is the same as that used with the 20 cm. Railway equipments.

The equipment is mounted on a fixed pedestal and is normally fitted within a turret.

The piece is of the loose liner type with tube and jacket assembly.

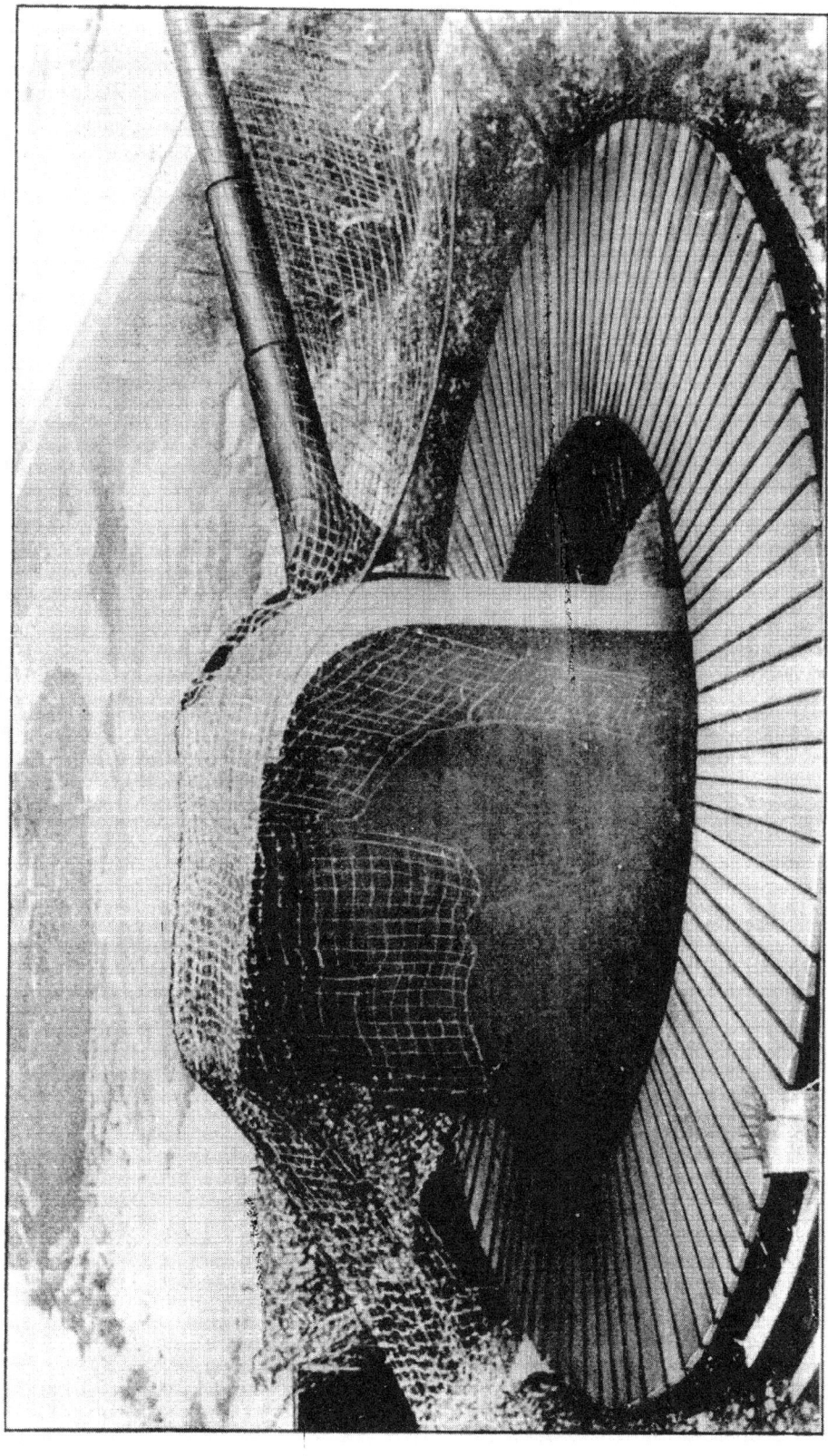

FIG. 48. 17 cm. S.K. L/40. (6.8in. Q.F. Gun, Model 1/40.)

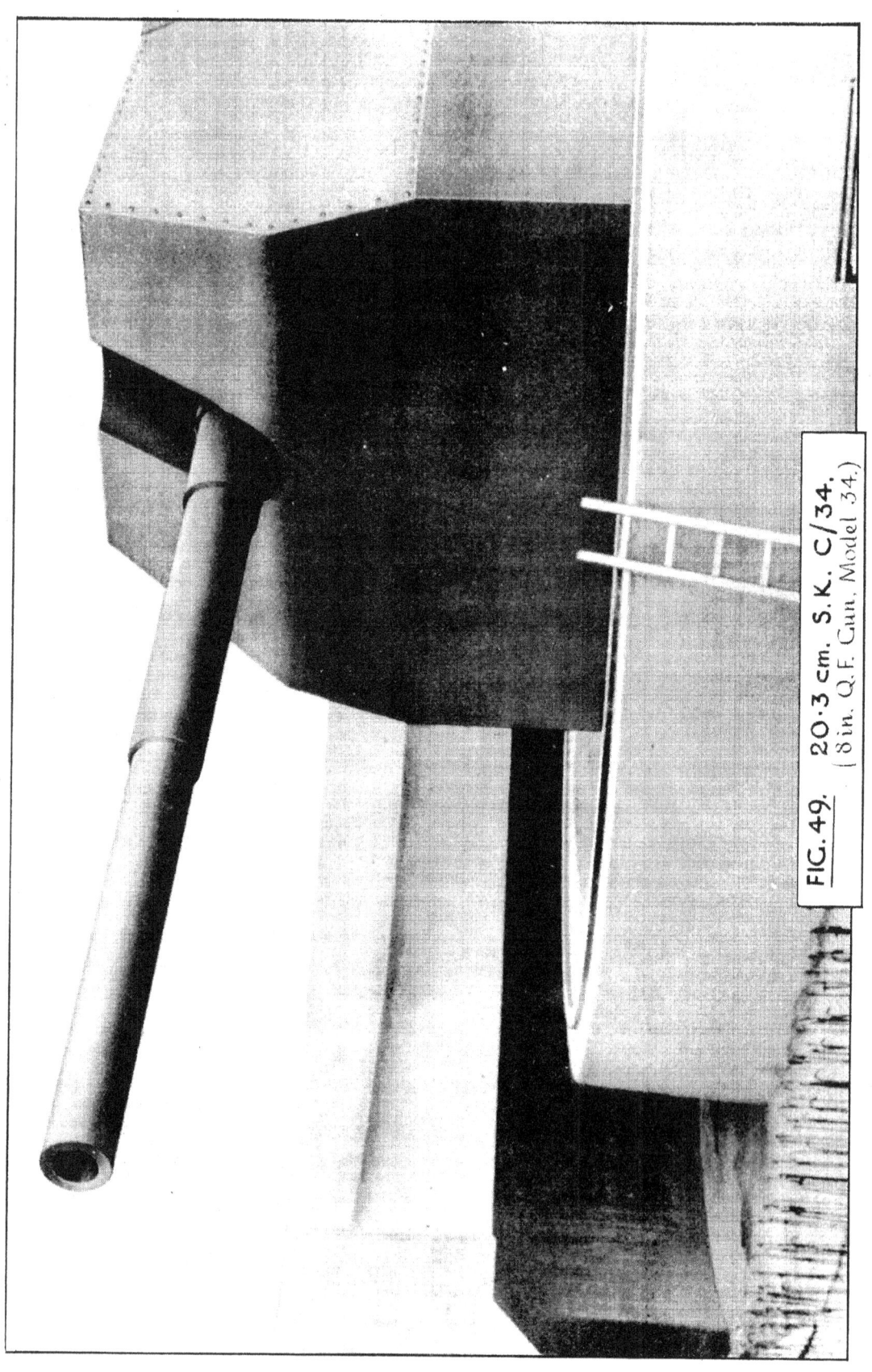

FIG. 49. 20·3 cm. S.K. C/34.
(8 in. Q.F. Gun, Model 34.)

The removeable breech ring is fitted with a horizontal sliding breech block, opening to the right.

The cradle is of the sleeve type with the recoil system fitted below the barrel. The buffer is hydraulic and the recuperator hydro-pneumatic.

The equipment is power operated for elevation, traverse and loading. Normal German type "follow the pointer" receiver dials are used.

2. Data:- 20.3 cm. S.K. C/34.

(a)
Calibre	203 mm.	(8 ins.)
Length of piece (60 calibres)	12150 mm.	(478.34 ins.)
Length of barrel	11587 mm.	(456.17 ins.)
Length of rifling	9527 mm.	(375 ins.)
Type of rifling - Increasing right hand twist	4° to 5°	
No. of grooves in rifling	64	
Elevation	- 5° + 40°	
Traverse (depends on local conditions)	up to 360°	
Weight of standard projectile (H.E.)	122 kg.	(268.4 lbs.)
Maximum range	37,000 metres	(40,465 yards)
Muzzle velocity	925 m.s.	(3,035 f.s.)
Chamber pressure	3200 atmospheres	(21 tons sq.in.)
Muzzle energy	5320 m.t.	
Rate of fire	1 r.p.m.	

(b)
Turret armour - top	220 mm.	(8.6 ins.)
sides	110 mm.	(4.3 ins.)
Front	220 mm.	(8.6 ins.)
rear	90 mm.	(3.5 ins.)

(c) Ammunition:

H.E. with ballistic cap:-	Weight of Projectile	Fuzes
20.3 cm. Sprgr.L/4.7. (m.Haube)	112.3 kg. (247 lbs)	KZ C/27 St or Dopp Z.28.K
20.3 cm. Sprgr.L/4.7 m Bdz (m.Haube)	122 kg. (268.4 lbs.)	Bd Z.C/38
A.P. B.C. H.E.:- 20.3 cm. Pzgr.L/4.4 (m.Haube)	125 kg. (275 lbs)	Bd Z. C/38

Cartridge Case:- 20.3 cm. Karth C/34 (Brass)

Primer:- C/12 nA (Brass) or C/12 nA.St (Steel)

Igniter:- 540 g (19 ozs.) Black Powder

Propellant Charge:- 35 kg. (7, lbs) C/32 Tubular.

24 cm. S.K.L/40. in Drh L.C/98. (9.4 ins. Q.F. Gun Model L/40 on Pivot Mounting Model 98.) See figs:- 50 and 51

1. The barrel and cradle assembly of this equipment was adapted for use on a railway mounting and known as the 24 cm. "Theodor" Kanone (E). The piece consists of a built up jacket and tube with a removable breech ring, fitted with a horizontal sliding breech block.

The recoil system has two hydraulic buffers and one spring type recuperator. These are housed in a cylinder block, secured to the cradle, and located below the gun barrel.

The elevating and traversing gears are operated manually, the elevating gear from the platform and the traversing gear from the pit, in which the pedestal of the mounting is secured. The traverse rollers at the rear of, and supporting the platform, travel over an exposed roller pathway.

The cradle follows normal German practice, being of the sleeve type.

2. **Data:- 24 cm. S.K. L/40.**

   (a)
Calibre	238 mm.	(9.4 ins.)
Length of piece	9550 mm.	(31.3 feet)
Length of barrel	8900 mm.	(29.16 feet)
Length of rifling	7820 mm.	(25.65 feet)
Length of chamber	1080 mm.	(42.5 ins.)
Rifling - Increasing right hand twist -	$3\frac{1}{2}°$ to 7° or 4° to 6°	
Elevation	- 5° to + 45°	
Traverse (depends upon local conditions)	up to 360°	
Maximum muzzle velocity	810 m.s.	(2657 f.s.)
Chamber pressure	2900 atmospheres	(19 tons sq.in.)
Muzzle energy	4966 m.t.	
Maximum range	26,750 metres	(29,250 yards)
Weight of standard projectile	148.5 kg.	(326.7 lbs)
No. of charges	2	

   (b) **Ammunition**

H.E. with Ballistic Cap	Weight of Projectile	Fuzes
24 cm. Sprgr. L/4.2 m Bd Z u KZ (m Haube) (Nose and Base Fuzes)	326.7 lbs (H.E. content 33.35 lbs)	E K Zdr f Sprgr. Dopp Z.16 n f Bd Z f Sprgr m Ko+
24 cm. Sprgr. L/4.2. m Bd Z u KZ (m Haube) ung (Nose and Base Fuzes)	326.7 lbs	K Z C/27 Bd Z C/38 Dopp Z S/90 St
24 cm. Sprgr L/4.1. m Bd Z (Base Fuze)	332.2 lbs	Bd Z f Sprgrm Ko+

   Primer:- C/12 nA or C/12 nA.St (Brass or Steel)

   Igniter:- 200 g (7 ozs.) Black Powder

   Propellant Charge:- (Both Tubular)
   Basic Charge. 82.8 lbs - RPC/32 (1040-12/6.6)
   (Includes 7 ozs. Igniter.)

   Increment Charge. 15.2 lbs - RPC/32 (346-12/6.6)

24 cm. S.K.L/35. (9.45 ins. Q.F. Gun Model L/35).

1. This equipment is of Krupp design and dates back to before the 1914 era.

The piece consists of a loose liner, jacket and removable breech ring. The latter is fitted with a horizontal sliding breech blocl of unusual design. The block is in the form of a half cylinder with curved surface facing towards the rear. The jacket is fitted with two longitudinal recoil slides, one on either side, which fit into grooves on the inner face of the sleeve cradle.

The recoil system comprises two hydraulic buffer cylinders, mounted within the cradle assembly above the gun barrel, and one recuperator cylinder, mounted below the barrel.

The normal German type centre pivot and pedestal mounting is used, with the platform supported on traverse rollers, which travel over an exposed roller pathway.

2. **Data:- 24 cm. S.K. L/35**

   (a)
Calibre	238 mm.	(9.4 ins.)
Length of piece (35 calibres)	8400 mm.	(27.5 feet)
Length of barrel	7800 mm.	(25.59 feet)
Length of rifling	6300 mm.	(20.67 feet)
Length of chamber	1500 mm.	(4.92 feet)
Elevation	-5° + 45°	

FIG. 50. 24 cm. S.K. L/40. in Drh L. C/98.
(9.4 in. Q.F. Gun, Model L/40, on pivot mounting, model 98.)

FIG. 51. 24 cm. S.K. L/40. in Drh L. C/98.
(9.4 in. Q.F. Gun, Model L/40, on pivot mounting, Model 98.)

2. **Data:- 24 cm. S.K. L/35 (contd.)**

        Traverse (Depends upon local conditions)   Up to 360°
        Muzzle velocity   675 m.s.   (2215 f.s.)
        Chamber pressure   2600 atmospheres (17 tons sq. in.)
        Muzzle energy   3450 m.t.
        Weight of standard projectile   148.5 kg.   (326.7 lbs)
        Maximum range   20,200 metres (22,100 yards)

  (b) **Ammunition:-**

H.E. with Ballistic Cap	Weight of Projectile	Fuzes
24 cm. Sprgr. L/4.5 m Bd Z (m Haube) (Base Fuze)	332.2 lbs	Bd Z f Sprgr m Kot. with gaine Gr Zdlg C/98
24 cm. Sprgr. L/4.2. m Bd Z u KZ (m Haube) umg. (Base and nose fuzes)	326.7 lbs	(KZ. C/27. (Dopp Z.S/90 (Bd Z.C/98.

Cartridge Case:-   Solid drawn brass - Kart.f.Th.Br.K.

Primer:-   Percussion C/12 nA (brass)

Propellant Charge:-
Igniter - 200 g (7 ozs. Black Powder (0.3 - 1.5)

Main Charge - approx. 68 lbs C/32 Tubular (1100 x 7.5/3.3 mm) or
                   62 lbs C/12 Tubular (550 x 8.75/4 mm)

Q. **28 cm. S.K. L/40.** (11 inch Q.F. Gun Model L/40). See figs:- 52 and 53

1. The gun is a 40 calibre naval piece, Model 1914, designed by Krupp and used on railway mountings, in addition to the fixed position coast defence role, during both wars. This barrel is the shortest of a series of four naval guns of 11 inch calibre, all used in similar roles.

The gun piece is of the built up type comprising tube, jacket and removable breech ring. The breech mechanism has a horizontal sliding breech block, which opens to the right.

The sleeve type cradle incorporates a structure for the housing of the recoil system. The latter is of the orthodox German type consisting of one hydro-pneumatic recuperator cylinder and two hydraulic buffers. The complete assembly is located below the barrel.

The elevating mechanism comprises two straight racks with a hand operated worm and wheel drive (also power driven).

The fixed mountings and emplacements vary in design, some mountings were modified railway mountings. In some cases, the equipments were emplaced in circular pits and at other times at ground level.

2. **Data:- 28 cm. S.K. L/40**

  (a) Calibre   283 mm   (11.14 ins.)
      Length of piece (40 calibres)   11200 mm   (36.75 feet)
      Elevation   - 5° + 45°
      Traverse (depends upon local conditions) Up to 360°
      Barrel recoil   690 mm   (27 ins.)
      Weight of standard projectile   240 kg   (528 lbs.)
      Maximum range   29,500 metres (32,250 yards)
      Muzzle Velocity   820 m.s.   (2690 f.s.)
      Chamber pressure   3000 atmospheres (19.7 tons sq. in.)
      Muzzle energy   8220 m.t.
      Rifling - No. of grooves   80
      Rifling - Increasing right hand twist - Angle 4° to 6°

FIG. 52. 28 cm. S.K. L/40.
(11in. Q.F. Gun. Model L/40.)

FIG. 53. 28 cm. S. K. L/40.
(11 in. Q.F. Gun, Model L/40.)

(b) Ammunition

H.E. with Ballistic Cap:-	Weight of Projectile	Fuzes
28 cm. Sprgr. L/4.1. KZ u Bd Z. (m Haube)	528 lbs (H.E. content 41.27 lbs.)	(KZ.C/27. Lm (Dopp Z S/90

Cartridge Case:-   28 cm. Karth C/95 (Brass)

Primer:-   C/12 nA.

Igniter:-   200 g (7 ozs) Black Powder

Propellant Charge: 67 kg (148 lbs.) C/32 Tubular or 64 kg (141 lbs.) C/12 Tubular.

R. **28 cm. S.K. L/45. (11 inch Q.F. Gun Model L/45)**

1. This equipment is similar to the L/40 coast defence equipment, except that the L/45 barrel is 5 calibres longer (i.e. about 4 feet 8 inches).

The piece is of built up jacket and tube construction with removable breech ring, fitted with a horizontal sliding breech block, opening to the right.

The sleeve type of cradle is so constructed that the recoil system, of two hydraulic buffers and one hydro-pneumatic recuperator, is housed below the barrel.

The equipment, like that of the L/40, was introduced into the Service during the 1914-18 war and used both railway and fixed coastal defence mountings.

2. Data:- 28 cm. S.K. L/45

(a)
Calibre	283 mm	(11.14 ins.)
Length of piece (45 calibres)	12735 mm	(41.8 feet)
Length of rifling	9698.5 mm	(31.8 feet)
Length of chamber	2192 mm	(86.3 ins.)
Capacity of chamber	150 litres	(33 galls)
Rifling - Increasing right hand twist - Angle 4° to 6°		
Elevation	- 5° + 45°	
Traverse (depends upon local conditions) Up to 360°		
Barrel recoil	860 mm	(34 ins.)
Muzzle velocity	875 m.s.	(2870 f.s.)
Chamber pressure	2900 atmospheres	(19 tons sq. in.)
Muzzle energy	11080 m.t.	
Weight of standard projectile	284 kg	(624.8 lbs.)
Maximum range	36,100 metres	(39,500 yards)

(b) Ammunition

H.E. with Ballistic Cap:-
(with Nose or Base Fuze)   Fuzes

28 cm. Sprgr. L/4.4.m Bd Z u KZ (m. haube) umg	(KZ. C/27. (Bd Z. C/38. (Dopp Z S/60.
28 cm. Sprgr. L/4.4 m Bd Z u KZ (m haube)	(EK Zdr f Sprgr. (Dopp Z.16 (Bd Z. f. Sprgr.

Primer:-   C/12 nA (brass)

Igniter:-   200 gr (7 ozs.) Gun Powder.

Propellant Charge:-   106 kg (233.2 lbs.) C/12 Tubular.

S. **28 cm. S.K. L/50.** (11 inch Q.F. Gun Model L/50)

1. This 50 calibres long gun barrel is one of the series of 11 inch naval guns, which were developed for both naval and coast defence purposes.

The piece follows normal German practice and comprises a tube, barrel jacket and removable breech ring. The latter is fitted with a breech block of the horizontal sliding type, opening to the right.

The cradle is of the sleeve type and has a form of construction, which permits of the two hydraulic buffers being housed above the barrel and the hydro-pneumatic recuperator below the barrel.

The platform, extended to the rear, is traversed on rollers, which travel over an exposed roller pathway.

The equipment, as a whole, is somewhat similar to that used with the other 11 inch equipments.

2. <u>Data:-</u> 28 cm. S.K. L/50

   (a) Calibre   283 mm   (11.14 ins)
       Length of piece (50 calibres)   14150 mm   (46.4 feet)
       Length of barrel   13304 mm   (43.65 feet)
       Length of rifling   11112 mm   (36.5 feet)
       Length of chamber   2192 mm   (86.3 ins)
       Chamber capacity   150 litres   (33 galls)
       Rifling - Increasing right hand twist - $3\frac{1}{2}°$ to $5°$
       Elevation $-4°$ to $+50°$
       Traverse (depends on local conditions)   Up to $360°$
       Weight of standard projectile   284 kg   (625.8 lbs)
       Maximum muzzle velocity   905 m.s.   (2970 f.s.)
       Maximum range   39,100 metres (42,760 yards)

   (b) <u>Ballistic Data</u>

       (i) <u>H.E. with Ballistic Cap</u> (Fitted Nose or Base Fuze)

           28 cm. Sprgr. L/4.4 m Bd Z u KZ (m Haube).
           Wt of Projectile 284 kg (626 lbs).
           Muzzle velocities 905-786 m.s. (2970-2580 f.s.)
           Range at 45° elevation (M.V. at 905 m.s.) 39,100 metres
                                                      (42,760 yards)
           Range at 45° elevation (M.V. at 786 m.s.) 30,200 metres
                                                      (33,500 yards)

       (ii) <u>Armour Piercing Projectile or H.E. with Base Fuze</u>

           28 cm. Pzgr. L/3.2 m Bd Z or Sprgr. L/3.6 m Bd Z
           Wt of projectile 302 kg (666 lbs).
           Muzzle velocities 890-770 m.s. (2920-2526 f.s.)
           Range at 45° elevation (M.V. at 890 m.s.) 31,000 metres
                                                      (33,880 yards)
           Range at 45° elevation (M.V. at 770 m.s.) 25,000 metres
                                                      (27,300 yards)

T. <u>30.5 cm. S.K. L/50.</u> (12 inch Q.F. Gun Model L/50). See fig:- 54

1. This Krupp equipment, of modern design, was considered a very efficient equipment. Special characteristics claimed were long range and accuracy, rapid traversing and elevation, and a high rate of fire due to the modern loading and firing gear. A number of equipments were built by Skoda and these differed in minor respects from the standard German weapon, but were ballistically the same.

The gun piece is of typical Krupp design and consists of a built up barrel and jacket with removable breech ring. The horizontal sliding breech block opens to the right. (Some of the Skoda production equipments were fitted with a breech screw and carrier mechanism). The cartridge case extractors are in one solid piece.

The recoil system, consisting of two hydraulic buffers and one hydro-pneumatic recuperator, is located below the gun barrel. The cradle follows normal German practice being of the sleeve type.

The elevating and traversing gear can be operated manually or by power. The elevating gear is of the twin rack and pinion type, as found in the 21 and 28 cm railway equipment weapons. A hand crank gives fast traverse and a handwheel slow traverse. Round the ramp is a bearing scale, graduated for 180° traverse. Casemate opening restricts the traverse to approximately 180°.

The sighting mechanism is placed on the right side of the cradle and consists of the sight, housing the range scale plate, the range cursor and individual gun correction mechanism. The range scale fits into a housing; on it are plotted ranges against elevation and against various muzzle velocities, corresponding to increasing states of wear of the gun. The cursor is operated for range and angle of sight by movement upwards or downwards and to the left or right, to correspond to the various muzzle velocities. There is also the gun correction scale, against the appropriate correction on which, the zero of the main scale must be adjusted. Two displacement converters are used - the range converter C.29 and the bearing converter C.26.

During indirect fire, orders are transmitted electrically from the battery plotting-room to the turret. Elevation and traverse are adjusted either electrically by universal transmission or by hand-gear.

During direct fire, the telescopic elevation sight on the right side of the gun and the traversing sight, in the form of a periscope on the left side of the gun, are used. Elevation and traverse are adjusted either electrically or by hand-gear.

2. The Mounting

The gun is mounted in a revolving turret, which rests on the revolving upper half of a ball-race. The fixed lower-half of the ball-race rests on an anchor-ring bolted to the bed of the circular concrete emplacement. The turret is further supported by a circular walled-support-platform, on which it rests by a system of leaf-springs running round the whole circumference. Thus the turret, if hit by an enemy shell, descends on the circular mantlet of the support platform and strain is taken off the ball-race. Between the inner-wall of the support-platform and the surrounding concrete wall of the emplacement is a gallery, along which the turret ammunition trolleys run.

3. The Turret

Inside the turret, there are three compartments, one above the other.

(a) The upper compartment contains the gun and gun-cradle, the sights, the traversing and elevating gear controls, the loading mechanism, and the upper opening of the ammunition hoist-shaft.

(b) The centre compartment contains the ammunition hoist and motor and ancillary gear, the electric elevating motor and the compressed-air system.

(c) The lower compartment comprises the magazine.

4. The Magazine and Ammunition Supply

The magazine is a rectangular concrete chamber built underground in rear of the gun-emplacement. Its capacity is about 200 shells with the requisite charges. Two trolleys on rails, each carrying one shell and two charges, transport the ammunition through revolving doors in the end-wall nearest the gun, to the magazine hoist. Ammunition is then transferred to the hoist and carried up to the level of the gallery, which runs round the support wall (see para.2 above). It is again transferred to a trolley and passes through revolving doors into the gallery. It is then pushed along the gallery to the revolving doors in the centre compartment of the turret, through which it passes to the turret ammunition hoist and is raised up to the gun-platform (upper compartment). It should be observed that at each stage the revolving doors "seal" off the turret, gallery, magazine-hoist and magazine from each other, so that the risk of flash or flame reaching the gallery or magazine is reduced to a minimum. The thickness of armour laid down for the mantlet over the gallery is 300 mm.

5. Battery Organisations

Batteries of 30.5 cm. guns may consist of one, two, three or four guns. The battery command post may be up to 2,500 yards from the centre of the battery. The battery plotting room, containing the predictor, is in the centre of the battery if possible, but may be up to 500 yards from the individual guns. Individual guns may be up to 950 feet above sea-level. The distance between predictor and guns and the height of the guns above sea-level is limited by the adjustments possible on the parallax-correctors for individual guns on the predictor.

6. Observation Posts

(a) Battery

The battery observation-post (B-stelle), which will be in most cases in the same building as the command post (Leitstand), is equipped with a vertical base range-finder, from which data is transmitted electrically or by telephone to the predictor in the plotting-room (Answertestelle).

(b) "Fortress"

When observation is on the "fortress" system, a number of F.O.P's (Mess-stellen) (generally two or three per battery) are used. These are sited along the coast; the total length of the "base" thus formed is not likely to be less than 15,000 yards. The type of F.O.P. used is probably the revolving armoured cupola type. Bearings are transmitted to the predictor, probably by telephone.

7. The Battery Plotting Room

The predictor in the plotting room works out the data transmitted from the B.O.P. or F.O.P's and applies all necessary corrections, including corrections for individual guns. Ranges and bearings are then transmitted electrically to the guns. The command "fire" is given direct to the guns by the officer in charge of the plotting room, as ordered by the battery commander.

8. Gun Detachment

1. The chief loading number and firer.
2. Breech operator.
3. Range convertor and reporter of orders.
4. Cursor operator and range telephonist.
5. Operator of electrical elevating mechanism.
6. to 9. Operators of the manual elevating mechanism.
10. to 14. Rammer numbers.
15. Operator of the electrical traversing mechanism and bearing telephones.
16. Bearing convertor.
17. and 18. Operators of the bearing coarse handwheel.
19. Operator of the secondary charge hoist.
20. Operator of the secondary charge davit.
21. Operator of the main charge hoist.
22. Operator of the main charge davit.
23. Operator of the projectile hoist.
24. Operator of the projectile davit.
25. Electrical switch operator.
26. to 37. Projectiles cart numbers.
38. to 45. Traversing mechanism operators.
46. to 54. Ammunition numbers.

9. **Data:- 30.5 cm. S.K. L/50.**

    (a)
Calibre	305 mm	(12 ins.)
Length of piece (50 calibres)	1525 mm	(50 feet 3/8 ins.)
Length of barrel	1418.5 mm	(46 feet 6¾ ins.)
Length of rifling	1149 mm	(37 feet 8¾ ins.)
Length of chamber	269.5 mm	(8 feet 10 ins.)
No. of grooves in rifling	88	
Grooves-Depth	3 mm	(.12 ins.)
-Width	4.2 mm	(.165 ins.)
Lands -Width	6.68 mm.	(.26 ins.)
Elevation	-4° to + 45°	
Traverse - depends on local conditions	Up to 360°	
Maximum recoil	650 mm	(25 5/8 ins.)
Trunnion pull with full charge	380-400 m.t.	
Trunnion pull with large front charge	340-360 m.t.	
Trunnion pull with small front charge	300-310 m.t.	
Liquid content of each buffer	60 litres	(105 pints)
Liquid content of recuperator	51 litres	(89 pints)
Air pressure in recuperator	120 atmospheres	(1764 lbs per sq.in.)
Total weight of gun and mounting - (without turret or protective armour)	177 tonnes	(174.2 tons)

    (b) The three range scales indicate the following details:-

        (i) H.E. with ballistic cap, and Base or Nose Fuze.
Sprgr. L/3.6. m Bd Z u KZ. (m Haube)
M.V.   1120-1050 m.s. (3674-3445 f.s.)
Wt. of projectile 250 kg. (551 lbs.)
Range 9-51 km (5½ - 32 miles)

        (ii) Armour Piercing, with Base Fuze.
Pzgr. L/3.4. m Bd Z.
M.V. 855-820 m.s. (2805-2690 f.s.)
Wt. of projectile 405 kg. (893 lbs.)
Range 1.2-32.5 km (¾ - 20 miles)

        (iii) Practice charges (3 scales)
gr Übg Ldg. M.V. 730-700 m.s. (2395-2297 f.s.)
               Range 2.5-24.5 km (1½-15 miles)

kl Übg Ldg. M.V. 575-545 m.s. (1886-1788 f.s.)
               Range 1.8-17.2 km (1-10½ miles)

Abk Ldg. M.V. 437 m.s. (1434 f.s.)
(for sub-calibre attachment) Wt. of projectile 7 kg. (15¼ lbs.)
             Range 1.3-8.3 km (¾-5 miles)

U. **38 cm. S.K. C/34. (Siegfried) (15 inch Q.F. Gun Model 34)**
See figs:- 55 and 56.

1. The gun barrel used in this equipment was originally developed as a main armament for new battleships. For use in a coast defence role, the guns were modified by increasing the length of the chamber and by use of a special light weight long range shell. The gun barrel and cradle of this equipment was also fitted into a railway mounting, having the nomenclature of 38 cm. "Siegfried" Kanone. (E).

    In the coast defence role, the gun was enclosed in a turret within a massive casemate (emplacement). Although a 1934 development, the mounting and fire control equipment, etc, were of thoroughly modern design. Power ramming, elevation, and traverse were employed, giving what was claimed to be a rapid rate of fire.

    The gun piece is of built up construction and comprises "A" and "B" tubes, hooped jacket, removable breech ring and a horizontal sliding breech block, opening to the right.

FIG. 54. 30·5 cm. S.K. L/50.
(12 in. Q.F. Gun, Model L/50.)

The gun recoils through a ring or sleeve type cradle. The main cradle casting is bored to house the cylinders of the recoil system. The single hydro-pneumatic recuperator and the two hydraulic buffers are located below the gun barrel.

2. **Data:-** 38 cm. S.K. C/34.

(a)
Calibre	380 mm	(15 ins.)
Length of piece (52 calibres)	19630 mm	(64 feet 4¾ ins.)
Length of bore	18405 mm	(60 feet 4 3/8 ins.)
Length of rifling	15748 mm	(51 feet 8 ins.)
Length of breech ring	1500 mm	(4 feet 11 ins.)
Length of chamber to base of shell	2479 mm	(8 feet 1 3/8 ins.)
Capacity of chamber	361.7 litres	(80 galls)
Rifling - Increasing right hand twise - angle 5° 0'19" to 5° 58' 42"		
- No. of grooves	90	
- Depth of grooves	4.50 mm	(.177 ins.)
- Breadth of grooves	7.50 mm	(.295 ins.)
Lands - Breadth	5.70 mm	(.224 ins.)
Normal recoil	1050 mm	(41.375 ins.)
Life of barrel	250-350 rounds	
Weight of piece	105300 kg.	(103.6 ins.)
Elevation	-4° to + 60°	
Traverse	Limited by casemate	

(b) **Ballistic Performance**

(i) with standard H.E. projectile, weight 495 kg.(1091 lbs.):-

	Reduced Charge	Full Charge
Weight of charge	213.25 kg.(470 lbs)	258.25 kg.(569 lbs)
Muzzle Velocity	920 m.s. (3017 lbs)	1050 m.s. (3445 f.s.)
Chamber Pressure	2400 atmospheres (15.75 tons sq.in.)	3200 atmospheres (21 tons sq.in.)
Maximum range	40,000 metres(43750 yds)	55700 m (61000 yds)
Muzzle Energy	21350 m.t.(68940 ft/tons)	27810 m.t.(89899 ft/tons)

(ii) With 800 kg (1764 lbs) projectile, full charge:-

Muzzle Velocity	820 m.s.	(2690 f.s.)
Maximum Range	42,000 metres	(46,000 yards)

(iii) With 425 kg (937 lbs) projectile:-

Muzzle Velocity	920 m.s.	(3018 f.s.)
Maximum Range	40,000 metres	(43,750 yards)

(c) **Ammunition**

38 cm. Pzgr. L/4.4. (m Hb)	- A.P. Shell L/4.4 with Base Fuze.
38 cm. Sprgr. L/4.4 Bd Z (m Hb)	- H.E. Shell L/4.5 with Base Fuze.
38 cm. Sprgr. L/4.6. KZ (m Hb)	- H.E. Shell L/4.6 with Nose Fuze.
38 cm. Si-Gr. L/4.5. Bd Z u KZ (m Hb)	- Long Range H.E. Shell L/4.5 with Base and Nose Fuzes.

(all with ballistic cap)

All weigh 800 kg (1764 lbs), with ballistics as shown in sub-para. (b) (ii) above, except the latter, which is classed as the standard projectile, described in sub-para. (b) (i) above.

(d) **Dimensional details of the APCBC shell**

The shell is a straightforward German APCBC, even to the contour of the penetration cap, which is the same as that found with the smaller calibres. The fuze employed appears to be the standard Bd Z.C/38 - it is possible that Bd Z m V u K may have been used.

There are three copper driving bands and a "zinnring" for decoppering.

Dimensions:-

Length overall	169.0 cm.	(5 ft. 6½ in.)
Base to "zinnring"	2.0 cm.	(0.78 in.)
Width of "Zinnring"	2.0 cm.	(0.70 in.)
Width of first driving band	3.0 cm.	(1.18 in.)
First to second driving band	2.2 cm.	(0.87 in.)
Width of second driving band	3.0 cm.	(1.18 in.)
Second to third driving band	2.0 cm.	(0.78 in.)
Width of third driving band	4.0 cm.	(1.57 in.)
Third driving band to base of penetrating cap	56.5 cm.	(22.24 in.)
Base of penetrating cap to base of ballistic cap	27.8 cm.	(10.94 in.)
Overall right length of penetrative cap	41.3 cm.	(16.25 in.)
Length of ballistic cap (cast Al.alloy: screw-on)	66.5 cm.	(26.18 in.)

(e) **Cartridge Case**

The cartridge case is of solid drawn brass; the design being the 38 cm 34. The number 6597 was stamped at 9 o'clock on the base, but it is not thought that this is a design No. The primer (screwing directly into the case) is a C/12 nA St.

Dimensions:-

Diameter of base	47.3 cm.	(18.62 in.)
Diameter of mouth	44 cm.	(17.32 in.)
Wall thickness at mouth	3 cm.	(1.18 in.)
Length overall	81.8 cm.	(32.20 in.)
Thickness of rim	1.4 cm.	(0.55 in.)
Width	1.2 cm.	(0.47 in.)

(f) **Charges**

Hauptkartusche (packed in cartridge case)
111 kg (245 lbs) R P C/38 Bu. (850/820 x 17/7)

Vorkartusche (mit Bleiring) = (with decoppering agent).
101 kg (223 lbs) R P C/38 Bu. (800 x 17/7)

Sondervorkartusche (Augmenting charge)
13 kg R P. 38   (400 x 17/7)

V. **40.6 cm. S.K.C/34 (Adolf)** (16 ins Q.F. Gun Model 34.)
See figs:- 57 and 58.

1. Like the 38 cm. weapon, the gun piece of this equipment was also designed originally for use on new modern battleships, being developed about the same time (i.e. 1934). In some cases, the same type mounting was used for both weapons. Power ramming, elevation and traverse were employed, giving a rapid rate of fire. (The latter is believed to be about 1 round per 1½ to 2 minutes.) Emergency hand controls for manual operation were provided.

The gun is of built up construction, consisting of "A" and "B" tubes with hooped jacket and removable breech ring. The horizontal sliding breech block opens, in some cases, to the right and in others to the left. This would appear to substantiate the information that the guns

FIG. 55. 38 cm. S.K. C/34. ("Siegfried").
(15in. Q.F. Gun, Model '34.)

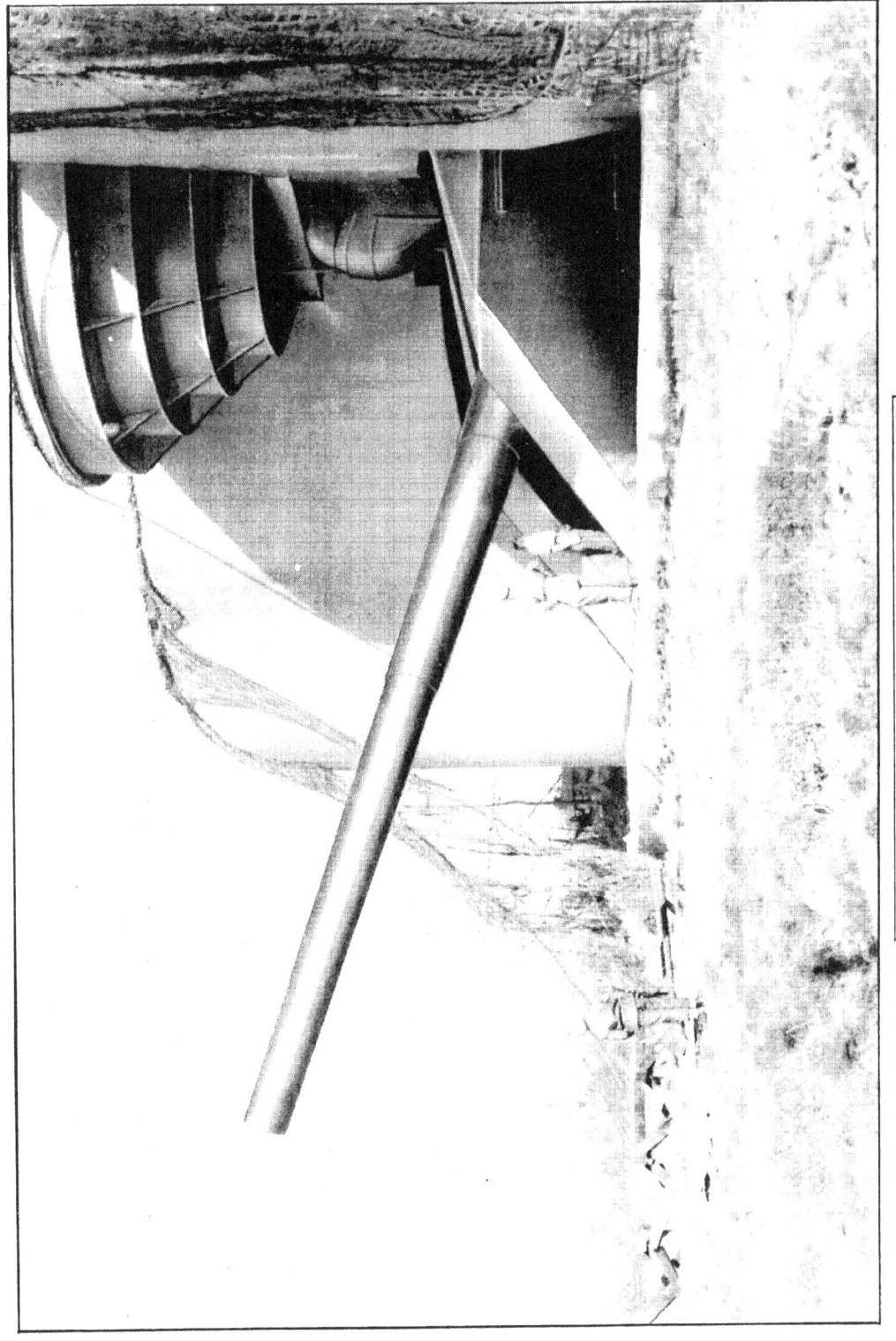

FIG. 56. 38 cm. S.K. C/34. (Siegfried).
(16in O.F. Gun, Model 34.)

were originally designed for naval gun turrets, twin or triple mounted.

The turret in this coast defence equipment was a single cupola with spaced armour. The cupola was mounted and pivoted on a solid conical concrete pedestal. The rear of the mounting traversed by means of bogie wheels over exposed traverse rails, the degrees of traverse being marked out along the rails.

The weapon was operated by electric power, except for the hydraulic ramming, provided by a diesel-electric plant in the casemate.

A feature of the sight, which is clearly of naval design, is that it is of the calibrating type, directly graduated in large curves on interchangeable steel scales. Corrections for variations in muzzle velocity are provided for by laying on different points on the range curves.

There were generally four magazines in the casemates, two for shells, and two for cartridges, connected by anti-flash double doors to the main turret chamber. From there the ammunition was conveyed on trollies, running on a circular track, to two electric hoists at the rear of the turret.

Fire control equipment varies slightly with the various defences. The fire commander was normally provided with a binocular periscope, the command post being located invariably below ground level. The 6 metre base rangefinder was mounted in a large armoured cupola. Giant Wurzburg radar installations were provided. Long base plotting boards, a mechanical meteor correction calculator and other calculating instruments were used. Modern electrical transmission gear was installed in most batteries.

2. **Data:- 40.6 cm. S.K.C/34.**

   (a) Calibre   406 mm   (16 ins.)
        Length of piece (50 calibres)   20300 mm   (66.6 feet)
        Elevation   - 0° to + 60°
        Traverse   Limited by casemate

   (b) **Ballistics**

        Full charge for Long Range H.E. shell:-
        Weight of projectile   600 kg   (1323 lbs)
        Muzzle velocity   1050-950 m.s. (3448-3115 f.s.)
        Maximum range   56,000 metres (61250 yards)
        Small charge for Long Range H.E. shells:-
        Muzzle velocity   970-870 m.s. (3180-2855 f.s.)
        Maximum range   46,700 metres (51,050 yards)
        Charge for Standard H.E. and A.P. projectiles:-
        Weight of projectiles   1030 kg   (2271 lbs)
        Muzzle velocity   810-730 m.s. (2655-2395 f.s.)
        Maximum range   42,800 metres (46,800 yards)

   (c) **Ammunition**

       (i) The following types of shell were fired:-

Nomenclature	Type
40.6 cm. Sprgr. L/4.6. m Bd Z (m Haube)	HE BC with nose fuze.
40.6 cm. Sprgr. L/4.8. KZ (m Haube)	HE BC with base fuze.
40.6 cm. Pzgr. L/4.4. (m Haube)	APCBC shell.
Adolf Gr. L/4.2. m Bd Z u KZ (m Haube)	HE BC with nose and base fuzes.

           The first three were unstreamlined of orthodox design and were classed as standard projectiles. Fuzes fitted were the KZ (or Kpf Z or E K Zdr). C/27 (Lm) or (Ms) or (St) and the Bd Z. C/38.

The latter was a special long range shell. It was fitted with 3 driving bands and a copper centering band at the shoulder. Fuzes fitted were the Bd Z 40 K and Hbgr Z 40 K or Dopp Z S/90 K.

(ii) The APCBC shells were standard type German projectiles and could be described as scaled-up versions of the 7.5 cm APCBC. The shells were fitted with a screw-on cast aluminium alloy ballistic cap and a base fuze Bd Z.C/38 under Gaine "A". Three copper driving bands were fitted, the shell base being square and not streamlined. The shells were painted yellow with all stencilling in black.

Dimensions:-

Overall length of shell	202.6 cm	(6 ft. 7¾ ins.)
Base to first driving band	4.5 cm	(1.77 in.)
Width of first driving band	3.0 cm	(1.18 in.)
First to second driving band	2.0 cm	(0.78 in.)
Width of second driving band	3.0 cm	(1.18 in.)
Second to third driving band	2.0 cm	(0.78 in.)
Width of third driving band	4.0 cm	(1.57 in.)
Approximate thickness of driving bands	1.0 cm	(0.39 in.)
Third driving band to base of penetrating cap	133.8 cm	(4 ft. 4½ in.)
Base of penetrating cap to base of ballistic cap	16.3 cm	(6.41 in.)
Length of ballistic cap	34. cm	(13.38 in.)

(iii) The H.E. shells were also fitted with three copper driving bands of the same dimensions and in the same position as on the APCBC shell. A screwed-in baseplate was fitted. The shells were fuzed with Kpf Z.C/27 (either in steel or light alloy), under a short ballistic cap. The fuze was actuated by a short "stossel" or hammer-rod, which terminated in a nose fitment screwed into the ballistic cap, and was closed with a wind shield (thin diaphragm). Certain of the shells were fitted with a slightly heavier nose fitment, which gave access to a small chamber in the nature of an exploder container. It is thought that this may have been for the use of a strike-indicating charge, which could have been fitted under the ballistic cap and detonated on impact by a nose fuze proper (the subsequent explosion giving the necessary blow to the striker of the shell fuze). This however cannot be confirmed.

The shells were painted yellow and stencilled in black.

Dimensions:-

Overall length	193.0 cm	(6 ft. 4 ins.)
Third driving band to base of ballistic cap	157.5 cm	(5 ft. 2 in.)
Length of ballistic cap	19 cm	(5 in.)
Protrusion of nose fitment	1 cm	(0.39 in.)

(iv) The practice shells were the same type, measurement and weight as the HE, but the shell colour was dull brick-red. Above the driving bands was stencilled "mit Kopfladung".

(v) Cartridge Case

The unusual thing about this was that, unlike all really heavy German cartridge cases, the case was of spirally fabricated steel construction. The case "design No" was 40.6 cm. W 34 St.

The full-length spiral was reinforced by a shorter outer spiral of steel. The primer, which screwed direct into the case and not (as in the railway guns) into a

Zündstrahlverstärker, was a C/12 nA St or C/12 K St.

Dimensions:-

Overall length	99.0 cm	(3 ft. 3 in.)
Thickness of rim	1.5 cm	(0.61 in.)
Width of rim	1.0 cm	(0.39 in.)
Rim to forward edge of base	1.5 cm	(0.59 in.)
Edge of base to end of lower spiral	15.4 cm	(6.06 in.)
Lower spiral to mouth	80.6 cm	(31.73 in.)
Diameter of base	47.8 cm	(18.82 in.)

(vi) Charges

There were two part charges: the Hülsenkartusche, packed in the cartridge case, and the Vorkartusche. The charges were packed in extremely efficient airtight metal cylinders. (Special charges were provided for the Adolf Gr.)

Hülsenkart:- 130 kg (287 lbs) R P 40. (865/825 x 12.5/4.2)
Igniter 600 gm (21 oz 2½ dr) grobk P (coarse-grain G P)

Vorkart:- 152 kg (335 lbs) R P 40 N. (1290/1275 x 12.5 /4.2)
Igniter 1200 gm (43 oz) grobk P

Vorkartusche:- 205 kg (452 lbs) Gu. R P. G. 5 (1290 x 10/3)
(Adolf Gr) Igniter 1200 g (43 ozs) schw P.

FIG. 57. 40.6 cm. S.K. C/34. ("Adolf").
(16 in. Q.F. Gun, Model 34.)

FIG. 58. 40·6 cm. S.K. C/34. ("Adolf").
(16 in. Q.F. Gun, Model 34.)

CHAPTER VI

THE DEVELOPMENT OF GERMAN RAILWAY ARTILLERY

General

1. Introduction

The earliest recorded use of railway artillery was during the American Civil War, when both sides mounted several types of muzzle loading guns and mortars on armoured trucks. The idea was quickly taken up by European countries. Experiments went on during the next fifty years, but there was little development till 1914. During the Great War, both sides produced many different types of carriages, mounting guns, howitzers and mortars of various calibres, up to a 52 cm. howitzer built by the French.

The main advantage of railway artillery is to give mobility to heavy guns, which would otherwise be virtually static. This means, on the one hand, that heavy guns can be concentrated quickly in the area where they are required, or switched at short notice from one area to another. On the other hand, it is possible to change the position of a gun after it has fired a few rounds, and so prevent the enemy from first locating it by sound-ranging or flash-spotting and then neutralising it by counter-battery fire or bombing.

Railway artillery may be classified according to the recoil system employed.

(a) Sliding mountings. The base is lowered till it rests on steel beams fixed parallel to the rails, so that most of the weight is transferred from the truck to the rails. The whole mounting slides to the rear in recoil, the recoil energy being absorbed by sliding friction. Usually, no traverse is possible on this type of gun, although sometimes the whole body may be traversed a few degrees. Traverse can be obtained only by moving the gun along the curved railway spur, from which it is fired.

(b) Rolling mountings. The carriage moves back on the track in recoil, on its own wheels. Part of the Recoil energy is absorbed by brakes and part by recoil cylinders on the gun. The gun is usually mounted on a cradle. It is fired from a curved spur, but in most types the gun itself can be traversed a few degrees. In many cases, a pit is dug below the track, leaving a free space to take the recoil of the gun.

(c) Platform mountings. This type is fitted with a recoil system to absorb the recoil, and does not move back on the rails. The necessary stability is provided by a special platform, from which, in most cases, two or four struts with spades are let down to the ground. According to the particular type, the platform can be traversed up to 360°. For these guns a curved spur is of course unnecessary.

It should be noted that for any railway gun, if a special track is not built, the existing tracks require special preparation.

Turntable positions for railway guns existed in nearly all strongly defended areas of the French and Belgian coasts. These turntables had all been built by the Germans since 1940. The structure was specially strengthened to take the weight of guns with calibres of 24 cm. to 32 cm. or more. There is some variation in the size of the turntables. They fall roughly into two groups, however, with diameters of 75 feet and 100 feet; the smaller type being the more numerous.

Generally speaking, the railway gun is designed for seige warfare and the bombardment of large targets. At great ranges, it is not a weapon of extreme accuracy, although the smaller guns on platform mountings may be regarded as more accurate than the heavier types on rolling mountings. It is accepted, however, that the accuracy of the heavier types is increased by firing them from turntables, rather than spurs.

The rate of fire will always be comparatively slow; roughly it may be estimated at one round in three or four minutes, except in the case of light calibres.

Krupp designed all the railway guns used by the German Army, although Rheinmetall-Borsig developed projects, which were never built, for 15 cm. and 24 cm. guns with all round traverses. The development of railway artillery falls into two distinct sections, firstly the long term design, and secondly an emergency programme, started in 1936. The latter will be considered first.

2. The Emergency Programme of 1936.

This programme called for the production of the maximum number of railway guns in the shortest possible time. In order to execute this order, old railway gun designs of the last war were extracted from the Krupp archives and reworked, in order to simplify production. The barrels, and, as far as possible, the cradle and recoil mechanisms were taken from ex-naval ordnance in stock in various depots.

Many of the barrels were constructed at the beginning of the century and all of them before 1918.

(a) The following list gives some details of the guns and the quantity produced:

(i) 15 cm. K. (E)

(5.9 ins)
(E) = Railway Mounting.

Based on the piece and cradle of the 15 cm. S.K. L/40. The carriage gave all round traverse. Four equipments were produced, construction starting in 1937 and finishing in 1938. Performance was as follows:-

Shell Wt.	M.V.	Max Range
43 kg (95 lbs.)	805 (2640 f.s.)	20000 metres. (21,870 yds.)

(ii) 17 cm. K. (E)
(6.7 ins.)

Based on the piece and cradle of the 17 cm. S.K. L/40. Same carriage as the 15 cm. K. (E). Six equipments were produced, construction starting in 1937 and finishing in 1938. Performance was as follows:-

Shell Wt.	M.V.	Max Range
62.8 kg (138 lbs)	875 m/sec (2870 f.s.)	27,000 metres. (29,300 yds.)

(iii) Theodor Bruno. K.(E)
(Calibre 24 cm.)
(9.45 inch)
Based on the piece of the 24 cm. S.K. L/35. Six equipments were produced, starting in 1937 and finishing at the beginning of 1939. Performance was as follows:-

Shell Wt.   M.V.   Max. Range

151 kg   670 m.s.   20000 metres
(232.2 lbs.)   (2200 f.s.) (21870 yds.)

(iv) Theodor. K.(E)
(Calibre 24 cm.)
(9.45 inch)
The original name for this gun was the Theodor Karl, but the latter part was dropped. The gun is based on the piece and cradle of the 24 cm. S.K. L/40. Three equipments were produced, starting in 1936 and finishing in 1937. Performance was as follows:-

Shell Wt.   M.V.   Max. Range

148.5 kg   810 m/s   26600 metres
(326.7 lbs.)   (2657 f.s.) (29,100 yds.)

(v) kurze Bruno K. (E)
(Calibre 28 cm.)
(11 inch)
Based on the piece of the 28 cm. S.K. L/40. Eight equipments were produced, starting in 1937 and finishing in 1938. Performance was as follows:-

Shell Wt.   M.V.   Max. Range

240 kg   820 m.s.   29500 metres
(529 lbs.)   (2690 f.s.) (32250 yds.)

(vi) lange Bruno. K. (E)
(Calibre 28 cm.)
(11 inch)
Based on the 28 cm. S.K. L/45. Three equipments were produced, starting in 1936 and finishing in 1937. Performance was as follows:-

Shell Wt.   M.V.   Max. Range

284 kg   875 m.s.   36100 metres
(624.8 lbs.)   (2870 f.s.) (39480 yds.)

(vii) schwere Bruno. K. (E)
(Calibre 28 cm.)
(11 inch)
Based on the 28 cm. Küst K. L/42. Two equipments were produced, starting in 1936 and finishing in 1938. Performance was as follows:-

Shell Wt.   M.V.   Max. Range

284 kg   860 m/s   36700 metres
(624.8 lbs.)   (2820 f.s.) (39050 yds.)

(b) Two other guns can be conveniently considered in this section, Bruno neue K. (E) and 20 cm. K. (E). Though not strictly part of the 1936 programme, they form nevertheless a continuation of the same trend and do not form part of the long term design.

(c) While the lange and schwere Br. K. (E) were still in production in the spring of 1938, the Heereswaffenamt expressed a desire for a greater range from the guns, possibly up to that of the 28 cm. K. 5 (E) (62,000 m). After due consideration of this project, Krupp replied that none of the guns could be modified, involving the construction of a new barrel, in the time available, while adhering to the very latest delivery date ordered of early spring 1939. Development of the new barrels was continued and the lg Bruno carriages were later modified to carry them. In all, three equipments were produced, one at the end of 1940, one in the middle of 1941 and one at the beginning of 1942. It had been intended to produce more, but this plan appears to have been cancelled owing to the better performance of the 28 cm. K. 5 (E); also the trouble caused by ossasional peak pressures in the barrel could not be accounted for. Performance was as follows:-

Shell Wt.	M.V.	Max. Range
255 kg	995 m/sec	46600 m.
(561 lbs.)	(3264 f.s.)	(51,000 yds.)

(d) The basic reason for the construction of the 20 cm. K. (E) (according to Krupp) was that eight 20.3 cm. S.K. C/34 were being made at Essen. These were taken over for railway mountings.

Since eight barrels complete with cradle were available, eight equipments were to be built, construction to be completed by the end of 1941. No sooner had the work on this project started than the Heereswaffenamt realised that these eight guns would be the only ones in the army with a calibre of 20.3 cm. It was decided therefore to convert them to the standard army calibre of 21 cm. This project proved impossible for the eight barrels, which were already completed, with a calibre of 20.3 cm.

The design of the new 21 cm. barrels, which would change the name of the gun to the 21 cm. K. (E), was undertaken with the intention that, as soon as the first set of 20.3 cm. barrels were worn out, the calibre of the 20.3 cm. would be dropped. The new gun, though externally the same as the 20.3 cm. barrel, was to be internally the same as the 21 cm. K.38, except for the fact that the bore of the 21 cm. K. (E) was to be 443 mm longer. The performance of the new gun was to be as follows:

Shell Wt.	M.V.	Max. Range
120 kg	940 m.s.	36000 m.
(264 lbs.)	(3083 f.s.)	(39370 m.)

Although this differs from the M.V. of the 21 cm. K. 38 (930 m.s.), the same range table was to be used. By July 1944, four of the new barrels had been made and production was continuing on a further four. None were ever fitted to a gun, since six, out of the eight, were captured in the Cherbourg and Brest areas by the Allied Armies.

3. Long Term Development

(a) Concrete work on two projects, the 21 cm. K.12. (E) (8 inch gun) and 28 cm. K.5 (E) (11 inch gun), was started in 1934. Although definite projects were not started until this date, a great deal of study had already been devoted to the consideration of various possible designs. In addition, the portable railway gun turntable, the "sine qua non" of all new designs, had already been tried out and was almost fully developed. One of the great incentives behind the development of the 21 cm. K. 12. (E) was the use of the Paris Gun in the last war. The latter had been developed and manned exclusively by the German Navy; the Army artillery branch considered this an intolerable slur on their capabilities. Initial work on this subject was started therefore immediately after the treat of Versailles.

Sub-calibre model barrels, for the early interior ballistic trials, were made for both the two new projects. The one for the 21 cm. K. 12. (E) being of 10.5 cm. calibre and that for the 28 cm. K. 5. (E). of 15 cm. calibre. „They were known as the K. 12. M and K.5. M (Suffix St = Stegführung, sometimes added) respectively. These two barrels were rifled for firing splined shell, with eight splines in the case of the K.12 and twelve in the case of K.5. In addition, two barrels were made with normal rifling, known as the K.12. M.Ku and K.5. M.Ku, to see if it was possible to develop a normal copper driving band to function at the high velocity required. The further development of each gun is best considered separately. In each case, the chronological order of development will be considered.

(b) 28 cm. K.5.(E). (11 inch Gun Model 5.(Railway Mounting)).

1934	Project started and model barrel constructed.
1936	First full calibre barrel proof fired.
1937	First trial equipment proof fired.
1940	A serious outbreak of split barrels occurred, in all about 5 inner tubes being split from one end to the other. After very careful consideration, no definite conclusions were reached as to the cause, but the depth of rifling was altered from 10 to 7 mm. in the hope that it would help to minimise the occurrence.
1940-43	Owing to the development of FEW soft iron driving bands, the project of employing a normal rifled barrel and driving band was reopened. Finally, by the end of 1943, the production version, known as the K.5. Vz, was produced with conical rifling grooves and a soft iron (not sintered) umbrella driving band. Very few of these barrels and their accompanying ammunition had been produced by the end of the war.
1942-45.	The development of the fin-stabilised sub-calibre projectile was applied very early to an experimental K.5 barrel, smooth bored to 31 cm. However, it was not until 1945 that the development of the projectile had progressed far enough for the equipment to be used in action and then only on an experimental scale.

It would seem best, before describing the further developments of the K.5, which were still under consideration at the end of the war, to review the situation at that date. In 1937, the first gun appeared, by Feb 1940 eight were in service and by the end of the war about 25 had been built. This means that the production during the war was about 3 a year and, in fact, was still continuing. An amusing point was that, owing to the popularity of the gun, it was renamed "schlanke Bertha" (Slim Bertha) in 1944. During the long period of service of the guns, a barrel life as high as 550 rounds and as low as 240 rounds had been achieved, discounting the split barrels.

During the war, four versions of the K.5 were all in use side by side. The nomenclature of these versions is somewhat vague. In order of appearance, they were as follows:-

(i) K.5.Tiefzug.10 mm, also known as K.5.St.
(St = Stegführung = rifled for splined projectiles.)
(Tiefzug = deep rifling groove)

(ii) K.5. Tiefzug. 7 mm.

(iii) K.5. Vielzug. (Normal rifled barrel). Krupp deny all knowledge of the nomenclatures K.5/1 and K.5/2, which appear in the Range Tables. The performance is as follows:-

Wt. of Shell	M.V.	Max. Range
255 kg (561 lbs.)	1120 m/sec (3675 f.s.)	61000 metres (66700 yds.)

A special Rocket Assisted Shell is also fired to a maximum range of 86000 metres. (94,060 yds.)

(iv) K.5. Glatt. (smooth bore). Calibre 31 cm.

Throughout the whole period, the carriage design remained unchanged, except for very minor modifications. On certain of the early carriages, the front of the cradle has four extra brackets formed on it, two above and two below the barrel. These can be seen on early photographs of the K.5. When originally designed, the piece included a cantilever barrel bracing structure, which was attached to these brackets. After the preliminary ballistic trials, it was realised that the bracing had no effect, even on the accuracy, and its inclusion in the design was dropped; but by then the first lot of cradles had been cast.

Various projects, connected with K.5, had been considered and dropped during the life of the gun; of these, two are of interest. The first was a B.L. breech mechanism of the interrupted screw-thread type. The contract for this project was given in 1943; the main incentive being the elimination of the use of cartridge cases. The supply of the latter was already a bottleneck at that date. In addition, Krupp considered that the new breech mechanism would be lighter, and also shorter, than the normal sliding wedge type. The latter point was of special advantage, since the barrel could then be moved to the rear, relative to the trunnions; this decreased the preponderance of the gun. First trials of the basic design, applied to a 21 cm. gun, resulted in complete failure and, with the prospect of the development of a suitable caseless sliding breech block mechanism, the subject was dropped to a very low priority.

The other project was for a muzzle brake, in order to permit an increase in the performance of the gun. After initial consideration, the subject was dropped.

In 1943, a far wider and more concrete project was started. This was based on the General Staff's appreciation that, with the mounting enemy air offensive, a railway gun must be made capable of traversing stretches of country where the railway bridges and track had been destroyed by bombing. A new specification was issued for the K.5 ERF. (Eisenbahn Runden Feld). Development of this specification had reached the point, where detailed design work on the final version had started.

The basic idea for the new project was for a railway gun, which could be lowered to the ground from its two bogies by hydraulic jacks in the bogie pivots. The centre section of the gun carriage, clear of the two bogies, was to carry a base plate, fitted with outrigger arms, and equipped with a turntable to give 360° traverse. In the lowered position, the two bogies would be run clear and the gun would be ready to open fire.

In order to make it capable of movement across country, the gun was designed so that it could be split up into several loads. A new tractor was being designed to carry these loads, based on the chassis of the Tiger II tank. In addition, special gear was being developed, so that two of the tractors could form bogies to carry one load between them.

The cradle of the equipment was to be capable of carrying either a 28 cm. gun or a 38 cm. howitzer. The 28 cm. gun was to be

ballistically identical with the K.5. Vz. The only change
made was the introduction of an interrupted screw thread joint
between the barrel and the breech ring, so that the two might
be separated for transport.

The idea of mounting a 38 cm. howitzer in the carriage of the
K.5. had been pressed by Krupp for some time, but it was not
until the new specification of the K.5. ERF. was issued, that
it received official approval. The new howitzer was to be
equipped with a sliding breech block, fitted with some form of
ring obturation. Performance was to be as follows:

Shell Wt.	M.V.	Max. Range
800 kg	540 to 600 m.s.	20 to 25000 metres
(1764 lbs)	(1770 to 1920 f.s.)	(21870 to 27340 yds.)

(c) 21 cm. K.12. (E) (8.3 inch Gun Model 12.(Railway Mounting)).

1934	Project started.
1935	Model barrel proof fired.
1937	First full calibre barrel proof fired.
1938	First equipment 21 cm. K.12 V. proof fired.
1939	21 cm. K.12.V. brought into service in the spring.
1940	21 cm. K.12.V. brought into service in the summer.

The original trials with the 10.5 cm. K.12. M. barrel showed
that there was no hope of any form of rifling, other than that
employing splines. No further developments for a soft iron
driving band as for the K.5. Vz. have ever been attempted.
The original barrel was known as the K.12. St., but the "St"
was later dropped as no other form of rifling was attempted.

When the carriage design was started, the designers were very
worried at the excessive muzzle preponderance of the barrel.
In order to reduce this as far as possible, the whole carriage
was raised about 1 metre in the firing position, so as to give
an increased clearance above the rails and thus allow the
barrel to be mounted further to the rear in the cradle. The
carriage was raised by two hydraulically operated jacks,
situated in the bogie bolsters. The sequence of operation
was as follows:- load, raise carriage, elevate gun, fire,
depress gun, lower carriage, open breech.

The first carriage produced to this design was known as the
K.12.V. and it operated reasonably well. In the firing
position, it was mounted in a special version of the standard
railway gun turntable. The main disadvantages were the
additional complication of the carriage raising gear, the great
diameter of the turntable required and the number of movements
required in firing.

As a result of the above difficulties, a new design known as the
K. 12. N. was started, before the construction of K.12. V. had
been completed. From the experience with the first design, it
was clear that balancing presses could be operated at far
higher pressures than had hitherto been thought possible. In
the new design, therefore, the barrel was mounted in the cradle
as far forward as possible. The resulting disequilibrium was
compensated for by a single hydro-pneumatic balancing press.

In all, one of each type of carriage was built; the two barrels
were almost identical. The performance was as follows:-

Wt. of Shell	M.V.	Max. Range	Life of Barrel
107.5 kg	1630 m.s.	120 km	about 100 to
(236.5 lbs.)	(5315 f.s.)	(75 miles)	150 rounds.

Krupp were of the opinion that as a gun, the project was a complete waste of money; but as a piece of ballistic and carriage research, it was amply justified.

(d) 38 cm. Siegfried. K.(E). (15 inch Siegfried Gun. (Railway Mounting)).
40 cm. Adolf. K. (E) (16 inch Adolf Gun (Railway Mounting)).

In 1938, as a result of the experience with the guns already tried out, it was decided to construct heavier railway guns. In order not to waste time in the development of a new barrel, the current 38 and 40.6 cm. naval gun designs were to be used. These two guns, the 38 cm. S.K. C/34 and 40.6 cm. S.K. C/34 had originally been designed as the main armament for new battleships. For use in a coastal artillery role, the guns were modified by increasing the length of the chamber and by the use of a special light-weight long-range shell. The C.D. version of the guns was used.

The projects were therefore developed, one for a 38 cm. and one for a 40.6 cm. railway gun. During the design of the 40.6 cm. equipment, it became clear that it would be difficult to design a suitable carriage and at the same time clear the railway loading gauge. The 40.6 cm. project was therefore postponed and all energies concentrated on the 38 cm. Siegfried. In 1939, the production of eight equipments was ordered, but it was not until the middle of 1943 that the first was put into service. Only three had been completed by the end of the war.

The performance of the 38 cm. Siegfried. K. (E) is as follows:

Wt. of Shell	M.V.	Max. Range
495 kg (1092 lbs.)	1050 m/sec (3445 f.s.)	5500 metres (60,150 yds.)

(e) A further grandiose project resulted in the production of two 80 cm. guns on railway mountings. These were given the code names of "Gustav Gerät" or "schwere Gustav" and "Dora Gerat". One of these guns fired against Sebastopol. These equipments weighed some 1350 metric tons in action and operated from a specially constructed four-track railway mounting. The barrel of 40.6 calibres length has a two-piece liner, secured by means of a locking nut. The breech block is of the horizontal sliding-wedge type, hydraulically operated. Performance is as follows:-

	Wt. of Shell	M.V.	Max. Range
Anti-concrete (standard)	7100 kg (7 tons)	700 m/sec 2296 f.s.)	38000 metres (41,560 yds.)
H.E. (light)	4800 kg (4.72 tons)	820 m/sec (2690 f.s.)	47000 metres. (51,400 yds.)

Rate of fire is recorded as one round in 20 mins. The gun detachment numbered some 3000 men, commanded by a Major General.

(f) A further project was for the construction of a 52 cm. gun 87 calibres long, to be known as the "lange Gustav". (Firing a rocket assisted shell of 1580 kg with a muzzle velocity of 1240 met/sec.). It was hoped to attain a max range of 150 kilometres.

4. It is interesting to record that the demand for increased performance of these super-heavy equipments led to projects for the development of specialised long range projectiles, of which the PPG seemed to offer the most satisfactory solution. This was part of the

programme sponsored by the Commission for Long Range Firing, which, in addition to the high priority given to V1 and V2 development, also pressed for increase in artillery range up to 150 km.

5. The following list contains comparative basic data for the more important projects for increased range, which were being considered early in 1944.

EQUIPMENT	PROJECTILE	CALIBRE (cms)	WEIGHT (kg)	M.V. (m.s.)	MAX. RANGE AT 52° ELEVATION (km)
"lange Gustav"	HE (normal)	52	1420	1290	110
	HE SABOT	52/38	1580	1560	150
	HE SABOT (rocket assisted)	52/38	1680	1490 + 180	190
"schwere Gustav"	P.P.G.	80/32	2000	1375 / 1280	160 / 140
	P.P.G.	80/30.5	1730	1385	160
K.12.	HE	21	107.5	1625	117
K.5. (rifled)	P.P.G.	28/12	149/114	1430	135
K.5. (smooth bore)	P.P.G.	31/12	172/125	1460	147

B. 15 cm. Kanone. (Eisenbahn). (5.9 inch Gun (Railway Mounting)). See Fig:- 59.

1. This railway mounting equipment, designed and produced by Krupp of Essen before 1937, was introduced into service during that year. It was one of the earliest of modern German designs and only a very limited number were made, the gun being quickly superceded by the heavier 17 cm. and other equipments. The gun is the naval S.K. L/40, used formerly in a coast defence role.

The piece was of the built-up multi-tube and jacket type. The open jaw breech ring is fitted with a vertical sliding breech block. Two recoil slides are fitted to the jacket, one on either side.

The muzzle preponderance of the gun is balanced by the breech counterweight.

The cradle is of the sleeve type with side plates, which carry slide ways for the piece recoil slides and the trunnions. The upper and lower fabricated sections of the cradle carry the hydraulic buffer below the barrel and the recuperator above the barrel. The recuperator consists of two cylinders one eccentrically inside the other, the inner one forming the liquid cylinder and the outer one the oil and air cylinder. The pistons of the recoil system are connected to the recoiling band of the piece.

The saddle is of orthodox design and is extended, to the rear and sides, to form a platform for the gun detachment.

The saddle is mounted on a ball race, which rests on the bottom plate of the truck.

The sighting is of the standard German type with sight and elevation reader arms.

The truck mounting consists of two three-axled bogies, on which are mounted the well platform. The springs of all six axles are locked in the firing position by screw jacks, which are fixed to the bogie body and screw down on to the top of the springs. In action, the platform is supported against tipping thrusts by four outriggers, which hinge out from the side of the truck and have screw jacks at their outer ends. In addition four screw jacks, mounted below the well of the platform, bear on the rails whilst in action. Horizontal stresses along the rails are taken by screw clamps, which grip the rails underneath the well of the platform, and by dogs, which lock the bogie wheels.

2. Data: 15 cm. K. (E).

	Metric	British
(a)		
(i) Piece		
Calibre of Barrels Nos. 5, 7 & 8.	149.1 mm.	5.87 in.
" " " No. 23	149.3 mm.	5.88 in.
Length, (40 calibres) with breech ring	5690 mm.	234.6 in.
Depth of breech opening	389 mm.	15.32 in.
Length of bore	5571 mm.	219.5 in.
Length of rifling (30 calibres)	4470 mm.	176.0 in.
Number of grooves	44	
Depth of Rifling:- Barrels Nos. 5, 7 & 8	1.5 mm.	0.059 in.
" No. 23	1.4 mm.	0.055 in.
Width of grooves	7.15 mm.	.281 in.
" " lands	3.5 mm.	.138 in.
Length of chamber	1101 mm.	43.4 in.
Capacity of chamber	21.1 litres	1281.5 cu.in.
Weight of Piece. (incl. slides and balancing weights)	5800 kg.	1279 lbs.
Weight of Breech Mechanism	110 kg.	243 lbs.
(ii) Mounting:-		
Elevation	10° to 45°	
One turn of main elevation handwheel	1° 11.5'	
Traverse	360°	
One turn of main traversing handwheel	1° 22.5'	
Height of axis of bore	3200 mm.	126.0 in.
Recoil Normal	590 mm.	232.3 in.
" Maximum	620 mm.	244.1 in.
" To beating faces	650 mm.	225.9 in.
Capacity of Buffer	31.51 litres	6 gall. 7½ pt.
Capacity of Recuperator - liquid	44.1 litres	9 gall. 5¼ pt.
" " - gas	33.1 litres	7 gall. 2½ pt.
Initial Recuperator Pressure	50 kg. sq. cm.	711 lb. sq. in.
Minimum permissible elevation of 10° =	11,300 metres	12350 yards.
(iii) Truck:-		
Wheel base of three-axle bogie	2 x 1,500 mm.	4 ft. 11 in.
Wheel base of two bogies (centre to centre)	12,800 mm.	42 ft. 11 in.
Overall length, buffer to buffer	20,100 mm.	65 ft. 11¼ in.
Weight less piece	53,400 kg.	52 ton. 11 cwt.
" incl. piece	74,000 kg.	72 ton. 16 cwt.
Axle load, uniform	12,200 kg.	12 ton.

(b) Ballistic Performance   Metric   British

		Metric	British
Muzzle Velocity	with 15 cm. K. Gr. 18	805 m.s.	2640 f.s.
Maximum Range		22,500 m.	24,610 yds.
Chamber Pressure		3,150 atmospheres	
Muzzle Energy		1420 m.t.	

(c) Ammunition

(i) Shell:-

Nomenclature	Range table wt.	Wt. of H.E. filling	Fuzes fitted
15 cm. K.Gr.18	43.0 kg. (95 lb)	5.688 kg. (12.5 lb.)	A.Z.23v.(0.15) Dopp.Z. S/90.
15 cm. Gr.19 Be.	43.5 kg. (96.2 lb)	3.144 kg. (6.92 lb.)	Bd. Z. für 15 cm. Gr.19. Be.

The 15 cm. K. Gr. 18 is a normal H.E. shell.

The 15 cm. Gr. 19. rot Be. is an anti-concrete (S.A.F.) shell with ballistic cap and base fuze.

(ii) Fuzes:-

A.Z. 23v (0.15) is a nose D.A. and graze action nose fuze with an optional delay of 0.15 secs.

Dopp. Z. S/90 is a mechanical time and graze action fuze with a maximum running time of 90 secs.

Bd.Z. für 15 cm. Gr.19 Be. is a base graze action fuze with a fixed delay of 0.05 secs. and optional delay of 0.5 secs.

(iii) Propelling Charges:-
Make up of Charges:-

               Muzzle Velocities

Small Charge = Grundladung + Sonderkart 1 600 m/s (1970 f.s.)
Middle Charge = Grundladung + Teilkart 2 725 m/s (2380 f.s.)
Full Charge = Grundladung + Teilkart 2 + 3 805 m/s (2640 f.s.)

Name	Weight kg.	lbs.	Propellant and Granulation
Grundladung (Basic Charge)	0.1 / 0.4	.22 / .88	Nz. Man. N.P. (1.5 x 1.5) (Igniter) Ngl. R.P. - 9.5 - (10 x 10/4)
Sonderkart 1 (Special Charge 1)	7.2	15.8	Ngl. R.P. - 9.5 - (495 x 6.5/3)
Teilkart 2 (Part Charge 2)	11.8	26	Ngl. R.P. - 9.5 - (750 x 10/4)
Teilkart 3	1.5	3.5	Ngl. R.P. - 9.5 - (750 x 10/4)

(iv) Propellant:-

Nz. Man. N.P. is a porous double base propellant containing D.E.G.N. in the form of chopped cord, the dimensions being given in brackets in mm.
Ngl. R.P. - 9.5 - is tubular cordite incorporating 9.5% Potassium sulphate, the dimensions being given in brackets in mm.

FIG. 59. 15cm. K.(E).
(5·9 in. GUN on RAILWAY MOUNTING.)

(v) Cartridge Case:-

Three types of cartridge case, of the same dimensions, are available:-

Solid drawn brass, with case design No. 6352

Solid drawn steel, brass plated with case design No. 6352 St.

Built up, wrapped steel case, oxide protected - case design No. 6352/75C.

(vi) Primer:-

The standard German primer C/12 n.A. or E/12 n.A. St. is used.

C. 17 cm. Kanone. (Eisenbahn). (6.8 inch Gun (Railway Mounting)). See Fig 60.

1. Mounted on the same railway mounting as that used with the 15 cm. Kanone. (E), the piece and cradle is that of the 17 cm. S.K. L/40 (Naval and coast defence gun, 40 calibres long). Six equipments were produced, construction commencing in 1937 and being completed in 1938.

The gun is of the multi-tube and jacket built-up type. The open jaw breech ring is fitted with a sliding breech block. Two recoil slides are fitted to the jacket, one on either side.

The cradle is of the sleeve type with a fabricated structure above and below, which houses the recoil system. The hydraulic buffer is located below the barrel and the twin spring recuperator above the barrel.

The remainder of the superstructure and also the railway mounting are of similar design to that used with the 15 cm. K. (E).

2. Data: 17 cm. K. (E).

	Metric	British
(a) Calibre	172.6 mm.	6.8 ins.
Length of piece (40 calibres)	6900 mm.	271.6 ins.
Length of rifling	4991.5 mm.	196.5 ins.
Type of rifling. Increasing right hand twist $4°$ to $6°$.		
Chamber capacity	31.7 litres	7 galls.
Elevation	$+10° + 45°$	
Rate of Elevation. 1 Turn of handwheel	$1°$	$11\frac{1}{2}'$
Traverse	$360°$	
Rate of Traverse. 1 Turn of handwheel	$1°$	$22\frac{1}{2}'$
Gun Barrel recoil.	340 mm.	13.4 ins.
Height of axis of bore	3250 mm.	128 ins.
No. of charges		One
Weight of standard projectile	62.8 kg.	138 lbs.
Muzzle velocity	875 m/s	2870 f.s.
Chamber Pressure	3100 atmospheres	20.35 Tons sq.in.
Muzzle Energy	2637 m.t.	
Maximum Range	26800 metres	29,300 yds.
Minimum permissible elevation of $10°$ =	13,350 metres	14,750 yds.
Weight in action	80,000 kg.	78.74 Tons
Overall length of railway mounting.	20,100 mm.	65 feet. 11 ins.

(b) Ammunition

Shell:- H.E. 17 cm. Sprgr. L/4.7 KZ. (m.Haube). Weight = 138 lbs.
Fuzes:- E.K. drf. Sprgr or M.Dopp. Z.S/90.
Primer:- C/12 n.A or C/12 n.A. St.
Igniter:- 200 g. (3086 grains) Black Powder.

(c) Propellant Charges
C.32 Tubular   C.12 Tubular
33.6 kg. (52 lbs.)   22.6 kg. (50 lbs.)

FIG. 60. 17 cm. K. (E).
(6·8 in. GUN on RAILWAY MOUNTING.)

D.   20 cm. Kanone. (E). (8 inch Gun (Railway Mounting)). See Fig:- 61.

1.   The basic reason for the construction of the 20 cm. K.(E) (according to Krupp) was that eight 20.3 cm. S.K. C/34 were being made at Essen. These were taken for railway mountings. The gun is of naval design and naval ammunition was used.

As for the earlier guns developed in 1936, an old design for the carriage of a great war gun, known as "Peter Adalbert" was reworked.

Since eight barrels complete with cradle were available, eight equipments were to be built; construction to be completed by the end of 1941. Actually the equipments were delivered to service in 1940. No sonner had the work on this project started than it was realised that these eight guns would be the only ones in the army with a calibre of 20.3 cm. It was therefore decided that it would be better to convert them to 21 cm., a standard army calibre. This project proved impossible for the eight barrels, which were already completed with a calibre of 20.3 cm.

The piece is of jacket and tube with loose liner construction. The breech ring is fitted with a horizontal sliding breech block.

The cradle is of the sleeve type with provision for housing the two hydraulic buffers below the barrel and the single hydro-pneumatic recuperator above the barrel.

The firing carriage is supported on two four-axle bogies.

Traverse of 360 degrees is provided by using a portable turntable. This is composed of a circular track, set over the main track, which supports a power traversing element. The gun and carriage are rolled on to the turntable by using a ramp.

For fire control, a long base plotting board is used with the data telephoned to the guns, when used in a coast defence role.

The minimum curve radius for travelling is 180 inches.

It was intended to replace the 20.3 cm guns, when worn out, with new 21 cm. guns, which had been designed for railway mounting. The new gun, though externally the same as the 20.3 cm, would be internally the same as the 21 cm. K.38, except that the bore of the 21 cm. K. (E) was to be 443 mm longer.

The performance of the 21 cm. K. (E) was to be therefore:-
Projectile Weight = 120 kg (264 lbs). Muzzle Velocity = 940 m/s
3085 f.s.) Max Range = 39,400 yds.

2.   Data: 20 cm. Kanone. (E)

	Metric	British
(a) Calibre	203 mm.	8 ins.
Length of piece (60 calibres)	12150 mm.	478.34 ins.
Length of barrel	11587 mm.	456.17 ins.
Length of rifling (64 grooves)	9527 mm.	375 ins.
Type of rifling - Increasing right hand twist. 4° to 5°.		
Chamber Capacity	70 litres	15.4 galls.
Height of the axis of the bore	3000 mm.	118 ins.
Barrel recoil	680 mm.	24.8 ins.
Weight of piece	20700 kg.	20.37 tons
Elevation	+ 10° to + 47°	
Traverse. No carriage traverse.	360° Turntable	
Weight of standard projectile	122 kg.	268.4 lbs.
Maximum Range	36,400 metres	39,800 yds.
Muzzle velocity	925 m/s	3035 f.s.
Chamber pressure	3200 atmospheres	21 Tons sq.in.
Muzzle Energy	5320 m.t.	
Rate of Fire	1 round per 3 minutes.	
Overall length of equipment	19445 mm.	765.55 ins.
Weight in action	86100 kg.	84.75 Tons.
Minimum permissible elevation of 10° = 13,700 metres.		

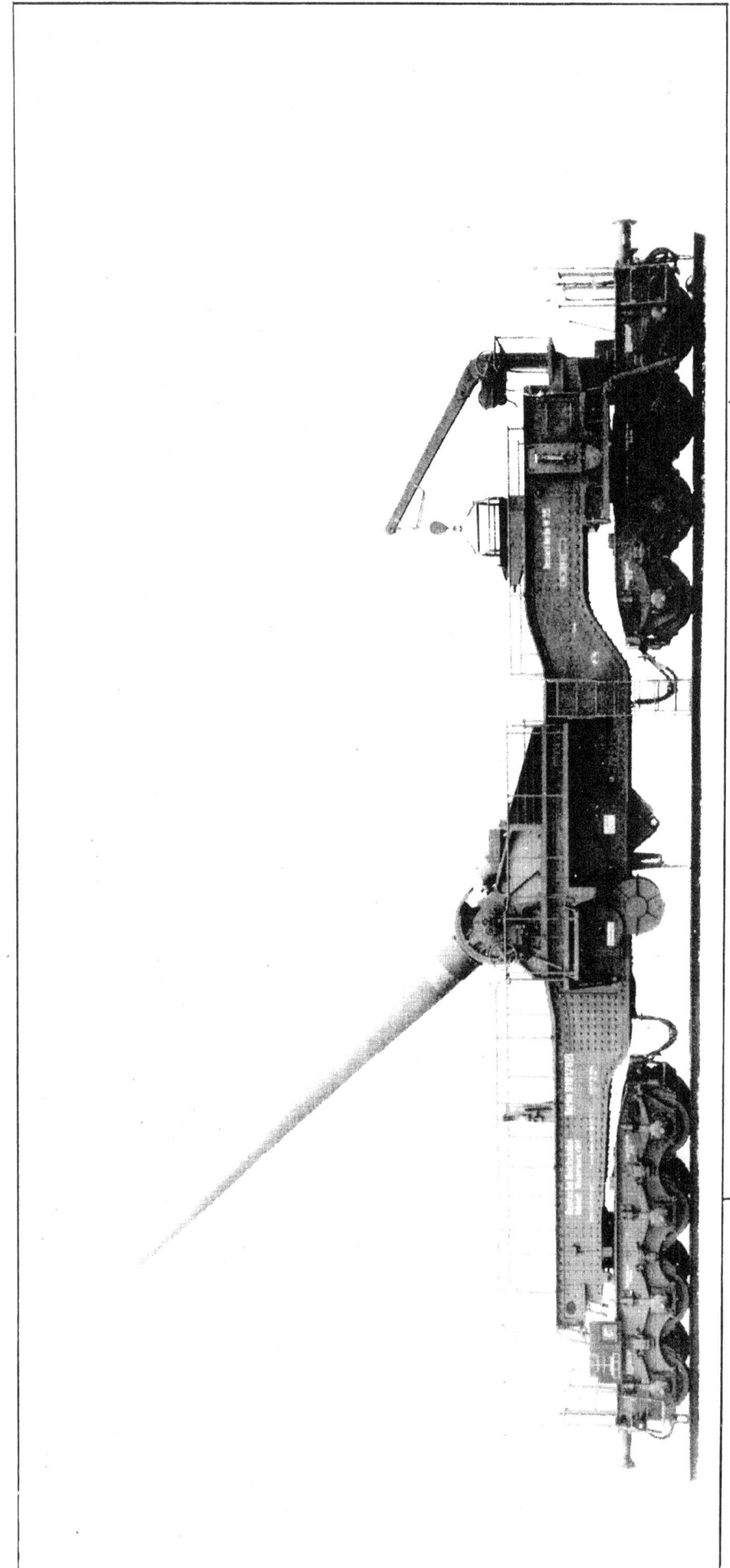

FIG. 61. 20cm. K. (E).
(8in. GUN on RAILWAY MOUNTING.)

(b) Ammunition

HE. Shell		Weight	Fuzes
20.3 cm.	Sprgr. L/4.7 (m.Haube)	247 lbs.	(.C/27. Stor Lm. (M.Dopp.z.28 K.
20.3 cm.	Sprgr.L/4.7 in Bd.Z (m.Haube)	268.4 lb.	Bd Z. C/38.

Cartridge Case:- 20.3 cm. Kart C/34 (Brass)
Primer:- C/12 n.A (Brass) or C/12 n.A St. (Steel).
Igniter:- 540 g (19 ozs. Black Powder.
Propellant Charge :- 35 kg. (77 lbs) C/32 Tubular.

21 cm. Kanone.12.(E). (8.3 inch Long Range Gun Model 12 (Railway Mounting)).
See Figs:- 62, 63 & 64.

1. General

Concrete work on two projects, 21 cm. K.12.(E) and 28 cm. K.5.(E), was started in 1934. Although definite projects were not started before this date, a great deal of consideration had been given to various possible designs. In addition, the portable railway gun turntable, the essential part of all new designs, had already been tried out and was almost fully developed. One of the great incentives behind the development of the 21 cm K.12.(E) was the use of the Paris gun in the last war. The latter had been developed and manned exclusively by the German Navy and the Army artillery branch considered this an intolerable slur on their capabilities. Initial work on this subject was started therefore immediately after the treaty of Versailles.

Sub-calibre model barrels for the early interior ballistical trials were made for both of the new projects. The one for the 21 cm. K.12. (E) was of 10.5 cm. calibre and known as the K. 12. M.

Trials with the model barrel and the full scale barrel were carried out between 1934 and 1939, when the first equipment was introduced into service.

The original trials, with the 10.5 cm. K.12.M. barrel, showed that there was no hope of any form of rifling other than that of employing splines. The original barrel was known as the K.12.St (Stegführung = rifled for spline projectiles), but the "st" was later dropped as no other form of rifling was attempted.

When the carriage design was started, the designers were very worried at the great muzzle preponderance of the barrel. In order to reduce this as far as possible, the whole carriage was raised about 1 metre in the firing position, so as to give an increased clearance above the rails and thus allow the barrel to be mounted further to the rear of the cradle. The carriage was raised by two hydraulically operated jacks, situated in the bogie bolsters. The sequence of operation was as follows:- load, raise carriage, elevate gun, fire, depress gun, lower carriage, open breech.

The first carriage produced to this design was known as the K. 12.V. and operated reasonably well. In the firing position, it was mounted in a special version of the standard railway gun turntable. The main disadvantages were the additional complication of the carriage raising gear, the great diameter of the turntable required and the number of movements required in firing.

As a result of the above difficulties, a new design known as the K.12. N. was started before the construction of the K.12. V. had been completed. From the experience with the first design, it was clear that balancing presses could be operated at higher pressures, than had hitherto been thought possible. In the new design therefore, the barrel was mounted in the cradle as far forward as possible. The resulting disequilibrium was compensated for by a single hydro-pneumatic balancing press.

In all, one of each type of carriage was built, the two barrels being almost identical.

The equipment consists of an unusually long braced barrel, carried on an extremely strong gun carriage.

The outstanding feature of the equipment, apart from the novelty of design, is the clear evidence that no cost was spared in order to achieve great strength and lightness, combined with a very high order of workmanship and finish. The complexion of certain of the design features, and the layout of the electrical equipment tended to show that considerable experimental work had been carried out before the design of the gun was finally arrived at.

The piece, which weighs 99,708 kg (98.1 Tons), consists of a barrel, jacket, breech ring fitted with horizontal sliding breech block and the barrel bracing. The jacket is in two sections, inner and outer.

The barrel is 33112 mm (105 Feet $4\frac{1}{4}$ inches) long. The jacket is about 35 feet long. The chamber is prepared to take the same cartridge case as that used with the 28 cm K.5. The bore is rifled with 8 grooves to take the splines of the projectiles.

The firing mechanism is of the percussion type, with provision for firing by lanyard or by electricity through an electromagnetic or solenoid fitting.

The barrel bracing is designed to give vertical support to the barrel, forward of the jacket.

The cradle is of the sleeve type, of massive construction and contains cylinder blocks for the recoil system of the gun.

The gun recoil system consists of two hydraulic buffers and one hydro-pneumatic recuperator.

In transport, the whole piece is pulled to the rear in the cradle by some 150 cm. (5 feet) and held in this position by two bolts. An electrically driven oil pump is provided and is connected to the front side of the recuperator piston, this portion of the cylinder being used as a hydraulic ram cylinder for moving the piece.

The sighting arrangement is of the normal German "follow the pointer" sight and elevation reader arm, together with the standard German railway gun sight.

The carriage is mounted on two recoil systems, which carry the pivots connecting the carriage to the bogie units. The two recoil systems are identical, each consisting of one hydraulic buffer and one hydro-pneumatic recuperator. The systems can be locked during transport of the equipment.

The carriage, in the well of which the weapon is mounted, is connected to two bogie units by two pivot bearings in ball races. The front bogie unit consists of two bogies with five axles and the rear bogie unit of two bogies with four axles.

The equipment can be bolstered up on a railway track for firing. It can also be fired from a turntable or a spur on the line. When firing on a spur, the weapon is brought forward after recoil by a locomotive.

2. Railway Mounting

(a) Bolsters.

    The two bolsters, each connecting the two bogies in a unit, are basically of normal railway design. They are identical in construction, except for the fact that the front bolster is somewhat longer to allow for the great length of the five-axled bogies, while the rear bolster has an ammunition crane mounted on the end.

Each bolster is fitted at front and rear with pivot bearings, which support it on the bogies. In addition, rollers are mounted on the bolster on either side, level with the pivot and resting on plates on the bogies. These provide increased lateral stability, which is necessary especially in the firing position. In the centre of each bolster is a socket, into which the carriage pivot lower race is bolted. A circular track around the pivot, is provided for the carriage side rollers.

The brake and stand pipes running along the bolster are connected by flexible rubber pipes to the inner of the two bogies. In addition, they are connected to pipes, running along the outside of the carriage to the other bolster, by the standard flexible connectors.

(b) Bolster Hydraulic System

Each bolster unit is equipped with a complete hydraulic system comprising, oil tank, oil pump, hydraulic jack, air pressure tank and a set of pressure gauges, together with the necessary valves.

The oil tank is mounted within the framework of the bolster. The oil pump, which is electrically driven, is mounted on the inner (non-buffing) bogie on the section not covered by the bolster. It is connected to the bolster by flexible pressure pipes. The air pressure tank, a vertical steel cylinder, is mounted inside the framework of the bolster.

The hydraulic jack is mounted in the centre of the bolster, vertically beneath the carriage pivot. The three pressure gauges, together with valves 1 - 7, are mounted in a single panel. Valves 8 - 10 and an oil level gauge, which indicates the oil level in the tank, are mounted on a second panel. A flexible pipe leads to the valve block on the carriage controlling the supply to the slider units on the carriage recoil slides.

To jack up the bolster, carrying with it the carriage and the two bogies, the oil pump is run with valve 5 open and all other valves closed. To lower the bolster again, the pump is shut off, and valve 4 opened, all other valves remaining closed.

Before firing takes place, compressed air at a pressure of 55 atmospheres (782 lbs.sq.in.) is admitted into the air pressure tank through valves, 8, 9 and 10. When the tank is full, as indicated by the gauge connected by valve 6, valve 10 is closed. Oil is pumped into the air pressure tank, until the pressure as given by the pressure gauge is 220 atmospheres (3129 lb. sq.in.) for the rear bolster and 250 atmospheres (3556 lb.sq.in.) for the front bolster. Just before the gun is fired, valves 1, 8 and 9 are opened, together with the valves on the carriage controlling the flow of oil to the slider units. The carriage recoil slides thus float on oil at a constant high pressure as the gun recoils. Under certain circumstances, such that the thrust on the recoil slides will be uneven, only the valve, connecting with the two slider units on the heavily stressed side, is opened.

(c) Ammunition Crane

An ammunition crane is mounted on the rear of the rear bogie bolster. The mounting bracket is positioned so that the axis, about which the crane turns, lies at the centre of the rear edge of the bolster. A platform is fixed to the crane, about 88 cm. above the top of the bolster, for the two crane operators. The jib, about 5 metres long, is hinged at the joint with the crane body and can be lowered for transport. Electric motors, mounted at the top of the crane body, drive the winch and traverse gears. Auxiliary hand controls are also provided.

(d) Electrical Equipment

The gun is provided with a comprehensive set of electrical equipment; all the movements of the gun in laying and all the hydraulic gear being electrically driven. Unfortunately a large part of the equipment was damaged in the original explosion used to blow the gun carriage. In addition, the majority of the wiring and a large proportion of the switchgear had been looted by the local population.

The electrical installation consisted of a petrol electric generator set providing the main power supply. This was connected by various rubber connectors and switchgear to the following electric motors:-

Elevating Gear	- 2
Recuperator Pump	- 1
Bolster Hydraulic Pumps	- 2
Bogie Motors	- 4

(e) Electrical Generator

The petrol electric generator is built as a separate unit, mounted on rollers. In transport, it is carried on an ammunition flat. When coming into action, the unit is pulled on to the rear bogie. It is then jacked up on to a small built-in turntable and swung broadside on to the bogie. This is done so that it can clear the rear of the carriage extention as the gun traverses. The unit is then lowered on to brackets on the bogie and bolted down. The brackets are provided with anti-vibration rubber cushions.

The generating set consists of a V.12 Maybach petrol engine of 185 metric HP. This is directly coupled to two generators running in tandem. The first of these is rated:-

220 Volts DC.   136 Amps. 30 KW at 1800 rpm.

The generator includes its own exciter. The second generator is excited by a 12 amp supply taken from the first. It is rated:-

360 Volts DC.   (146 Amps. 53 KW)
                (80 Amps. 29 KW) at 1800 rpm
                (300 Amps.108 KW)

It is clear that all the circuits cannot be run at full capacity together, since the engine would thereby be overloaded. Whether all the circuits are run together, at well below their rated capacity, or one or more of the 360 volt circuits are provided as reserves, is not clear.

The connections, on the distribution panel of the generator set, provide for one large and one small twin connector and two very large single connectors.

(f) Wiring

The wiring on the equipment, as has already been stated, was in a very bad state. It is clear that the majority of the wiring on the carriage itself was of heavy single conductor braided cable. All joints, however, between the carriage, bolsters and bogies were made by flexible, multiple conductor, rubber cable. Multiple plugs and sockets were used to connect the cables at each end.

(g) Controls

A main switchboard was provided on the motor generator, this had been removed however. Other switch boxes were provided on each bogie bolster and at the front of the main carriage. The actual firing controls are mounted below the left trunnion. They consisted of a multiple, double throw switch, marked "Traverse" or "Elevation", and an electric motor control unit. In addition, a brake control unit, connected to the brake pipe on the carriage, is provided together with a pressure gauge. It appears therefore that laying for line and elevation could not be done simultaneously.

(h) Description of the Firing Tracks

Two special railway flats, carrying firing track, were included in the train with the gun. Both were carrying similar loads consisting of 9 track units and a ramp unit. In addition, one flat carried a rectangular track crossover. Of the 9 track units, 4 were fitted with clamps at the sides and 5 were fitted with rollers. All the units were numbered, in white paint, as follows:-

	Waggon 1.	Waggon 2.
Track units with rollers.	22A, 23A, 24A, 25A, 26A.	22B, 23B, 24B, 25B, 26B.
Track units with clamps.	27A, 28A, 29A, 30A.	27B, 28B, 29B, 30B.
Ramp units.	31A.	31B.
90° Cross Over.		27B.

(j) Track Waggons

The two track waggons are identical. Each is based on a standard railway flat, mounted on two 2-wheeled bogies. The length overall of the platform is 18 metres. An overhead monorail hoist track runs down the centre of the track, projecting some distance over the buffers at one end. The track is carried on two fabricated steel arches, attached to the sides of the platform by brackets. A hand operated winch is mounted on the platform at the end from which the monorail does not project. A slider fitted with pulleys is mounted on the monorail.

It appears that a hoist on the slider was operated by the winch at the end. When a load had been lifted clear, it could be pushed down to the end of the rail and lowered clear of the end of the waggon.

(k) Track Units

There are 18 straight track units, 8.20 cm. long. Of these, 10 are equipped with rollers and 8 with clamps. Basically however, all the units are identical and consist of a length of specially heavy standard gauge railway track. The clamp and roller fittings will be described in further paragraphs.

Each track unit consists of 15 fabricated steel sleepers and two straight lengths of fabricated rail. The rails are bolted to the sleepers by 4 bolts at each joint. Apart from these, no bolts or rivets are used in the construction.

The sleepers are each built up of two 60 mm x 140 mm steel channels, back to back. They are connected together by 6 short cross pieces and a thin base plate, running between the end cross pieces. The upper flanges are reinforced, where the rails cross them by two cross pieces, one on either side of the rail, joining the two channels.

The rail consists of two 'L' sections back to back, each with one flange horizontal. Welded along the top is a strip, which overlaps the top of each 'L'. A ridge is formed down each edge of this strip. One of these forms the rail bearing surface. The other is machined as a rack, with square section teeth and 23 mm. pitch.

The last sleeper, at each end of the unit, is mounted flush with the end of the rails. Two holes are drilled at each end of the rails for the fish plates, which are used in joining the track units together.

(1) Track Clamps

Track units number 27 to 30 in. each set are fitted with clamps. One clamp is mounted at each end of the 2nd, 5th, 8th, 11th and 14th sleeper on each of the units concerned. Each clamp is mounted so that it can be raised and housed for transport or lowered into the clamping position when in use.

In addition, two cross pieces, joining the two lower flanges of the channels forming the sleeper, are welded on each of these sleepers. The outside width over the cross pieces is the standard railway gauge. It thus appears that these track sections are intended to be mounted on existing standard gauge railway lines, with the cross pieces and clamps holding the track unit rigidly to the railway line below.

Each clamp consists of a frame and a clamping screw bearing in a nut, pivotted to the frame. The frame is built up from two flat plates, held apart by welded distance pieces. The block, containing the nut in which the clamping screw rests, is fixed in bearings at the outer end of the frame, so that the nut and the screw can rotate in a vertical plane. The clamping screw is screwthreaded throughout its length. A circular head with hinged handle is fitted at the outer end. A forked foot is mounted on a bearing at the inner end.

The inner end of the frame is hinged on a horizontal pin, joining the side channels of the sleeper. It is held in the clamped or housed postions by a loose locking pin passing through holes in the side channels. Bearing points for the pin are formed in the upper and lower edges of the side plates.

In the housed position, the bottom edges of the frame rest on the locking pin. The clamping screw is screwed right in, the shaft passing through a hole in the first cross plate of the sleeper. In the clamped position, the frame is prevented from swinging outwards and upwards by the locking pin, which bears against the upper edge of the frame.

(m) Track Rollers

Track units, numbered 22 to 26, are fitted with rollers. One roller is mounted at each end of the 2nd, 8th and 14th sleeper on each of the units concerned. Each roller is mounted so that it can be held in the down position, for transport and when in use for rolling the track unit, or lifted clear of the ground when laid.

Each roller consists of a frame, fitted with an axle on which the roller turns. The frame is built up from two plates held apart by welded distance pieces. They are tapered off and bent together at their outer ends. The axle is welded on to the ends of the side plates. The roller is a one-piece casting.

The inner end of the frame is hinged on a horizontal pin, joining the side channels of the sleeper. The roller is held in the down or lifted positions by a loose locking pin, passing through holes in the side channels. A hole is made through the side plates of the frame for the locking pin in the down position. Bearing points for the pin are made in the lower edge of the side plates in the lifted position.

(n) Ramps

The two ramps are numbered 31A and 31B respectively. They are built up from heavy section rails of normal type and a series of steel sleepers of varying height. Distance pieces are welded to the underside of each sleeper to fit over a standard gauge railway track.

The ends of the rails are tapered off to nothing at one end, the sleepers being arranged so that, when the ramp unit is placed on a section of normal railway line, the rails lead up from the surface of the underlying permanent way to the height of the standard track unit. The overall length of the ramp is 760 cm.

(o) Track Crossover

One track crossover unit, numbered 27B, is included with the track waggons. It is an entirely fabricated structure. The rails on it are similar in construction to those on the standard track units, but are without the rack along the outer edge.

The crossover is so constructed that it can be fitted over a section of normal railway track. A pyramid construction of steel plates rises in the centre of the crossover. It is provided with a flat top, having a curved depression in the middle suitable to receive the base of the hydraulic jack in the bogie bolster.

3. Method of Employment of the Gun in conjunction with the Firing Track.

First it must be clearly stated that, while the gun was found with this special track, it is equally obvious that the gun can also fire from the curved section of a railway spur or from a special railway gun turntable. No details of the method of employment of the firing track for the K.12. have been obtained from captured documents. However, from the construction of the various components, it is possible to arrive at a fair idea of the true method of employment.

The site required for the use of the firing track consists of a level section of single track railway line with flat firm ground on either side for about 50 metres. It is probable that a considerable number of standard sleepers are used in laying out the track sections.

First the two special track waggons, with their overhanging jibs facing inwards, are pushed to the centre of the proposed gun position. Then track units 22 to 26 are lifted from each truck by the special crane. They are run out, one set on each side, at right angles to the railway line, their rollers running on two rows of sleepers. When bedded into their final position, the rollers are lifted clear of the ground.

The track crossover unit, B 27, is then lowered on to the railway line and the units, already laid out, are aligned with it and connected up by the fishplates. Meanwhile, each of the two track waggons lays out track units 27 to 30 along the railway line, progressing away from the crossover at the centre, as each unit is laid. The two ramps, A 31 and B 31, are finally laid, leading up from the standard railway line onto the railway track on the track units. The clamps, on units 27 to 30 in each set, are then lowered and used to secure the track on the railway line below. The firing track is now laid out and the two empty track waggons are shunted away, one of them crossing over the firing track.

The gun, with the generator already mounted on the rear bogie, is now mounted up on to the firing track, so that the centre of either the front or rear bogie unit lies vertically over the track crossover. Normally it will be the front bogie unit, since the ammunition supply coming up on the railway line is lifted on to the gun by the crane on the rear bogie unit.

The whole front bogie unit is jacked clear of the rails, by the hydraulic jack in the bolster, and swung at right angles to the gun carriage. It is lowered then on to the section of track running at right angles to the railway line. The gun can be traversed now through some 300° by the electric drive on the bogies, pushing each bogie along its own section of track. A traverse of 360° is not possible, without jacking up the rear bolster as it comes to the centre of the cross, owing to the absence of clearance between the buffers on the bogies and the main girder.

In laying, the gun is propelled along the two tracks by its electric drive, controlled by the layer. When he has finished laying for line, he throws over the laying switch and proceeds to lay for elevation. It seems probable that the racks on the special rails of the track units are used as a grip for clamping dogs to secure the wheels. Before firing, the carriage slides are floated on oil by the air pressure in the bolster hydraulic system.

4. Data: 21 cm. K. 12. (N)

   (a) Ballistic Performance

   The following details of the ballistic performance have been taken from captured documents and various other sources:-

	Metric	British
Weight of shell	107.5 kg.	236.5 lbs.
Weight of charge	259 kg.	571 lbs.
Muzzle velocity	1500 m.s.	4920 f.s.
Maximum range (approx)	115 km.	126,000 yds.
Minimum range	45,000 m.	48,210 yds.
Chamber pressure	4,000 atmospheres	26.2 tons sq.in.
Muzzle energy		12,520 m.t.

   (b) Weights and Dimensions

   (i) Piece

	Metric	British
Calibre over lands at muzzle	211 mm.	8.31 ins.
Calibre over grooves at muzzle	229 mm.	9.02 ins.
Length of piece (158 calibres)	33.3 m.	109 ft. 3 ins.
Depth of breech opening	1175 mm.	3 ft. 4 ins.
Length of barrel	32.112 m.	105 ft. 4 ins.
Length of chamber	5 m.	16 ft. 5 ins.
Length of rifling	27.724 m.	90 ft. 11 ins.
Chamber capacity	343 litres	75½ galls.
Twist of rifling	5° 48'	
No. of grooves	8	
Depth of grooves	9 mm.	.35 ins.
Width of grooves	14.5 mm.	.57 ins.
Width of lands	68.4 mm.	2.70 ins.
Weight of piece	99,700 kg	98 tons
Maximum piece recoil	60 - 70 cm.	23½ - 27½

   (ii) Mounting

	Metric	British
Length overall (incl. muzzle overhang)	47.86 m.	157 ft.
Length over buffers	41.30 m.	135 ft. 6 ins.
Length over carriage main girder	27.62 m.	90 ft. 7 ins.

(ii) Contd.

	Metric	British
Wheel base	38.50 m.	126 ft. 4 ins.
Length of front bogie unit	16.36 m.	53 ft. 8 ins.
Length of rear bogie unit	13.36 m.	43 ft. 10 ins.
Clearance of main girders over rail	53 cm.	20.9 ins.
Height of bogies over rail	124 cm.	4 ft. 7/8 ins.
Height of bolster over rail	182 cm.	5 ft. 11 5/8 ins.
Height of carriage main girder over rail	341 cm.	11 ft. 2½ ins.
Height of trunnions above rail	328 cm.	10 ft. 9⅘ ins.
Weight of gun and mounting	302,000 kg.	297 tons
Maximum carriage recoil	98 cm.	38½ ins.
Elevation	+ 25° to + 55°	
Traverse (Fine 15 minutes to 25 minutes)	360°	

(iii) Track Waggons

	Metric	British
Length over buffers	20.10 m.	65 ft. 11 ins.
Weight loaded	40,000 kg.	39 tons
Weight empty	20,560 kg.	20 tons

(iv) Track Units

	Metric	British
Length of standard unit	8.20 cm.	26 ft. 11 ins.
Length of track on crossover	2.70 cm.	8 ft. 10½ ins.
Length of ramps	7.60 cm.	24 ft. 11½ ins.

(c) Ammunition

H.E. with ballistic cap	Weight of Projectile	Fuzes used
21 cm. Gr 35. (m.Haube)	107.5 kg (236.5 lbs)	(H bgr.Z.35.K. (Bd Z.36.K.4.

5. Data: 21 cm. K.12.(V)

This is the same as for the K.12.N., shown above, except for the following:-

	Metric	British
Height of axis of gun in action	5,000 mm.	196.8 ins.
Carriage recoil	1,500 mm.	59 ins.
Weight in action	318,000 kg.	313 tons
Weight travelling	309,000 kg.	304 tons
Overall length (in action)	49.75 m.	163 ft. 2½ ins.
Overall length (travelling)	44.95 m.	147 ft. 5½ ins.

F. 24 cm. THEODOR BRUNO. K.(E). (9.45 inch Gun (Railway Mounting)). See Fig. 65.

1. This equipment is from a design by Krupp of Essen, which was introduced into the German Army before 1939. The piece is the 24 cm. S.K. L/35, a naval Q.F. gun of the 1914 - 18 era. Six equipments were produced, starting in 1937.

The piece consists of a loose liner, jacket and removable breech ring. The breech mechanism is a horizontal sliding block of unusual design. The block is in the form of a half cylinder with the curved surface facing towards the rear.

The cradle is formed by two case plates, one on each side of the barrel, connected at the top and bottom by rivetted plates. The barrel has two splines formed on it, one on either side, which fit into grooves in the cradle side plates.

The recoil gear consists of two hydraulic buffer cylinders, mounted within the cradle above the barrel, and one recuperator cylinder, mounted below the barrel.

The carriage consists of two massive steel girders, reinforced by shallow webs connected together by transoms. The carriage is supported on two four-axled bogies. The platform for the gun detachment is extended on either side by means of hinged platforms.

The elevating gear is almost identical with that of a 28 cm. railway gun, used by the Germans in the last war. It consists of two elevating cranks, one on either side of the gun carriage, which, through gearing, operate diagonal shafts running down the outside of the carriage

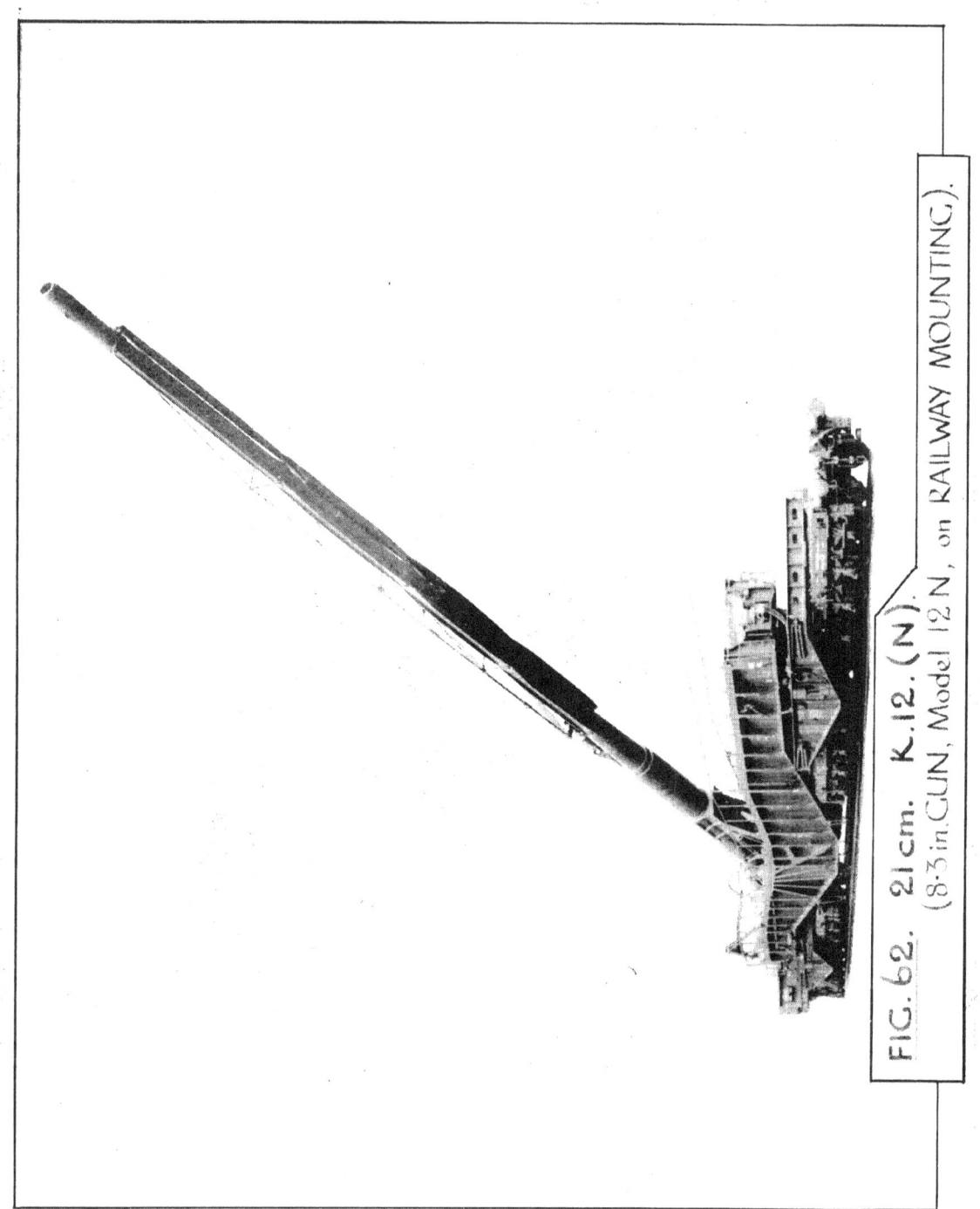

FIG. 62. 21 cm. K.12.(N).
(8·3 in. GUN, Model 12 N, on RAILWAY MOUNTING).

FIG. 63. 21cm. K.12.(v).
(8.3 in. GUN, Model 12V, on RAILWAY MOUNTING).

FIG. 64. 21 cm. K. 12. (v). (8.3 in. GUN, Model 12 V, on RAILWAY MOUNTING.)

side members. These shafts are connected by worm gears to a horizontal shaft, linking up the two elevating gear drives. Mounted on this shaft are two pinions, which engage with two straight racks about 12 ft. long. The racks are held in mesh with the pinions by rollers. The two racks are pivotted at their rear ends to a yoke piece, which projects downward from the rear end of the cradle.

Carriage traverse is employed. The rear pivot of the gun carriage, which engages with the rear bogie, is mounted in a slideway in the gun carriage, which is traversed by means of a screw.

2. Data: 24 cm. THEODOR BRUNO

		Metric	British
(a)	Calibre	238 mm.	9.4 ins.
	Length of piece (35 calibres)	8,400 mm.	27.5 ft.
	" " barrel	7,800 mm.	25.59 ft.
	" " rifling	6,300 mm.	20.67 ft.
	" " chamber to C. of R.	1,500 mm.	4.92 ft.
	Pressure in recuperator	70 atmospheres	995 lb. sq. in.
	Weight in action	94,000 kg.	92.5 tons
	Elevation	+ 10° to 45°	
	Traverse	1°	
	Maximum recoil	1,000 mm.	3.28 ft.
	Maximum Muzzle velocity	675 m.s.	2215 f.s.
	Chamber pressure	2,600 atmospheres	17 Tons sq. in.
	Muzzle energy		3450 m.t.
	Weight of standard projectile	148.5 kg.	326.7 lbs
	Maximum range	20,200 metres	22,100 yds.
	Minimum range	10,000 metres	10,930 yds.
	Height of bore	3,400 mm.	11.15 ft.
	Weight of piece	24,000 kg.	23.6 Tons
	Overall length	20,700 mm.	68 feet

(b) Ammunition

Nomenclature	Type	Weight	Fuzes fitted
24 cm. Sprgr. L/4.5 m. Bd Z.(m. Haube)	H.E. Base fuzed and ballistic cap	332.2 lbs.	Bd Z.f. Sprgr. m.Ko+ with gaine Gr. Zdlg.
24 cm. Sprgr. L/4.2 m. Bd Z.u Kz. umg (m. Haube)	H.E. Nose and base fuzed with ballistic cap	326.7 lbs.	(KZ.C/27.Lm (or St or Ma) (M.Dopp.Z.S/90 St (Bd.Z.C/98.

(c) Fuzes

Bd.Z.f. Sprgr.m.Ko+ and Bd Z.C/98 are base percussion fuzes with no delay. KZ.C/27 is a nose percussion fuze.

M. Dopp.Z.S/90 St is a nose mechanical Time and Percussion fuze with a maximum running time of 90 seconds.

(d) Cartridge Case

Solid drawn brass case - Kart.f.Th.Br.K(E).

(e) Primer

Percussion C/12 nA - Brass or C/12 nA St. - Steel.

(f) Propelling charge

Igniter:- 200 g. (7 oz.) Black powder (0.3 - 1.5)
Main charge:- approx. 68 lbs. C/32 Tubular (1100 x 7.5/3.3 mm.)
    or 62 lbs. C/12 Tubular (550 x 8.75/4 mm.)

FIG. 65. 24 cm. THEODOR BRUNO. K.(E).
(9.45 in. THEODOR BRUNO RAILWAY GUN).

G. 24 cm. THEODOR Kanone. (E). (9.45 inch Gun (Railway Mounting)). See Fig.- 66.

1. Three of these equipments were produced, starting in 1936, and completed the following year. The gun is an old naval type, being the 24 cm. S.K. L/40, approximately 4 feet longer than that used with the Theodor Bruno equipment, dealt with in the previous section.

The piece consists of a built-up jacket and tube. The removable breech ring is fitted with a horizontal sliding breech block.

The sleeve cradle is fitted with a counterweight to counteract the muzzle preponderance of the piece.

The recoil system, consisting of a single hydro-pneumatic recuperator and two hydraulic buffers in a single cylinder block below the piece, is of orthodox design.

The firing carriage is supported on two four-axled bogies, and, excepting for one or two minor differences, is of the same type as used with the Theodor Bruno equipment.

2. Data: 24 cm. THEODOR.K.

	Metric	British
(a) Calibre	238 mm.	9.45 ins.
Length of piece (40 calibres)	9,550 mm.	31.3 feet
Length of barrel	8,900 mm.	29.16 feet
Length of rifling	7,820 mm.	25.65 feet
Length of chamber	1,080 mm.	42.5 ins.
Rifling - Increasing right hand twist	(a) $3\frac{1}{2}°$ to $7°$ or (b) $4°$ to $6°$	
Elevation	$+ 10°$ to $+ 45°$	
Traverse	$1°$	
Height of bore	2,880 mm.	9.45 feet
Barrel recoil	530 mm.	21 inches
Maximum Muzzle Velocity	810 m.s.	2,657 f.s.
Chamber pressure	2,900 atmospheres	19 tons sq.in.
Muzzle energy	4,600 t.m.	
Maximum range	26,750 metres	29,250 yds.
Minimum range	13,700 metres	15,000 yds.
Weight of standard projectile	148.5 kg.	326.7 lbs.
No. of charges	?	
Overall length	18,450 mm.	60.5 feet
Weight in action	95,000 kg.	93.5 tons

(b) Ammunition. H.E. B.C.

	Weight of Projectile	Fuzes Used
Sprgr.L/4.2 m Bd Z u KZ(m. Haube)	326.7 lbs.	(E.KZ.dr f Sprgr. (Dopp.Z.16. (Bd.Z.f.Sprgr.m.Ko+
Sprgr.L/4.2 m.Bd.Z u KZ(m. Haube). ung.(Nose and Base Fuze)	326.7 lbs.	(KZ.C/27. (Bd.Z. C/38. (M.Dopp. S/90. St.
Sprgr.L/4.1 m Bd Z. (Base Fuze)	332.2 lbs.	Bd.Z.f.Sprgr.m.Ko+

Primer - C/12 n A or C/12 n A St. (Brass or Steel).

Igniter - 200 g. (7 ozs.) Black Powder.

(c) Propellant Charge:-
Basic Charge:- 82.8 lbs. - RPC/32 (346 - 12/6.6)
Increment Charge:- 15.2 lbs. - RPC/32 (346 - 12/6.6)

FIG. 66. 24 cm. THEODOR K.(E).
(9.45 in. THEODOR RAILWAY GUN)

H. 28 cm. kurze. BRUNO. Kanone.(E). 11 inch. short BRUNO Gun (Railway Mounting)).

1. This gun is one of a series of four 28 cm. models, which were used mounted on the same type of railway mounting. The four barrels of the models were of varying lengths. The barrel of the equipment dealt with here was the shortest of the four.

This equipment is based on the 28 cm. S.K. L/40, a Q.F. Naval Gun of 40 calibres length. Eight equipments were produced, starting in 1937 and finishing in 1938.

The barrel is of the built-up type consisting of a tube, jacket and removable breech ring. The latter is fitted with a horizontal sliding breech block, opening to the right.

The cradle, as is normally the case with railway equipments, is of the sleeve type.

The recoil system is contained in a single cylinder block, below the barrel; the block being an extension of the sleeve cradle. The recoil system is of orthodox type and is composed of two hydraulic buffers and one hydro-pneumatic recuperator.

The firing carriage is supported on two bogie units, each having five axles.

2. Data: 28 cm. kz. BRUNO

	Metric	British
(a) Calibre	283 mm.	11.14 ins.
Length of piece (40 calibres)	11200 mm.	36 ft. 9 ins.
Rifling - Increasing right hand twist - Angle $4°$ to $6°$		
Elevation	$+10°$ to $45°$	
Traverse	$1°$	
Height of bore	3400 mm.	11 feet 2 ins.
Barrel recoil	690 mm.	27 ins.
Weight of standard projectile	240 kg.	528 lbs.
Maximum range	29500 metres	32,250 yds.
Muzzle velocity	820 m/sec	2690 f.s.
Chamber pressure	3000 atmospheres	19.7 Tons sq. in.
Muzzle energy		8220 m.t.
Minimum range	14300 metres	15,640 yds.
Weight of piece	45300 kg.	44.57 tons
Weight in action	129,000 kg.	127 Tons.
Overall length of equipments	22800 mm.	74.8 feet

(b) Ammunition
	Weight of Projectile	Fuzes Used
H.E. Ballistic Cap. 28 cm. Sprgr.L/4.1 Bd Z u KZ.(m.Haube)	528 lbs.	(KZ.C/27.Lm. (M.Dopp.Z.S/90.St.

Cartridge Case	28 cm. Kart C/95 (Brass)
Primer	C/12 nA or C/12 nA St. (Brass or Steel)
Igniter	200 g (7 ozs) Black Powder.
Propellant Charge	67 kg (148 lbs.) C/32 Tubular. or 64 kg (141 lbs) C/12 Tubular.

J. 28 cm. lange BRUNO. Kanone.(E) (11.14 inch long BRUNO Gun (Railway Mounting)).
See fig:- 67.

1. This equipment is the second of the series of four types of barrel, mounted on the same type mounting. This long barrel is 45 calibres in length, which is 5 calibres (about 4 feet 8 inches) longer than the kurze (short) barrel, dealt with in the previous section.

The piece is of the built-up tube and jacket construction with a removable breech ring, in which is fitted a horizontal sliding breech block, opening to the right.

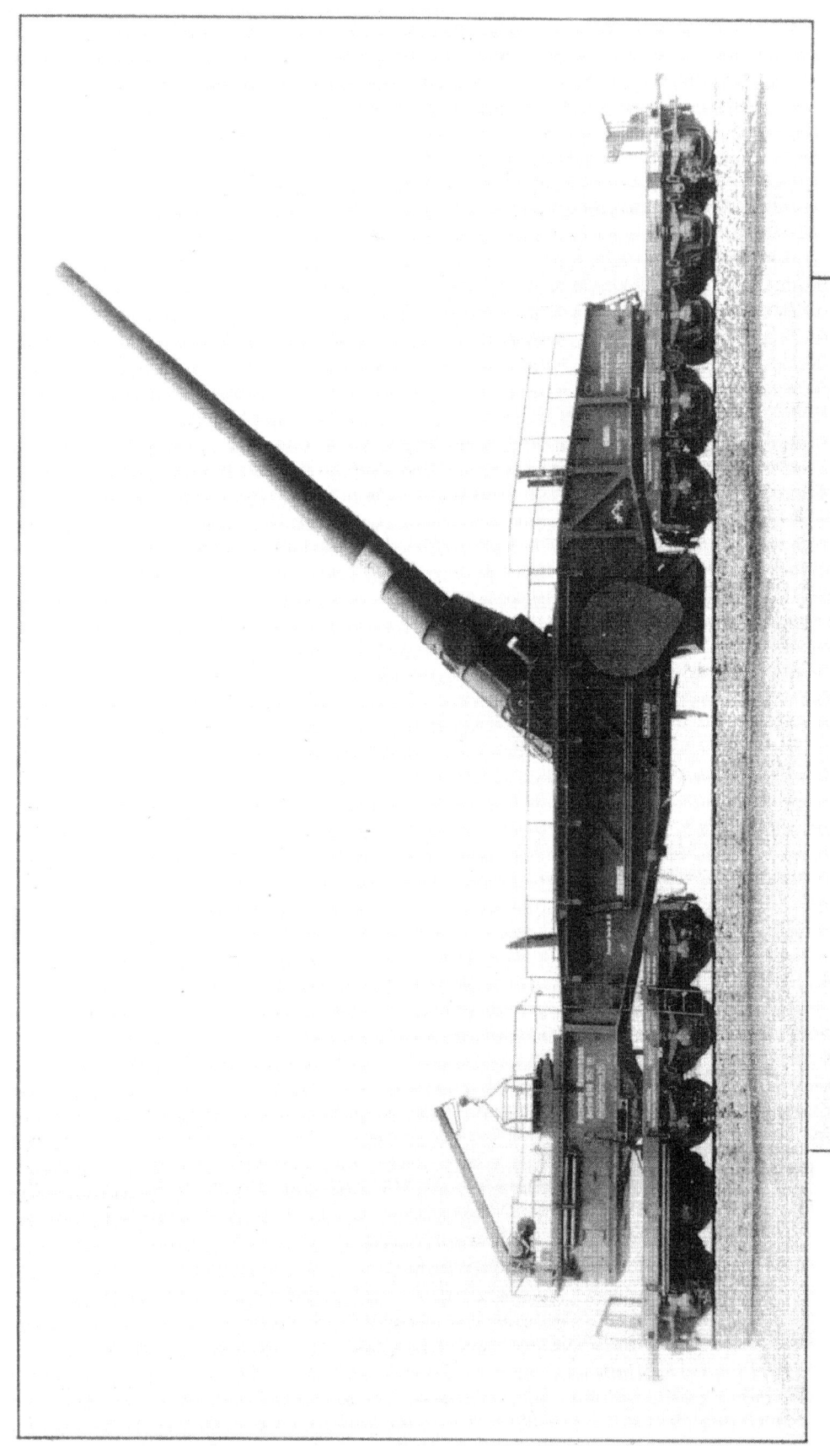

FIG. 67. 28 cm. Lange BRUNO. K.(E).
(11·14 in. Long barrelled BRUNO RAILWAY GUN).

The sleeve type cradle is so constructed that the recoil system, of two hydraulic buffers and one hydro-pneumatic recuperator, is housed below the barrel.

The firing carriage is supported on two five-axle bogies.

The naval gun S.K. L/45 is the basis for this equipment. Three weapons were produced, starting in 1936 and finishing in 1937.

2. Data: 28 cm. lg. BRUNO

	Metric	British
(a) Calibre	283 mm.	11.14 ins.
Length of piece (45 calibres)	12735 mm.	41.8 feet
Length of rifling	9698 mm.	31.8 feet
Length of chamber	2192 mm.	86.3 ins.
Capacity of chamber	150 litres	33 galls.
Rifling - Increasing right hand twist - Angle 4° to 6°		
Elevation	+ 10° to + 40°	
Traverse	1°	
Height of axis of bore	3645 mm.	12 feet
Barrel recoil	860 mm.	34 inches
Muzzle velocity	875 m.s.	2870 f.s.
Chamber pressure	2900 atmospheres	19 Tons sq. in.
Muzzle energy		11080 m.t.
Weight of standard projectile	284 kg	625.8 lbs.
Maximum range	36,100 metres	39,500 yards
Minimum range	16,800 metres	18,315 yards
Weight of piece	39,800 kg.	39.16 Tons
Weight in action	123,000 kg.	121 Tons
Overall length	22,800 mm.	74.8 feet

(b) Ammunition

H.E. Ballistic Cap (Nose or Base Fuze)	Weight of Projectile	Fuzes Used
28 cm. sprgr. L/4.4 m Bd Z u FZ. (m.Haube) umg.	624.8 lbs.	(KZ. C/27 (M.Dopp.ZS/60 (Dd Z. C/38
28 cm. Sprgr. L/4.4 m Bd Z u KZ (m.Haube)	624.8 lbs.	(E.KZ.dr.f. Sprgr. (Dopp.Z.16. (Bd Z.f.Sprgr. Ko+.

Primer - C/12. nA or C/12. nA St.
Igniter - 200 gr (7 ozs) Gun Powder
Propellant Charge - 106 kg. (233.2 lbs) C.12. Tubular.

28 cm. schwere. BRUNO. Kanone. (E).(11 inch heavy BRUNO Gun (Railway Mounting)).
See fig:- 68.

1. This equipment is based on the 28 cm. Küst. K. L/42, a coast defence gun of 42 calibres length. Two weapons were produced, starting in 1936, being completed in 1938. This is the third of the series of guns mounted on the same type mounting.

The barrel is of the orthodox built-up type, composing tube or barrel, jacket and removable breech ring, constructed to receive a horizontal sliding breech block, opening to the right.

The cradle is of the normal sleeve type construction, with provision for housing the two hydraulic buffers above the barrel and one hydro-pneumatic recuperator below the barrel.

The firing carriage is mounted upon two bogie units, each having 5 axles.

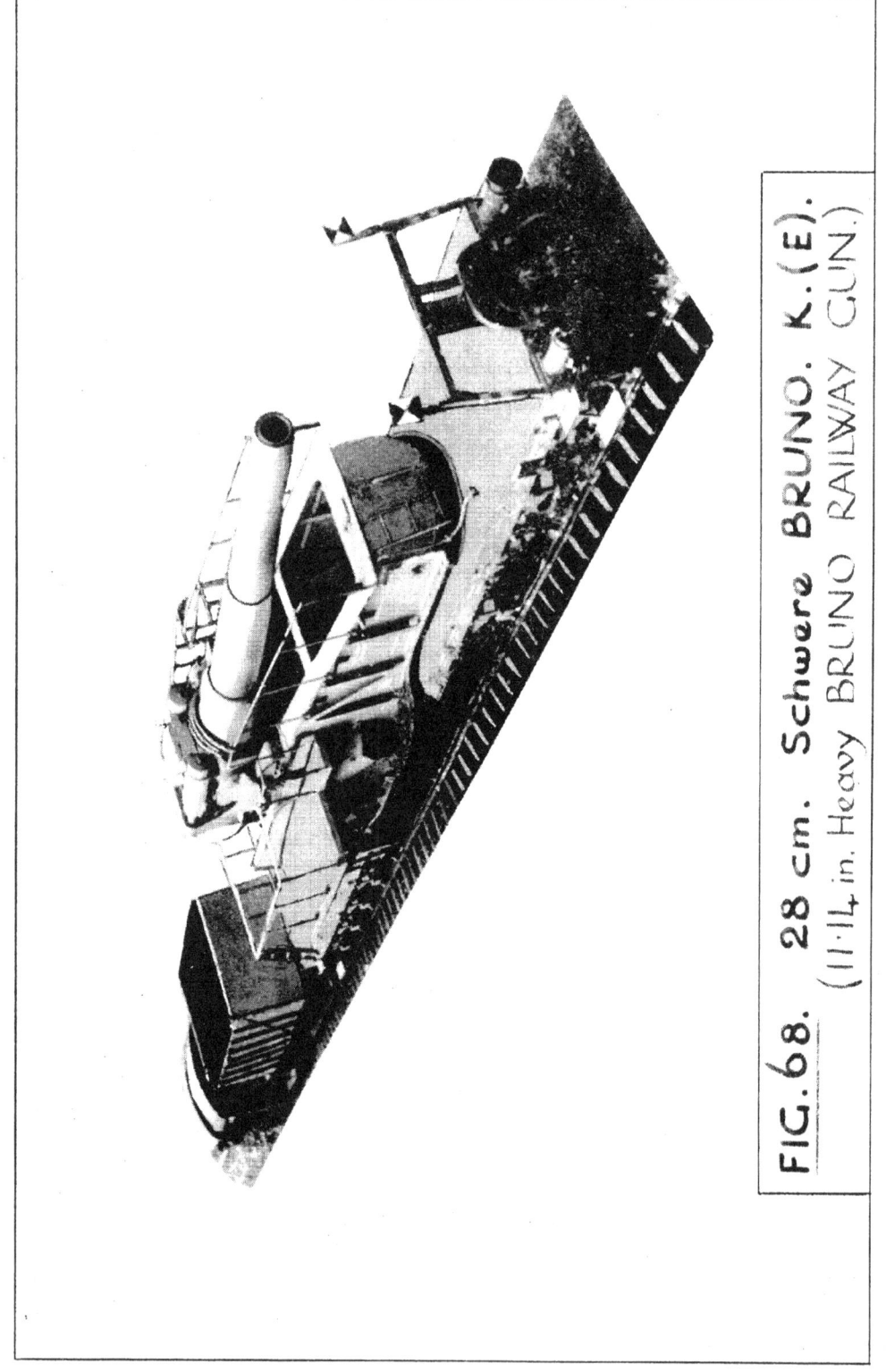

FIG. 68. 28 cm. Schwere BRUNO. K.(E).
(11·14 in. Heavy BRUNO RAILWAY GUN.)

2. Data: 28 cm. s. BRUNO.

	Metric	British
(a) Calibre	283 mm.	11.14 ins.
Length of piece (42 calibres)	11930 mm.	39.14 feet
Length of barrel	11084 mm.	36.36 feet
Length of rifling	8892 mm.	29.17 feet
Length of chamber	2192 mm.	86.3 ins.
Chamber capacity	150 litres	33 galls.

Rifling - Increasing right hand twist - angle $3\frac{1}{2}^{o}$ to 5°.
80 grooves.

	Metric	British
Elevation	+ 10° to 45°	
Traverse	1°	
Barrel recoil	700 mm.	27.5 ins.
Height of axis of bore	3400 mm.	11.15 feet
Weight of standard projectile	284 kg.	625.8 lbs.
Maximum muzzle velocity	860 m.s.	2821 f.s.
Chamber pressure	2900 atmospheres	19 tons sq.in.
Muzzle energy		10694 m.t.
Maximum range	35700 metres	39,050 yds.
Minimum range	16800 metres	18,375 yds.
Overall length of equipment	22800 mm.	74.8 feet
Weight of piece	40850 kg.	40.2 Tons
Weight in action	118000 kg.	116.13 Tons

(b) Ammunition

H.E. Ballistic Cap (Nose or Base Fuze)	Weight of Projectile	Fuzes Used
28 cm. sprgr. L/4.4 m Bd Z.u KZ. (m.Haube) umg.	625.8 lbs.	(KZ.C/27 (M.Dopp. Z.S/60 (Bd S.C/38
28 cm. Sprgr. L/4.4 m Bd Z.	625.8 lbs.	(E.KZ.dr f Sprgr. (Dopp. Z.16. (Bd Z.f. Sprgr Ko+.

Primer - C/12 nA or C/12 nA St.
Igniter - 200 g (7 ozs) Gun Powder.
Propellant Charge - 106 kg (233.2 lbs). C/12 Tubular.

L. 28 cm. BRUNO neue. Kanone.(E). (11 inch new BRUNO Gun (Railway Mounting)).
See fig:- 69.

1. While the lange and schwere Bruno equipments were still being produced in the spring of 1938, the Heereswaffenamt expressed a desire for a greater range from the guns, possibly up to that of the long range 28 cm. K.5.(E), i.e. 68000 yards. After due consideration of this project, Krupp replied that none of the guns could be modified, involving the construction of a new barrel, in the time available, and also adhere to the very latest delivery date ordered in early spring 1939. Development of the design for a new barrel was continued and lange Bruno carriages were modified later to carry the new barrels. In all, three equipments were produced, one at the end of 1940, one in mid 1941 and the last at the beginning of 1942. To identify them from the previous Bruno models, these equipments were designated "Bruno neue" i.e. Bruno new revised models. It had been intended to produce more than three equipments, but this appears to have been cancelled owing to the better performance of the 28 cm. K.5(E), and also to the fact that trouble caused by occassional peak pressures in the barrels could not be accounted for. The previous barrels in the Bruno series had been of old Naval designs, but these new ones were of modern design.

The piece comprised a barrel of jacket and tube construction with interchangeable liner sections. The removable breech ring is fitted with a horizontal sliding breech block, opening to the right.

An orthodox sleeve type cradle is used, with a fabricated construction secured to the lower portion, which houses the recoil system. The latter

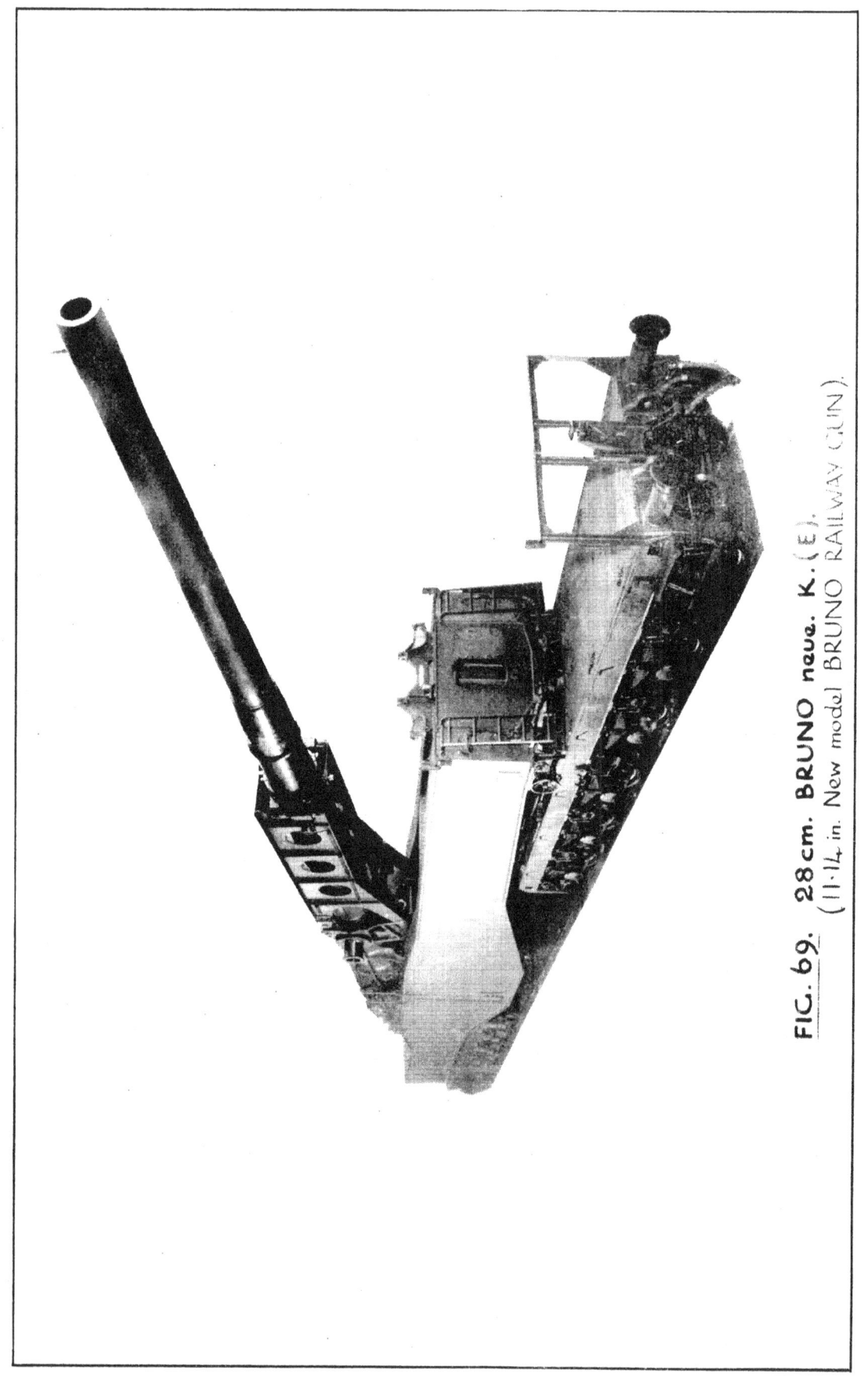

FIG. 69. 28 cm. BRUNO neue. K. (E).
(11·14 in. New model BRUNO RAILWAY GUN).

consists of hydraulic buffers and a single hydro-pneumatic recuperator.

The elevating gear can be operated by both manual and electrical means. Muzzle preponderence is compensated for by two hydro-pneumatic equilibrators. Limited fine traverse is obtained by manual operation. Provision is made for an electric or hand operated ammunition hoist. A separate power generating plant is included.

The weapon is fired from a curved track or a turntable. When firing from the turntable, controlled carriage recoil is employed. The firing carriage is supported on two bogies units, each having five axles.

2. Data. 28 cm. BRUNO. neue.

	Metric	British
(a) Calibre	283 mm.	11.14 inches
Length of piece (58 calibres)	16400 mm.	53.8 feet
Length of barrel	15247 mm.	50 feet
Length of rifling	12401 mm.	40.7 feet
Length of chamber	2845.5 mm.	112.02 ins.
Rifling - 80 grooves. Increasing right hand twist.	3° 59' 37" to	5° 7' 45"
Chamber capacity	229.7 litres	50 galls.
Height of the axis of bore	3580 mm.	11.75 feet
Barrel recoil	960 mm.	37.8 ins.
Traverse	1° and 360°	
Elevation	0° to 50°	
Weight of standard projectile	255 kg.	561 lbs.
Maximum muzzle velocity	995 m.s.	3264 f.s.
Chamber pressure	2900 atmospheres	19 Tons.sq.in.
Muzzle energy		12867 m.t.
Maximum range	46600 metres	51,000 yds.
Weight of piece	55260 kg.	54.4 Tons
Weight in action	150,000 kg.	147.6 Tons
Overall length	24880 mm.	81.627 feet

(b) Ammunition

H.E. with Ballistic Cap - 28 cm. Gr.39.(m.Haube).
Nose fuzed - Hbgr.Z.35.K. or Dopp.Z.28.K.
Weight of projectile - 255 kg. (561 lbs.)
" H.E. content - 34.3 kg. (75.46 lbs.)
Primer - C/12 nA or C/12 nA St. (Brass or Steel)
Propellant - Weight 163.8 kg. (360.4 lbs.)

M. 28 cm. Kanone.5.(E). (11.14 inch long range Gun Model 5 (Railway Mounting)).

See figs:- 70 & 71.

1. Development

This gun, in its various sub-marks, became the standard German heavy gun. It was originally developed as one of the super-long range guns, firing pre-rifled projectiles. Together with the 21 cm. V.L.R. (very long range) class, they were the only railway gun pieces specifically developed by and for the army, all the others being naval designs.

The project fot the 28 cm. K.5.(E) was commenced in 1934 and a model barrel constructed. The chronological order of development is most interesting. During 1936, the first full calibre barrel proof was fired and, in the following year, the first trial equipment fired its proof series of rounds. The first equipment was introduced then into the German service. By the end of February 1940, eight equipments were in service and, by the end of the war, about 25 equipments had been built. This means that, during the war, the production was about 3 per year. In fact, production was still being continued at the end of the war.

During 1940, trouble was encountered with the K.5. in the form of a serious outbreak of split barrels; in all, about 5 inner tubes were split from end to end. Pre-rifled projectiles were being used and the number of grooves in the rifled barrel was twelve. After very careful consideration, no definite conclusions were reached as to the cause, but the depth of rifling was altered from 10 to 7 mm, in the hope that it would help to minimise the occurrence of splits.

During the period 1940-43, owing to the development of FEW soft iron driving bands, the project of employing a normal rifled barrel was reopened. Finally, by the end of 1943, the production version, known as the K.5. VZ, was produced with conical rifling grooves and soft iron (not sintered) umbrella driving band. Very few of these barrels and their respective ammunition had been produced by the end of the war.

In 1942, work started on fin-stabilised sub-calibre projectiles. Experiments were carried out in a K.5 barrel, smooth bored to about 31 cm. By 1945, the development had progressed far enough for the equipment to be used in action, but only on an experimental scale.

2. Types

The 28 cm. K.5.(E) became quite popular and it was renamed "schlanke Bertha" (Slim Bertha) in 1944. During the long period of service of the guns, a barrel life as high as 550 rounds and as low as 240 rounds had been achieved (discounting the split barrels).

During the war, four versions of the K.5. were all in use side by side. The nomenclature of these versions is somewhat vague. In order of appearance, they were as follows:-

(a) K.5. Tiefzug 10 mm. (Depth of rifling groove 10 mm (.3937 ins.)). Also known as the K.5, St (St = Stegführung - Spline rifling)

(b) K.5. Tiefzug 7 mm. (Depth of rifling groove 6.75 mm. (.265 ins.)).

(c) K.5. Vielzug (VZ). Normal rifled barrel.

Wt. of Shell	Muzzle Velocity	Maximum Range
155 kg. (562 lbs.)	1120 m/sec (3675 f.s.)	61000 m (66,700 yds.)

A special Rocket Assisted Shell was also fired to a maximum range of 86,000 m (94,060 yds).

(d) K.5. Glatt. A smooth bore with a calibre of 31 cm. approximately.

(Krupp denied all knowledge of the nomenclatures K.5/1.(E) and K.5/2(E), which appear in the range tables, and claimed that the correct nomenclatures were as shown above).

Throughout the whole period, the carriage design remained unchanged, except for minor modifications. On certain of the early carriages, the front of the cradle has four extra brackets on it, two above and two below. These can be seen in early photographs of the K.5. When originally designed, the piece included a cantilever barrel-bracing structure, which was attached to these brackets. After the preliminary ballistic trials, it was realised that the bracing had no effect, even on accuracy, and its inclusion in the design was dropped. By then the first lot of cradles had been produced however.

Various projects connected with the K.5. had been considered and dropped during the life of the gun. Of these, two are of interest. The first was a B.L. breech mechanism of the interrupted screw thread type. The contract for this project was given in 1943, the main incentive being the elimination of the use of cartridge cases. The supply of the latter was already a bottleneck at that date. In addition, Krupp considered that the new breech mechanism would be lighter in weight and also shorter than the normal sliding wedge type. The latter point was of special advantage, since the barrel could then be moved to the rear relative to the trunnions, thus decreasing the preponderance of the gun. First trials of the basic design, applied to a 21 cm. gun, resulted in complete failure. With the prospect of the development of a suitable caseless sliding breech block mechanism, the subject was dropped to a very low priority.

The other project was for a muzzle brake, in order to permit an increase in the performance of the gun. After initial consideration, the project was dropped.

In 1943, a far wider and more concrete project was started. This was based on the General Staff's appreciation that, with the mounting enemy air offensive, a railway gun must be made capable of traversing stretches of country, where the railway bridges and track had been destroyed by bombing. A new specification was issued for the K.5. ERF. (Eisenbahn Runden Feld). Development of this specification had reached the point, where detailed design work on the final version had started.

The basic idea for the new project was for a railway gun, which could be lowered to the ground from its two bogies by hydraulic jacks in the bogie pivots. The centre section of the gun carriage, clear of the two bogies, was to carry a base plate, fitted with outrigger arms and equipped with a turntable to give 360° traverse. In the lowered position, the two bogies would be run clear and the gun would be ready to open fire.

In order to make it capable of movement across country, the gun was designed so that it could be split up into several loads. A new tractor was being designed to carry these loads, based on the chassis of the Tiger II tank. In addition, special gear was being developed, so that two of the tractors could form bogies to carry one load between them. The new tractor was to weigh about 25 tons. The gun was split up into the following loads:-

Load 1. Breech Mechanism and Breech Ring on one tractor.

Load 2. Barrel on two tractors.

Load 3. Carriage on two tractors.

Load 4. Base plate on two tractors.

The maximum loaded weight of any two tractors was to be kept down to 130 tons.

The cradle of the equipment was to be capable of carrying either a 28° cm. gun or a 38 cm. howitzer. The 28 cm. gun was to be ballistically identical with the K.5.Vz. The only change made was the introduction of an interrupted screw thread joint, between the barrel and the breech ring, so that the two might be separated for transport.

The idea of mounting a 38 cm. howitzer in the carriage of the K.5. had been pressed by Krupp for some time, but it was not until the new specification of the K.5. ERF. was issued, that it received official approval. The new howitzer was to be equipped with a sliding breech block, fitted with a form of ring obturation. Performance was to be as follows:-

Calibre	Shell Wt.	Muzzle Velocity	Maximum Range
380 mm.	800 kg.	500 to 600 m/s	20 - 25000 metres
(15 inches)	(1764 lbs.)	(1640 to 1970 f.s.)	(22 - 27350 yards)

This equipment was still in the project stage, when the end of the war came.

3. Train transport

The outstanding feature of the equipment is the revolutionary development in railway gunnery of carrying a portable turntable with the gun itself. In this connection it is interesting to study the make up of the two trains, which together formed a battery of one gun.

(a) 1st Train
    Engine   Heated magazine truck
    +Gun   Covered truck for personnel

(a) (contd.)

+Ammunition hoist car.	Covered truck for equipment.
Diesel shunting locomotive.	" " " armoury.
Shell truck with 113 shells.	" " " kitchen.
Shell truck with 113 shells	Flat wagon with blast hut
Cartridge truck	Open truck for A.A.
Cartridge truck	Three living coaches.

(b) 2nd Train

Engine.	Covered truck for equipment.
+Turntable car.	Open truck for A.A.
+Truck fitted with crane for turntable segments.	Covered truck for personnel.
	9 Platform trucks for M.T.
Three ammunition trucks.	

(The items essential for gun and platform are marked +).

4. Description

(a) Piece and Cradle

The barrel consists of a jacket and removable liner. It recoils in a cylindrical sleeve, 20 ft. 4½ in. long, which surrounds the jacket and forms part of the cradle. Two trunnions are mounted on the sleeve portion of the cradle, which has two curved arms projecting downward, one on either side of the buffer - recuperator, connecting up with the equilibrator and elevation mechanisms.

(b) Breech ring and block

The breech ring is cylindrical with a traverse opening at the rear for the breech block. The breech block is of standard Q.F. Krupp design. The firing mechanism is operated by a lanyard passing through the centre of the right trunnion.

(c) Gun Buffer and Recuperator

There is one hydro-pneumatic recuperator cylinder, charged at 95 atmospheres (1050 lb. sq.in.), with a buffer cylinder on either side; all three cylinders are mounted on the cradle below the barrel.

(d) Equilibrator and Elevating Mechanisms

The single hydro-pneumatic pusher type equilibrator, charged at 95 atmospheres, is mounted in horizontal trunnions and pushes forward against the centre of the traverse beam. The electrical elevating gear operates two pinions, which mesh with two racks. Safety switches cut out the electric motor, when the maximum safety limit of elevation is reached.

(e) The gun carriage frame is box shaped and supported on two pintles, which rest in bearings in the centre of two six-axled bogies. The pintle bearing in the front bogie rides in a guideway and can be traversed up to 6 inches either side of the centre, thus giving a total carriage traverse of about 1°. The traversing gear is operated by two electric motors, one on either side of the bogie.

(f) Turntable

The turntable equipment consists of two main portions, the turntable and the circular track. The table, on which is a length of standard gauge railway track, is fitted at each end with four rollers, which ride on the circular track, the inner two rollers at each end being electrically driven. There are five hydraulic jacks mounted on the table. One is mounted below the centre and incorporates the central pivot. The other four are mounted, two on each side, 14ft 10 ins. from the rollers at each end. The turntable is transported on two six-angled bogies with central pivots, similar to the bogies of the gun carriage. At the front of the turntable is a curved bracket carrying a recoil mechanism, consisting of a hydraulic buffer and a hydro-pneumatic recuperator, charged at 40 kg/sq.cm. (440 lb/sq.in.). This recoil mechanism is connected to the front of the gun carriage by a special bracket and permits a limited recoil by the gun carriage on the table.

The circular track is built up of 16 curved segments, each 17 ft. $11\frac{1}{4}$ in. long, transported on a special truck; two segments, used to straddle the main railway track, each 8 ft. long, are carried on the bogies of the platform wagon.

(g) Ammunition hoist truck

This is in the form of a flat truck, 29 ft. 3 in. long. A small four cylinder petrol engine is fitted centrally under the truck and geared through a reverse gear box and differential to the front axle. The engine is operated from a cab on top of the car; however, a reverse lever is mounted on the right side of the frame, so that it can be controlled by a man standing on the ground. The truck is used for moving shell and charges from the ammunition trucks to the gun.

Mounted on top of the truck for transport are a petrol-electric generator and an electric ammunition hoist. This unit is pushed off the truck on to the rear bogie of the gun carriage, when the gun goes into action. The petrol electric plant supplies all the power for the gun carriage; it compresses a V.12 petrol engine and an electric generator. The electric ammunition hoist lifts the ammunition on to a small trolley, mounted on rails, which join up with rails (on the top of the gun carriage) running up to the loading tray.

(h) Air Conditioned Cartridge Truck

This is a covered truck, which has an air conditioned equipment compartment at one end and a compartment at the other for housing an auxiliary petrol-electric generating plant. The truck is used for bringing cartridges to the required temperature and humidity before firing.

(j) Diesel Locomotive

The diesel locomotive is used for shunting ammunition trucks and for bringing the gun to and from the rest position to the firing position. It was a six cylinder diesel-electric locomotive Type C 14, gauge 1435 mm, weight 40 tons and speed 30-60 k.p.h.

5. Bringing Gun and Turntable into Action

All that is required in the way of a platform for the turntable is a firm flat space, astride the railway track, large enough to take the circular truck. No pit is needed.

(a) The truck carrying the 16 curved segments is brought to the centre of the position, where the turntable is to be erected, and the segments are unloaded and laid out in a rough circle bisected by the railway truck. The empty truck is then removed.

(b) The truck carrying the turntable is shunted centrally on to the position; the five jacks are lowered to lift the table clear of the bogies, which are then run clear.

(c) The two special segments are placed over the railway truck and a circular track is then bolted together. The platform is lowered so that the rollers rest on the two sections of the circular track.

(d) Meanwhile, the petrol electric generating unit is run off the ammunition hoist truck on to the rear bogie of the gun carriage.

(e) The difference in height between the track on the turntable and the railway track is 2 ft. 3¾ ins. In order to bridge this gap, an inclined track about 40 ft. long, formed of 6 track sections 6 ft. 6¾ ins. long (carried with the train), is used. The gun is pushed up on to the table and the inclined track removed.

(f) The buffer and recuperator at the front of the turntable are connected up to the front of the gun carriage.

(g) To rotate the turntable and traverse the gun, the four side jacks are raised clear of the ground and the turntable turned electrically. Before firing, weight is again taken on the four side jacks.

6. Data: 28 cm. K.5. (Tiefzug 7 mm.)

	Metric	British
(a) Piece		
Calibre	283 mm.	11.14 in.
Length of Barrel (76 calibres)	21539 mm.	70 ft. 8 in.
Length of liner tube	20548 mm.	67 ft. 5 in.
Length of Rifling	17374 mm.	56 ft. 11 in.
No. of grooves		12
Width of grooves	15.88 mm.	5/8 in.
Depth of grooves	6.75 mm.	.265 in.
Twist of rifling: Constant RH - angle		approx 5°
Length of chamber	3175 mm.	10 ft. 5 in.
Diameter of chamber at broach	333 mm.	13⅛ in.
Diameter of breech ring	1308 mm.	4 ft. 3½ in.
Length of breech ring	1054 mm.	3 ft. 5½ in.
Weight of breech block	1553 kg.	3425 lbs.
Weight of barrel	80545 kg.	84 tons
(b) Carriage		
Maximum Elevation approx		50°
Traverse approx		1°
Length of cylindrical cradle	6210 mm.	20 ft. 4½ in.
Recoil - Maximum	1187 mm.	46.8 in.
" - Normal	813 mm.	32 in.
Overall length of carriage	21234 mm.	69 ft. 8 in.
" " " "(including overhang of barrel and projecting rear bogie)	21934 mm.	95 ft. 7 in.
Overall width	2655 mm.	8 ft. 8½ in.
Overall height	4191 mm.	13 ft. 9 in.
Height of trunnions above rails	3480 mm.	11 ft. 5 in.
Weight of carriage and piece	209550 kg.	206 tons
Weight in action	218000 kg.	215 tons
(c) Turntable	Metric	British
Overall length	36779 mm.	120 ft. 8 in.
Effective length of track	31547 mm.	103 ft. 6 in.
Diameter of circular track	29464 mm.	96 ft. 8 in.
Height of turntable rails above ground	857 mm.	2 ft. 9¾ in.

(d) Ammunition hoist truck

Overall length	11963 mm.	39 ft. 3 in.
Wheelbase	7010 mm.	23 ft.
Weight	22732 kg.	22 tons

(e) Air Conditioned Cartridge Truck

Weight	21000 kg.	20.6 tons

(f) Diesel Locomotive

Weight	40,000 kg.	39.4 tons

7. Ammunition

   (a) Shell (Prerifled)

   28 cm. Gr. 35.m Bd Z.35 K+. ⎫
                                        ⎬ H.E. with Bal: Cap. Weight 561 lbs.
   28 cm. Gr. 35.(Ei).   ⎭

   (These two shells are identical ballistically, the only difference being that the "Ei" shell is a ranging shell and presumably contains a large smoke box or other indicator device).

   28 cm. R.Gr.4331. Weight 547 lbs.

   (This rocket assisted shell is reported to increase the range by 50%).

   These three shells are all prerifled and fitted with only one copper band as a gas check. The rifling strips are formed of a steel separate from the shell and are pressed into grooves in the shell body.

   (b) Cartridge and Charge

   The design number of the brass cartridge case is:- 6309.

   The charge is made up of Diglycol G.5 (Tubular propellant).

   Primer:- G.12. K.St.

8. Ballistic Performance

Gun	Projectile	Weight of shell	M.V. f.s.	Max. Range
(a) K.5.	H.E. with Ballistic Cap. GR.35.(Ei). Gr.35.m Bd Z. (pre-rifled)	561 lbs.	3675	68,000 yds.
(b) K.5.	H.E. with Ballistic Cap. R.Gr.4331 (pre-rifled and rocket assisted)	547 lbs.	3710	94,600 yds.
(c) K.5./Vz.	H.E. with Ballistic Cap. GR.42. (not pre-rifled)	561 lbs.	3675	68,000 yds.
(d) K.5. Glatt.	H.E. Sub-calibre Shell (smooth bore)	300 lbs. (approx)	4600 - 5000	75 miles(effect) 100 miles(max)

Notes:-

    (i) Rangetables H.Dv.119/643 serve for both the K.5 and the K.5.Vz. firing normal type H.E. projectiles (serials a and c).

(ii) Rangetables H.Dv.119/648 serve for the K.5 firing the rocket-assisted projectile.

(iii) A non-prerifled rocket-assisted projectile, the R.Gr.4341, was also known to have existed. Although no documentary evidence is available, there is no reason to doubt that it was fired from the K.5. (Vz.).

(iv) It must be borne in mind that whereas the figures given in serials (a) to (c) are taken from German rangetables, those given in serial (d) are only approximate and unconfirmed.

N. Notes on the projectiles used in 28 cm. K.5(E)

1.
H.E.(B.C.) 28 cm. Gr.35.	255.5 kg.	(561 lbs.)
H.E.(B.C.) 28 cm. Gr.35.(Ei).	"	"
H.E.(B.C.) 28 cm. R.Gr.4331.	248 kg.	(547 lbs.)

All the above shell are of the pre-rifled type, having 12 longitudinal splines let into the outer wall of the shell. Certain changes, however, have taken place during the development of this equipment, and these are summarised below:-

(a) 28 cm. Gr. 35.

(i) The original 28 cm. Gr.35 was fitted with both a nose fuze (Hbgr. Z.35 K) and a base fuze (Bd.Z.35 K). The base fuze was then abandoned and shell prepared for base fuze were fired with a plug (Ersatzstück) instead. The latest type of Gr.35 is prepared for nose fuzing only.

(ii) Three types of nose fuze were used on the earlier Gr.35:- Hbrg. Z.35 K., A.Z.23 (0.8) umg. St., or A.Z.35 K with star or white ring. For the later models, only three types of the Hbgr. Z.35 K are provided, varying in the amount of delay, 0.10, 0.15 or 0.05 sec. The fuze now known as the Hbgr.Z.35 K.(0.15) is identical with the fuze earlier referred to as the Hbgr.Z.35 K.

(iii) As an alternative to the percussion fuze, a time and percussion fuze, the Dopp.Z.45 K, is also employed with the Gr.35. The Dopp.Z.45 K is identical with the fuze previously known as Dopp.Z.S/45 - 125. (Maximum setting 125 secs.)

(b) 28 cm. Gr.35. (Ei).

This is a ranging shell (Einschiessgeschoss). In weight and external appearance, it is similar to the 28 cm. Gr.35; it differs internally in weight of H.E. filling (21 lb. instead of 67.25 lb. in the Gr.35) and in being designed to produce a column of thick smoke rising to a height of 130 ft. and lasting about 2 minutes. The remarks in sub-paras (i) to (iii) above, concerning fuzes, also apply to the Gr.35. (Ei).

(c) 28 cm. R.Gr.4331.

The next development was the application of the principle of rocket assistance in the design of projectiles for the 28 cm. K.5.(E) and, some time in late 1943, there appeared the 28 cm. Rocket-assisted shell, known as the 28 cm. R.Gr.4331. According to the range tables (dated January 1944), the 50% zone of this projectile at 56,000 m. (61,250 yds.) is 750 m. x 31 m. (820 yds. x 33 yds.) and at 86,000 m. (94,060 yds.) is 2210 m. x 200 m. (2416 yds. x 218 yds.).

(d) General

   (i) All the above projectiles are provided with a gas sealing ring (Dichtung 28) of graphited asbestos, which is located behind the copper band at the base of the driving splines. This ring may be already fitted to the shell when delivered, or may have to be fitted by the gun detachment, in which case it is tamped into position after the shell has been loaded. Two thicknesses of Dichtung 28 are provided, one of 301 mm. and one of 304 mm; the 304 mm. type to be fitted according to the degree of wear in the shot seating.

   (ii) As there are two different types of liner provided for the 28 cm. K.5.(E), one with slightly deeper grooves (10 mm.) than the other (7 mm.), the above projectiles may be found with two different types of driving splines. For the earlier or deep-grooved type of liner, projectiles have driving splines with raised portions at the forward and rear ends of the splines. To correspond with the increased overall diameter of the splines a slightly thicker sealing ring (Dichtung 28) is provided, all in two sizes, 305 mm. and 308 mm.

(e) 28 cm. Gr. 42

   Weight 561 lbs. An HE shell of normal design, provided with a driving band of conventional type. It is used with the 28 cm. K.5.Vz. The same fuzes are used as with the 28 cm. Gr.35.

(f) 28 cm. Gr. 42 Ei.

   No details of this projectile are available, but presumably it is a ranging round, fired by the K.5. Vz, corresponding to the Gr. 35 Ei, fired by the K.5.

(g) 28 cm. Gr. 39/42.) No details of these projectiles
(h) 28 cm. Gr. 39/44.(Ei).) are available.

(j) Sub-Calibre shell

   Information about this projectile is still incomplete, but the following description is thought to be a fair approximation. The projectile is fired from a smooth bore liner of 31 cm. calibre (the gun is then known as the 28 cm. K.5. Glatt); to make the shell (which has a body diameter of 16 cm.) fit the 31 cm. liner, a discarding steel ring, 2 in. wide and weighing 54 lb., is fixed to the body. Fins, at the rear end of the projectile, stabilise it in flight. Range dispersion is reported to be 2% with a negligible lateral dispersion. The weight of the projectile is 300 lb. The M.V. and range attained with this shell are respectively 4600 - 5000 f.s. and 100 miles. As the guns, equipped with smooth bore (glatt) liners, are known as "Versuchsrohre" (experimental barrels), it would appear that this type of projectile is still in the experimental stage, though a number have in fact been fired in action.

2. 28 cm. R.Gr.4331. (Rocket assisted shell for 28 cm. K.5.(E).)

   (a) General

   This shell, which is rocket-assisted and pre-rifled, is fired by the 28 cm. K.5.(E). (11 inch Railway Gun). The shell is fired with the top charge for the K.5.(E) and, after 19 seconds flight, a mechanical time fuze initiates the rocket mechanism in the nose; the base closing plate of the shell is blown off and the venturi in the base exposed. The duration of burning is not known. The HE filling is provided with 2 internal percussion fuzes, which are armed by the heat of burning of the rocket element. A tracer plug is screwed into a central hole in the base plate. This can be replaced with a tracer No.5, if it is desired to measure the muzzle velocity.

(b) Construction

The shell consists of three main sections:- the front body, main body and base closing plate. The front body is screwed to the main body. The main body is provided with 12 steel ribs, set at the angle of the rifling, which are pressed into undercut slots in the shell wall. The ribs are extended to the rear by short extension pieces to join up with the front of the copper obturating band. The latter is in the form of an equilateral triangle in cross section. Behind the copper band is a shallow groove, into which a graphited asbestos obturator band (Dichtung 28) is pressed shortly before firing. This band ensures gas sealing and it is forbidden to fire any shell without it. On the base edge of the main body are two diametrically opposed slots, which are engaged by the loading device, to ensure that the rifling in the gun and on the shell marry up on ramming.

(c) Rocket Mechanism

The nomenclature of the rocket propellant is "Treilsatz.T.28/4.7". It is contained in the front body of the shell. Shells are only allowed to be fired when the temperature of the rocket propellant is between +5° to +15°C. The rocket mechanism is initiated by a Zt.Z.S/30 fuze mounted in the nose. This is set at the graduation 225 to give a time of flight of 19 seconds. On initiation of the rocket mechanism, the base closing plate, weighing 10 kg (22 lbs), is blown off to expose the venturi. The plate falls to the ground 10 - 16 km in front of the gun.

(d) Fuzing

Two graze action percussion fuzes, AZ 4331, are mounted on an adapter inside the shell. This fuze is armed by the heat of burning of the rocket propellant. There is no delay incorporated in the fuze.

(e) Ramming

The shell is rammed with a special rammer "Ansetzer für die 28 cm. Gr.35", which is modified by fitting two special sleeves. The latter have two lugs which engage in the slots in the base of the shell. After securing the shell to the front of the rammer and testing that it is securely fixed, the nut on the ram-rod is released and pushed forward as far as the front stop ring. The ram-rod, together with the shell, is then pushed forward slowly, until the arms on the nut engage in the slots in the rear face of the breech ring. The rammer is then aligned with the axis of the bore and the shell is rammed home. The length of the ram is read off on the ram-rod, before withdrawing it. After withdrawing the ram-rod, the graphited asbestos obturator ring is tamped in with three blows of a ring hammer.

(f) Safety Precautions

Properly rammed shells are not allowed to be unloaded. Shells with dented or damaged nose caps are not allowed to be fired.

On initiation of the rocket mechanism, the base plate is blown off and falls in an area (4 km wide by 6 km long) whose nearest edge is 10 km from the gun along the axis of fire.

If the time fuze fails to work, or the rocket mechanism does not work for any other reasons, the shell ranges in a similar manner to the 28 cm. Gr.35. This is ullustrated in the following table:-

Range to Target	Range at which "Dud" lands.
km.	km.
55	45
60	48.4
65	51.4
70	54.2
75	56.8
80	59.6
85	62

An area, 8 km. wide within these maximum ranges, must therefore be regarded as a danger area.

(g) Marking

The shell is painted dark green and stencilled "R". The weight of the rocket propellant in kg. is marked in red. The weight of the shell in kg. is stencilled in black. Between the ribs, information is stencilled (in black) regarding the gauging limits over the ribs and the obturator band.

(h) Data: 28 cm. R.Gr. 4331

	Metric	British
Range Table Weight of Shell	248 kg.	547 lbs.
Weight of Rocket propellant	19.5 kg.	43 lbs.
Weight of Gun Propellant	183 kg.	403 lbs.
Weight of Base Closing Plate	10 kg.	22 lbs.
Muzzle Energy	16140 m.t.	52100 ft.tons
Maximum Chamber Pressure	3200 atm.	20.3 tons. sq.ins.
Muzzle Velocity	1130 m.s.	3710 f.s.
Time of flight before rocket mechanism operates	19 secs.	
Maximum Range	86500 m.	94600 yds.
Basis of Range Table Temperature	10°C	
Air Density	1.22 kg/cu.m.	

Range (km)	Elevation (mils)	50% Zone (metres) Length	50% Zone (metres) Width	Drift Right (mils)	Time of Flight (secs)	Remaining Velocity (m.s.)	Angle of Descent (mils)
55	537	-	-	22	93.1	445	847
56	549	730	31	23	94.9	449	854
57	559	-	-	23	96.7	454	861
58	569	830	32	24	98.5	458	867
59	580	-	-	25	100.2	462	873
60	590	910	34	25	102.0	466	879
61	601	-	-	26	103.7	470	884
62	611	990	36	27	105.4	475	889
63	621	-	-	27	107.1	479	894
64	631	1070	39	28	108.7	484	898
65	641	-	-	29	110.3	488	901
66	651	1160	43	29	112.0	493	905
67	661	-	-	30	113.6	497	908
68	670	1250	48	31	115.2	502	911
69	680	-	-	31	116.9	507	914
70	690	1340	54	32	118.5	512	917
71	700	-	-	33	120.2	517	920
72	710	1440	61	33	121.9	522	924
73	720	-	-	34	123.6	527	927
74	730	1540	71	35	125.3	533	930
75	740	-	-	35	127.1	538	934

Range (km)	Elevation (mils)	50% Zone (metres) Length	50% Zone (metres) Width	Drift Right (mils)	Time of Flight (secs)	Remaining Velocity (m.s.)	Angle of Descent (mils)
76	751	1640	83	36	128.8	543	937
777	762	-	-	37	130.7	549	941
78	773	1750	97	38	132.6	555	945
79	785	-	-	39	134.5	561	948
80	797	1860	116	40	136.6	567	952
81	811	-	-	41	138.7	574	957
82	825	1970	140	42	141.0	581	962
83	840	-	-	43	143.5	588	969
84	858	2090	168	45	146.3	597	977
85	880	-	-	47	149.7	607	987
86	911	2210	200	49	154.5	621	1004
86.5	960	-	-	54	160.0	638	1030

(Source: German Range Table H. Dv.g. 119/649 dated Jan 44)

3. **28 cm. R.Gr.4341.** (11 in. Rocket Assisted Shell)

The information on this shell is based on a picture of it in the ammunition pamphlet of the 28 cm. R.Gr.4331. for the K.5 (E). From this, it is presumed that the same charge is used for both shells.

The 28 cm.R.Gr.4331 and 4341 are identical in appearance and weight, except for the omission in the latter of the rifling ribs and the substitution of two centering bands and an iron driving band of complicated shape instead of the copper obturator band.

No definite evidence can be offered as to what gun fires this shell. There are two alternatives:- 28 cm.Br n.K.(E) or the 28 cm.K.5/1.(E). Of these, the former seems more probable for the following reasons:

(a) It is known to fire normal shell, whereas there is no definite evidence for the K.5/1 though it is thought to fire pre-rifled shell.

(b) It uses the same charge and cartridge case as the K.5.(E).

(c) The other shells for it resemble these for the K.5.(E), in the same way as the two shells in question.

4. **Cartridge Case and Propelling Charge for the 28 cm. K.5.(E)**

(a) Cartridge Case

The only cartridge cases, so far reported, are of solid drawn brass.

Case design No. 6309 K 5

Dimensions:- Overall length of case   787 mm.

Overall length to cap (with main charge and cap inserted) 860 mm.

Outside diameter of mouth   326.8 mm.

Outside diameter of rim   360 mm.

(b) Primer

The primer, C/12.K.St, is screwed into a primer magazine (Zündstrahlverstärker), which is in turn screwed into the base of the cartridge case. The primer C/12.K.St is similar to the C/12.n.A. The primer magazine is filled with an igniting composition and has one main forward vent and a ring of inclined radial vents.

(c) Part Charges

The charge for the K.5.(E) is made up of 4 separate part-charges. All the part charges have igniters and are built round a large central tube of propellant, which allows the flash of the primer to penetrate throughout the charge. Secondary charges 1 and 2 include 4 large propellant tubes, in addition to the central one, which are used to house small incremental charges. (See below).

The weight of the part charges are as follows:-

Type of Propellant and Granulation in mm.	Main charge	Secondary charges 1	2	3
Nz Man N P (1.5 x 1.5). (Igniter)	0.180 kg.	0.200 kg.	0.200 kg.	0.100 kg.
Digl RP-G5-($\frac{675}{800}$ (A) x (B) 12.7/5.6))	60.0 kg.(C)	-	-	-
Digl RP-G5-(820 x 12.7/5.6)	-	50.0 kg.(D)	50.0 kg.(D)	-
Digl RP-G5-(300 x 12.7/5.6)	-	-	-	22.0 kg.(E)

Notes:-

(A) Length of central bundle.

(B) Length of outside bundle.

(C) Including central flash tube of Digl RP-G5-(683 x 42/35), charge spacing plates and covering of pressed propellant.

(D) Including central flash tube of Digl RP-G5-(828 x 58/51), incremental charge tubes of Diagonal RP-G5-(820 x 104/97) and charge spacing plates etc.

(E) Including central flash tube of Digl RP-G5-(300 x 152/145) and charge spacing plates etc.

(d) Make up of charges

The 28 cm. K.5.(E) fires with two charges, large and small, which give muzzle velocities of 1120 m.s. (3620 f.s.) and 990 m.s.(3650 f.s.) respectively, with the 28 cm. Gr.35.

Small charge = Main + secondary charges 1 + 2 = 160.58 kg. (353.3 lb.)
Large charge = Main + secondary charges 1 + 2 + 3 = 182.68 kg. (401.9 lb.)

(e) Loading

The required secondary charges are loaded on to the loading tray, one behind the other in descending order, with their base igniters to the rear. They are then pushed into the chamber, until the mark on the cartridge rammer comes in line with the rear face of the barrel; the rammer is then withdrawn. After removing the screwed primer protective cap from the base of the cartridge case, the cartridge case with the main charge inside is pushed into the breech. The latter movement causes all the secondary charges to be pushed slightly further forward, so that on firing all part-charges are in contact, and the flash from the primer can reach the whole of the charge.

(f) Conditioning of Charges.

Charges for the 28 cm. K.5.(E) are carried in an air-conditioned truck, which brings them to within 1°C of the standard temperature of 10°C. This consistency in charge temperature ensures minimum variation in MV between one round and the next. However, if the air-conditioned truck is not available, the charge can be adjusted for variations in temperature.

(g) Adjustment of Charges for Variation in MV

The muzzle velocity of each round fired by the K.5.(E) is normally measured. After continued use, the MV tends to drop due to barrel wear. If the last 10 rounds have a mean MV 10 m.s. or more below the standard MV of the charge, incremental charges of Digl RP-G5-(820 x 12.7/5.6) are added. The charge must never be increased to such an extent that the MV of the large charge exceeds 1126 m.s., otherwise bore prematures are liable to occur. Incremental charges in excess of 15 kg are never used with the small charge.

To calculate the necessary incremental charge, the mean MV of the last 10 rounds is subtracted from the range table MV of the charge. The charge is calculated from the approximate relation:-

$$1 \text{ kg. } (2.2 \text{ lb}) \text{ incremental charge} = 6 \text{ m.s. increase in M.V.}$$

The required incremental charge is placed in the four large propellant tubes of the secondary charges 1 and 2, but not in the central flash tube. To do this, the top of the charge bag is untied, upper igniter and perforated propellant plate removed, and the incremental charge divided equally among the tubes. The igniter etc., are replaced and the charge bag tied up again.

With the same barrel and under the same conditions, the incremental charge for both charges, to bring them up to range table MV, is taken to be the same.

(h) Calculation of variation in MV when the temperature is not standard

If the air-conditioned truck is not available, the charges can still be used. Precautions should be taken, however, to ensure that all the charges are of the same temperature. It is strictly forbidden to increase the MV variations, caused by low charge temperature, by incremental charges since this is liable to cause bore prematures.

The calculation of the variation in MV for both charges is based on the following approximation:-

$$\text{Variation of charge Temperature } 1° \text{ C} = 1 \text{ m.s. variation in MV.}$$

To correct for the effect of low charge temperature, the elevation is increased in accordance with the meteor correction table in the Range Tables. With high charge temperatures, the same procedure is followed, except that the powder temperature with the large charge (unreduced) must never exceed 25°C. If this temperature is exceeded, the charge is reduced by removing propellant from the secondary charges 1 or 2 in the following proportions:-

Charge Temperature	+ 26° to + 30° C	1 kg to be removed.
" "	+ 31° to + 35° C	2 kg to be removed.
" "	+ 36° to + 40° C	3 kg to be removed.

FIG. 70. **28 cm. K.5.(E).**
(11·14 in. GUN, Model 5, on RAILWAY MOUNTING).

FIG. 71. 28 cm. K.5. (E). (11¼-in. GUN, Model 5, on RAILWAY MOUNTING).

The MVs to be expected with various charge temperatures are as follows:-

Charge Temperature °C	Large Charge m.s.	Small Charge m.s.
- 30°	942	1072
- 20°	954	1084
- 10°	966	1096
0°	978	1108
+ 10°	990	1120
+ 20°	1002	1132
+ 30°	1014	1138) Adjusted
+ 35°	1020	1138) charge.

(j) Adjustment of charge to correct for worn barrel and charge temperature

If the barrel is worn, the charge can be adjusted (even if the charge temperature is not normal) to give an MV the same as would be expected from a new gun, with charge at the same temperature. It is forbidden however to increase the large charge by more than 15 kg.

If no MV measuring section is available, the increasing wear can to some extent be corrected for by increasing the charge (large or small) by 1 kg for every 40 rounds fired. The temperature of the charge must be taken into account however.

(k) Packing of the charges

The main charge, together with the cartridge case, and secondary charges 1-3 are packed in four separate labelled steel boxes. The packed weights are as follows:-

Main charge and cartridge case	125 kg. (275 lb.)
Secondary charge. 1.	70 kg. (154 lb.)
Secondary charge. 2.	70 kg. (154 lb.)
Secondary charge. 3.	30 kg. (66 lb.)

N.B. (Source: German Range Table H.Dv.g 119/649 dated Jan 44 and "Vorläufige anweisung für das zuladen bei K.5").

O. 38 cm. SEIGFRIED.Kanone.(E). (15 inch SEIGFRIED Gun (Railway Mounting)).
See fig:- 72.

1. In 1938, as a result of the experiences with the guns already tried out, it was decided to go ahead with the design and construction of heavier railway guns. In order not to waste time in the development of a new barrel, the current 38 cm and 40.6 cm naval gun designs were to be used. These two guns, the 38 cm. S.K. C/34 and the 40.6 cm. S.K. C/34, had originally been designed as the main armament for new battleships. For use in a coastal artillery role, the guns were modified by increasing the length of the chamber and by use of a special long range shell.

The projects were therefore developed, one for a 38 cm. and one for a 40.6 cm. railway gun, the latter to be named Adolf Kanone (E). During the design of the 40.6 cm. equipment, it became clear that it was impossible to design a suitable carriage and at the same time clear the railway loading gauge. The 40.6 cm. project was therefore postponed and all energies concentrated on the 38 cm. Seigfried. In 1939, the production of eight equipments was ordered, but it was not until the middle of 1943 that the first was put into service and only three had been completed by the end of the war.

The gun piece consists of a liner, an "A" tube, a "B" tube, a jacket consisting of 4 hoops, a breech ring and a horizontal sliding breech block, opening to the right.

The percussion firing mechanism is operated by a lanyard through the right trunnion.

The piece recoils through a ring or sleeve type cradle. A complicated system of grease nipples is provided for the lubrication of the bearing surface within the sleeve. The main cradle casting is bored to carry the recoil system cylinders. The single hydro-pneumatic recuperator and the two hydraulic buffers are located below the barrel.

For travelling, the piston rods of the recoil system are disconnected and the gun barrel moved to the rear in the cradle by some 6 metres (20 feet approx). This is effected by an electrically driven oil pump, working in conjunction with two ram cylinders on the top of the cradle.

The gun carriage is of an elongated box shape, cranked in the middle to form a well for the gun and superstructure. The carriage is mounted on two pintle or pivot bearings, which rest on two sixteen-wheel bogie units.

The sighting gear is of the "match the pointer" type elevation and sight reader arm, together with the standard German railway gun dial.

The piece is elevated by applying a horizontal force to the ends of the cradle arms, causing the cradle to pivot about the trunnions. The elevating gear is power operated by electric motors, housed in the front part of the gun carriage.

As is usual in German heavy railway guns, elevation is assisted by hydro-pneumatic pusher type equilibrators. These equalise out the effects required to elevate and depress a gun with muzzle preponderance in weight.

No carriage traverse is provided. Traverse is obtained, either by movement along a spur in the railway truck under the power of the electric motors, mounted on the bogie units, or by means of a portable turntable.

The two bogie units are identical, each having eight axles mounted on semi-eliptical springs. In action (i.e. in the firing position), the movement of the springs is locked by screw clamps. Two axles in each bogie are provided with a geared electrical drive.

The bogie units are unusual owing to their long wheel base, and, in order to give a smaller turning radius, only two of the axles in each bogie are rigidly mounted. The axles at each end of the bogie are pivotted about a vertical axis at the mid point of the axle. The next axle at each end is rigidly mounted and the inner four axles can slide sideways in the bogie frame.

A petrol driven generator mounted on the rear bogie, to the rear of the gun carriage, supplies the electrical power for laying and for the hydraulic and self-propelling gear.

2. Ballistic Performance

	Reduced Charge	Full Charge
(a) Weight of charge	213.25 kg. (470 lbs)	258.25 kg. (569 lbs.)
Muzzle velocity	920 m.s. (3017 f.s.)	1050 m.s. (3445 f.s.)
Chamber pressure	2400 Atmospheres (15.75 Tons sq.in.)	3200 Atm. (21 Tons sq.in.)
Maximum range	40,000 m. (43,750 yds)	55,700 m. (61,000 yds.)
Weight of standard projectile	495 kg (1091 lbs)	
Muzzle energy	21350 m.t.	27810 m.t.

(b) With 800 kg. (1764 lb) shell:-

Muzzle Velocity	-	820 m/s (2690 f.s.)
Maximum range		42 Km (46,000 yds.)

3. Data: 38 cm. SEIGFRIED. K.

	Metric	British
(a) Calibre	380 mm.	15 ins.
Overall length of piece (52 cals)	19630 mm.	64 ft. 4¾ ins.
Length of bore	18405 mm.	60 ft. 4 3/5 ins.
Length of rifling	15748 mm.	51 ft. 8 ins.
Length of breech ring	1500 mm.	4 ft. 11 ins.
Length of chamber to base of shell	2479 mm.	8 ft. 1 3/8 ins.
Capacity of chamber	361.7 litres	79 galls.
Rifling - Increasing right hand twist.	- angle 5°0' 19" to 5°58' 42"	
- No. of grooves	90	
- Depth of grooves	4.50 mm.	.177 ins.
- Breadth of grooves	7.50 mm.	.295 ins.
- Breadth of lands	5.70 mm.	.224 ins.
Normal Recoil	1050 mm.	41.375 ins.
Maximum permissible recoil	1100 mm.	43.75 ins.
Weight of piece	105300 kg.	103.6 tons
Weight of breech	2800 kg.	2.75 tons
Elevation	0 - 813 mils	45°44'
Traverse. (top - Nil.) Turntable	6400 mils.	360°
Recoil of carriage	Up to 1500 mm.	59 ins.
Stability of elevation above	180 mils	10°17'
Height of trunnions above rail	3270 mm.	10 ft. 8¾ ins.
Clearance of main girder over rail	560 mm.	1 ft. 10 ins.
Length over buffers in travelling position	31320 mm.	112 ft. 2½ ins.
Length of carriage main girder	24000 mm.	78 ft. 8 7/8 ins.
Length of bogie unit buffers	12300 mm.	41 ft. 6 ins.
Weight of gun and mounting in action	294000 kg.	289.3 tons

(b) Ammunition - H.E. standard round.

Nomenclature	38 cm. Sprgr L/4.5.(Ei)
Projectile weight	1091 lbs. (495 kg.)
Length (w/ballistic cap)	5 ft. 5¼ ins.
Length of ballistic cap	2 ft. 7½ ins.
Width over driving band	397 mm.
Width at shoulder	379.8 mm.
Number of rotating bands	3 (copper)
Base Fuze	Bd Z.40 K.
Nose Fuze	Dopp.Z.S/45-125
Percussion primer	C.12.nA.

Army System Colour:- field grey, white band at centre.
Naval System Colour:- yellow, with black nose, double-headed black arrow at nose, white band at centre of gravity.

(c) Propelling charges:-

Large and small charges are fired - these are made up in each case in two parts with a main charge (Hauptkartusche), and a secondary charge (Vorkartusche). The latter can be varied.

Weights:

Type of propellant	Hauptkartusche	Vorkartusche
Gunpowder igniter (grob Pulver)	1.250 kg.	1.000 kg.
Gu R P - G5 - (820x10.5/3.5) (850	approx. 133 kg.	-

(c) (Contd.)

Type of propellant	Hauptkartusche	Vorkartusche
Gu R P - G5 - (1300x10.5/3.5)		approx. 123 kg.

Included in the Vorkartusche are:

3 adjusting tubes, each with a 10 kg. bag, and
3 adjusting tubes marked "T", each with 5 kg. of Gu R P - G5 - (1300 x 10.5/3.5).

The large charge consists of the "Hauptkartusche" and the "Vorkartusche" with three adjusting tubes and three smaller adjusting tubes, all complete with adjusting bags.

The small charge consists of the "Hauptkartusche" and the "Vorkartusche" with all six adjusting tubes emptied.

No adjustment charges for correction of M.V., due to barrel wear, are provided.

Charges are maintained at + 15°C. ($\pm$ 1°C.) in the charge waggon. In the event of the temperature controlled charge waggon not being available, or failing to function as such, adjustment of charges is made for variations in charge temperature above 20°, when firing the large charge.

(i) Variations from + 16° to + 20° C. are dealt with according to the correction table in the Range Tables.

(ii) At higher variations, the small adjusting bags "T" are removed as follows:

from 21° to 25°C. - 1 adjusting bag removed.
from 26° to 30°C. - 2 adjusting bags removed.
from 31° to 35°C. - 3 adjusting bags removed.

(d) In this way, with a standard range table barrel, (i.e. M.V. 1050 m.s. at 15°C.) the following M.V. will be arrived at:

Charge Temp. °C.	M.V. m.s.	Charge Temp. °C.	M.V. m.s.	Charge Temp. °C.	M.V. m.s.
21	1039	26	1028	31	1016
22	1040	27	1029	32	1017
23	1040	28	1029	33	1017
24	1041	29	1030	34	1018
25	1042	30	1031	35	1019

(e) 50% Zones. (extracted from Range table 119/670).

	Small charge			Large charge	
Range m.	Length m.	Breadth m.	Range m.	Length m.	Breadth m.
1000	74	0	1000	103	0
10000	74	1	10000	103	0
20000	78	5	20000	105	3
30000	123	15	30000	130	10
40000	304	42	40000	213	22
41000	392	56	50000	391	44
			55000	610	65

FIG. 72. 38 cm. SEIGFRIED. K.(E).
(15 in. SEIGFRIED RAILWAY GUN)

P   40.6 cm. Kanone.(E) (16 inch Gun (Railway Mounting))

1. Reports on the existence or otherwise of this weapon were very conflicting, but it is now generally accepted that a few equipments were used operationally. These equipments were manufactured by Krupp apparently.

The barrel was the Naval S.K. C/34, the same type piece that was used in the coast defence role along the French coast and elsewhere. It was known as the "Adolf" Kanone.

The railway mounting was very similar to that used with the 38 cm. It is probable that it was a strengthened version of it. The elevating gear is power operated. Hydro-pneumatic equilibrators compensate the muzzle preponderance of the piece. No carriage traverse is provided. Traverse is obtained either by movement along a spur in the railway track or by means of a portable turntable.

A petrol driven generator mounted on the rear bogie, to the rear of the gun carriage, supplies the electrical power for laying and for the hydraulic gear, operating the movement of the gun from the travelling to the firing position and vice-versa.

The following limited data cannot be guaranteed for accuracy.

2. Data: 40.6 cm. K.(E)

		Metric	British
(a)	Calibre	406 mm.	16 inches
	Length of gun (50 cals)	29300 mm.	66.6 feet
	Muzzle velocity	850 m.s.	2790 f.s.
	Weight of projectile	960 kg.	2100 lbs.
	Maximum range	45000 metres	49000 yds.
	Elevation	0° to + 40°	
	Traverse	Nil.	
	Weight in action	323000 kg.	318 Tons.

(b) In addition, it is thought probable that the following projectiles were used:-

H.E. L/4.6. Weight 2271 lbs. Muzzle Velocity 2655 f.s.
                                        Max.Range 46,800 yds.
H.E. L/4.8.   "   "   "   Muzzle Velocity 2655 f.s.
                                        Max.Range 46,800 yds.
A.P. L/4.4.   "   "   "   Muzzle Velocity 2655 f.s.
                                        Max.Range 46,800 yds.
H.E. L/4.2.   "   1323 lbs.   Muzzle Velocity 3445 f.s.
                                        Max.Range 61,250 yds.

Q. 80 cm. Kanone.(E). (31.5 ins.Gun (Railway Mounting)) See figs:- 73 & 74.

1. In 1937, work commenced on a gradiose project resulting in the production of two 80 cm. guns on railway mountings. These two mammoth weapons were given the code names of "Gustav Gerät" or "schwere Gustav" and "Dora Gerät", more commonly known as "Gustav" and "Dora".

One of these guns fired against Sebastopol. Some idea of its destructive effect can be gauged from the fact that the heavy weight projectile weighed 7100 kg. (15,655 lbs.) and the light weight projectile 4800 kg. (10,584 lbs.) i.e. 7 tons and 4.72 tons respectively.

The gun detachment numbered some 3000 men, commanded by a Major General. The rate of fire is recorded as one round in 20 mins.

The weapon is operated from a specially constructed double track (four rails) railway carriage.

The barrel (40.6 calibres long) has a two piece liner, secured by means of a locking nut. The construction of the piece is completed by a jacket and a removable breech ring. A horizontal sliding breech block, opening to the right, is employed; movement is effected by hydraulic methods.

The cradle of the weapon, which is of the sleeve type, is attached to the somewhat massive trunnions by twelve large bolts.

The recoil system comprises four cylinders, two for the hydraulic buffers below the barrel. The piston rods are secured in the piston rod yoke, attached to the piece, and therefore recoil with the piece.

The cradle and piece pivot within the trunnion bearings, secured in the saddle or upper portion of the firing carriage.

The platform, for the detachment serving the gun, is fitted on the upper portion of the firing carriage.

The lower portion of the firing carriage is supported on two twin-bogie units, each of the twin-bogie units are fitted with five two-wheeled axles.

The equipment, when assembled ready for action, runs on two parallel tracks, i.e. four rails.

2. In the travelling position, the equipment runs on a normal type railway track. To enable this to be done the equipment travels as follows:-

(a) Breech ring, Barrel, Barrel Jacket, Cradle, Trunnions, and Trunnion bearings are all carried on separate railway trucks.

(b) The remainder of the equipment comprising the upper firing carriage, lower firing carriage and the twin bogie units are uncoupled tranversely into a right half section and a left half section, so that the two half sections can travel separately on normal two rail tracks.

To bring the equipment into action, a four rail track is laid, with branch tracks on the outside for the cranes. The right and left half sections are run along side each other on the inner tracks and coupled together by swing and transverse couplers. The remainder of the components are then brought alongside and lifted into position by the attendant cranes in the following order. First the trunnion bearings are lifted into position on the upper portion of the firing carriage and bolted down. The trunnions are assembled to the cradle, which is then placed in the trunnion bearings. The barrel jacket is then inserted in the sleeve cradle. The barrel tube is then inserted from the rear into the barrel jacket through the piston rod yoke. The breech ring is then inserted into the piston rod yoke and is locked to the barrel and piston rod yoke by the interrupted threads.

3. Data: 80 cm. K.(E)

	Metric	British
Calibre	800 mm.	31.5 ins.
Length of piece (40.6 calibres)	32480 mm.	106 feet
Length of barrel	28957 mm.	95 feet
Rifling	96 grooves	
Elevation	65°	
Traverse (fired from a spur in the track)	zero	
Weight of H.E. projectile	4800 kg.	4.72 tons
Weight of Anti-Concrete projectile	7100 kg.	7 tons
Maximum range with H.E. projectile	47 km.	51,400 yds.
Maximum range with Anti-Concrete projectile	38 km.	41,560 yds.
Muzzle velocity with H.E. projectile	820 m.s.	2690 f.s.
Muzzle velocity with Anti-Concrete projectile	700 m.s.	2296 f.s.
No. of charges	3	
Muzzle velocity with small charge	500-700 m.s.	1640 - 2300 f.s.
Chamber pressure with small charge	2000-2300 atmospheres	13.1 - 15.2 tons per sq.in.
Maximum range with small charge	23 km.	30,520 yds.

FIG. 73. 80 cm. K. (E).
(31·5 in. RAILWAY GUN – "GUSTAV & DORA")

FIG. 74. 80 cm. K. (E).
(31·5 in. RAILWAY GUN – "GUSTAV & DORA")

3. (Contd.)

	Metric	British
Maximum rate of fire	1 round in 15 minutes	
Weight in action	1350 tonnes approx.	1329 tons.
Overall length	42976 mm. approx.	141 feet.
Overall width	7010 mm. approx.	23 feet.

R. Ammunition for the 80 cm. (31.5 in.) Super Heavy Gun (Gustav and Dora)

See fig:- 75.

1. General

This Q.F. separate ammunition is designed for the "schwere Gustav", which is a super-heavy gun mounted on double railway track and is described in the previous section. The calibre of the guns has been variously reported as 80 cm. and 82 cm.

Each shell and cartridge is stencilled with a number. It is believed that there are individual serial numbers enabling a specific shell to be fired with its own ballistically adjusted charge. (e.g.:- All part charges used with shell '81' would likewise be stencilled '81').

2. Projectiles

Two types have been encountered - Anti-concrete (Be.Gr) and H.E. (Sprgr).

Projectiles and ballistic caps are stored separately in substantial wooden crates. It has not been possible to weight the complete projectile, but the weight mentioned in documentary evidence is 7100 kg. (over 7 tons).

(a) Anti-concrete shell (Be.Gr.)

This is an H.E. projectile of conventional APCBC appearance, plugged to take a base fuze. The outer edge of the penetrative cap is screw-threaded to receive the ballistic cap.

Length (w/o ballistic cap)	240 cm. (94.5 ins.)
Diameter at base	80 cm. (31.5 ins.) approx.
Colour	Olive drab.
White stencillings	10 cm. white band at centre of gravity. A number below the centre of gravity band (e.g. 168 - This is believed to be the serial number of the shell). A number in Roman numerals (e.g. II - This normally refers to the weight class). A four figure number above the driving bands (e.g. 7090 - The meaning of this serial is probably the weight in kilograms).
Driving bands	Three double driving bands of iron, with a single band at the rear of greater diameter for obturation purposes. All driving bands are varnished for protection. Breadth (total):- 27 cm. (10.63 ins.)

(b) Ballistic Cap for anti-concrete shell

Length	153 cm. (60.24 ins.)
Diameter at base	72 cm. (28.3 ins.)
Colour	Olive drab

(b) (Contd.)

    White stencilling   Letter 'B' followed by a number (e.g. B.147). (It is assumed that B = Beton (Concrete), as this marking is not present on ballistic caps for H.E. Shell. The number is taken to be the shell serial number.)

The top of the cap is sealed by a screwed plug, which it is assumed is replaced by a lighter plug (Stösselschraube), when the projectile is fired. (This is a common arrangement for large calibre German nose-fuzed shell with ballistic cap; a rod, leading from the top plug to the closing disc of the fuze, forms an extended striker).

There are four equally spaced key slots placed circumferentially around the outside of the cap, 11 cm. from the base. The inside of the cap is screw-threaded in a similar manner to the cap used with the anti-concrete shell.

3. Charges

There are three part charges, each stored separately in a large wooden crate fitted with iron wheels. A label, affixed to the outside of the crates, gives the abbreviated nomenclature of the equipment (s.G.), charge weight and propellant details. Each crate is stencilled in white with a number followed by the letters 'a' 'b' or 'c'. It is assumed that the number is the individual serial number already referred to. From examination, the letters 'a' 'b' and 'c' seem to refer to the type of part-charge. Numbers followed by 'a' were found to contain the main charge housed in the cartridge case (Hauptkartusche), those followed by 'b' the secondary charge No.1 (Vorkartusche 1) and those followed by 'c' the secondary charge No.2 (Vorkartusche 2).

   (a) Hauptkartusche. (Cartridge case and main charge.)

      This is the part-charge housed in the cartridge case. The charge was not removed, but all relevant details were stencilled on the cartridge case.

   (i) The cartridge case is of steel, plated with brass, and of conventional one-piece design.

Length	130 cm. (51.18 ins.)
Width of base	96 cm. (37.8 ins.)
Width at mouth	89 cm. (35 ins.) (inside measurements)

      The base of the case houses a transit plug of the same dimensions as the C/12 nA percussion primer. This plug is screwed into an adaptor, which in turn is screw into a cylindrical adaptor approximately twelve inches long.

      It is assumed that the latter would take a 'sausage' igniter to boost the primer.

   (ii) Black stencilling on base of case

H.Nr. 172	See note 1 below.
0, 54 kg.	" " 2 "
Gu.R.P.-G5-$\frac{103}{128}$.2,5/1,5	" " 3 "
Dbg.42/10626 a-b	" " 4 "
H.P1. 11.42 Lu	" " 5 "

(ii) (Contd.)

    2 Messeier Nr. 52,54   See note 6 below.
    Tab. No. 1271   " " 7 "

(iii) Black stencilling on side of case

Repetition of marking on the base of case, except that the last two lines are omitted.

In addition there is a narrow black band around the case, indicating the centre of gravity.

Interpretation of stencillings

    Note 1. Probably refers to shell and cartridge serial number.

    Note 2. Refers to weight of part-charge, but the figure is not understood (i.e. 0.54 kg. is approx. 1 lb. 3 oz., whereas the part-charge housed in the cartridge case would presumably weigh nearer one ton).

    Note 3. Gu.R.P. = Flashless tubular propellant.
            G.5. = Probably refers to calorific value.
            $\frac{103.2,5/1,5}{128}$ = Measurement of tubular propellant in centimetres.

    Note 4. dbg. = Propellant manufacture (Düneberg?).
            42 = Year.
            10626 a-b = Not known.

    Note 5. Cartridge filling details.

    Note 6.)
) Not understood.
    Note 7.)

(iv) Stampings on base of cartridge case

    At 12 O'clock   b wm (Manufacturer of case).
    At 3 O'clock   1942 (year).
    At 9 O'clock   172 (This appears to be an individual serial number, already referred to.) See Note 1 above.

(b) Vokartusche 1. (Secondary charge No.1)

This part-charge is 156 cm. long and the propellant is contained in a white cylindrical bag.

Stencilling in black.

für Sprgr. (or Be.Gr.)   for H.E. shell (or anti-concrete - as applicable.)

Black band at centre of gravity.
V.K. 1.   Vorkartusche 1.
0,535 Kg.   Charge weight (?)
Gu.R.P.-G5-151-2.5/1,5   Nature, shape and size of propellant.
Dbg. 42/106260   Manufacturer of propellant.
H. Pl. 5.43 Lü   Cartridge filling details.

The outside of the crate, containing the specimen examined, was stencilled '125 b'.

(c) Vorkartusche 2. (secondary charge No.2)

    This differs mainly from the Vorkartusche 1 in the stencilling and in having a slightly heavier charge to weight.

    Stencilling in black

    für Sprgr.
    Black band at centre of gravity.
    V.K. 2.
    0,655 Kg.
    Gu.R.P. -G5-151-1,4/0,4.
    Dbg. 43/11490.
    H.Fl. 5.43 Lü.

    The outside of the crate containing the specimen examined was stencilled '125 c'.

C.5/14/7/48.

THE BIGGEST SHELL IN THE WORLD

Shell and cartridge case for 80cm. (31·5in.) German gun "SCHWERE GUSTAV"

FIG. 75.

DATA FOR GERMAN ARTILLERY EQUIPMENT

HEAVY A.A. GUNS

APPENDIX A

Nomenclature	Calibre (ins.)	Length of Ordnance (ins.)	Length of Rifling (ins.)	Number of Grooves	Elevation	Recoil (ins.)		Firing System (Electrical/Mechanical)	Transmission System (Übertragungsgerät)	Fuze Setter (Zünderstellmaschine)	Rate of Fire (r.p.m.)	Ceiling (ft.)	Overall Dimensions (in draught)			Weight in draught (lbs.)	Weight of HE Projectile (lbs.)	M.V. (f.s.)
													Length	Width	Height			
Flak 18 8.8 cm. Flak 36 Flak 37	}3.465	194	162$^7/_{16}$	32	-3° +85°	(at 0° (at 25° (at 85° (Max.	41.34) 33.46) 27.75) 42.5)	M	}30 37	}18 (19 (37	15-20	34770	25ft.	7ft. 7ins.	7ft. 11ins.	15129	20	2690
8.8 cm. Flak 41	3.465	257¾	213	32	-3° +90°	at 0° at 90°	47 35¼	E	37	41	15	49200	31ft. 8ins.	7ft. 10ins.	7ft. 9ins.	24784	20½	3280
10.5 cm. Flak 38 Flak 39	}4.13	261½	217¾	36	-3° +85°	(at 0° (at 85° (Max.	35.4) 32.7) 35.8)		38 39	38	10-15	42000	33ft. 10ins.	8ft. 4½ins.	9ft. 8ins.	32193	33¼	2886
12.8 cm. Flak 40	5.04	308½	255	40	-3° +88°	at 0° at 85°	51.27 39.37	E	37	40	12	48500	49ft. 2ins.	-	13ft.	59535	57½	2886
12.8 cm. Flakzwilling 40 (Twin barrel)	5.04	308½	255	40	0° +88°	at 0° at 85°	51.27 39.37	E	37	(40 (41	20-25	48500	STATIC EQUIPMENT ONLY 29ft. 11ins.	16ft. 6¾ins.	9ft. 6¾ins.	59535	57½	2886

APPENDIX B   PERFORMANCE DATA OF GERMAN A.A. GUNS

Weapon (Number of Guns per Bty./Tp.)	Muzzle Velocity (Metres per Sec.)	Max. Range (Metres)	Max. Ceiling (Metres)	Max. Range (Metres) ∅	Rate of Fire:- (r.p.m.):- (a) Theoretical (b) Practical	Limits of:- (a) Q.E. (b) Bearing
2 cm. Flak 30 (15 and 3)	900 (2,950 f.s.)	4,800 (5,250 yds.)	3,780 (12,460 ft.)	2,000 (5.5 secs.)	280 / 120	$-10°$ to $+90°$. No limits
2.5 cm. Flak 28 (Hotchkiss) (15 and 3)	830 (2,723 f.s.)	4,400 (4,812 yds.)	2,800 (9,200 ft.)	2,100 (6 secs.)	280	$-15°$ to $+90°$. No limits
2 cm. Flak 38 (15 and 3)	900 (2,950 f.s.)	4,800 (5,250 yds.)	3,780 (12,460 ft.)	2,000 (5.5 secs.)	450 / 220	$-20°$ to $+90°$. No limits
2 cm. Vierling Flak 38 (15 and 3)	900 (2,950 f.s.)	4,800 (5,250 yds.)	3,780 (12,460 ft.)	2,000 (5.5 secs.)	1,800 / 800	$-10°$ to $+100°$. No limits
3.7 cm. Flak 18 (12 and 3)	820 (2,690 f.s.)	6,600 (7,217 yds.)	4,800 (15,750 ft.)	2,500 - 3,300 (6 - 9 secs.)	160x / 80 and 120x	$-8°$ to $+85°$. No limits
3.7 cm. Flak 36 and 37 (12 and 3)	820 (2,690 f.s.)	6,600 (7,217 yds.)	4,800 (15,750 ft.)	3,500	160x / 80 and 120x	$-8°$ to $+85°$. No limits
3.7 cm. Flak 43 (12 and 3)	840 (2,757 f.s.)	6,600 (7,217 yds.)	4,800 (15,750 ft.)	2,500 - 3,300 (6 - 9 secs.)	250 / 150+	$-10°$ to $+90°$. No limits
3.7 cm. Flakzwilling 43	840 (2,757 f.s.)	6,600 (7,217 yds.)	4,800 (15,750 ft.)	2,500 - 3,300 (6 - 9 secs.)	500 / 300+	$-10°$ to $+90°$. No limits
5 cm. Flak 41	840 (2,757 f.s.)	8,000 (8,750 yds.)	5,600 (18,370 ft.)	4,000	200 / 130	$-10°$ to $+90°$. No limits
8.8 cm. Flak 18, 36 and 37 (6 or 8)	820 (2,690 f.s.)	14,860 (16,270 yds.)	10,600 (34,750 ft.)	10,600	15 - 18	$-3°$ to $+85°$. 2 x 360° in each direction
8.8 cm. Flak 37 (with increased performance) (6 or 8)	1,000 (3,281 f.s.)	19,800 (21,650 yds.)	15,000 (49,200 ft.)	12,350	15 - 18	$-3°$ to $+85°$. 2 x 360° in each direction
8.8 cm. Flak 41 (6)	1,000 (3,281 f.s.)	19,800 (21,650 yds.)	15,000 (49,200 ft.)	12,350	15 - 20	$-3°$ to $+90°$. No limits
10.5 cm. Flak 38 and 39 (6)	800 (2,866 f.s.)	17,700 (19,350 yds.)	12,800 (42,000 ft.)	11,800	12 - 15	$-3°$ to $+85°$. No limits
12.8 cm. Flak 40 or Flakzwilling 40 (4)	880 (2,886 f.s.)	20,000 (22,850 yds.)	14,800 (48,500 ft.)	12,800	10 - 12	$-3°$ to $+87°$ No limits

Notes:- ∅ Depending on self-destroying element or time limit of the fuze.

x With extended loading trays.

+ Allowing for barrel changing. Rounds per barrel prior to change = 80 - 100 rounds.

PERFORMANCE DATA OF GERMAN A.A. EQUIPMENT

APPENDIX C

Equipment	Nomenclature	Performance		
		Normal Range/Effective Search Radius		Day/Night Accurate Range Measurement
Radar set (Flak)	39 T(C) and (D) (WÜRZBURG)	15 - 20 km/20 - 35 km. (9½ - 12½ miles/12½ - 22 miles)		10 - 12 km/12 - 20 km. (6 - 7½ miles/7½ - 12½ miles)
	39 T(D) Riese (WÜRZBURG)	30 - 40 km/40 - 70 km. (19 - 25 miles/25 - 44 miles)		20 - 24 km/24 - 40 km. (12½ - 15 miles/15 - 25 miles)
	41 T (MANNHEIM)	20 - 25 km/25 - 40 km. (12½ - 15½ miles/15½ - 25 miles)		20 - 25 km/25 - 40 km. (12½ - 15½ miles/15½ - 25 miles)
		Range Measurements		Magnification
Range finder	EM 6 m R 41 and 43 (19.7 ft. base)	1,580 - 1,000,000 m. (4,900 - 3,281,000 ft.)		40 or 20 times, but only 40 times with type 43
	EM 4 m R 40 (13.1 ft. base)	1,200 - 100,000 m. (3,900 - 328,100 ft.)		32 and 20 times
	EM 4 m R (H) 36 (13.1 ft. base)	620 - 50,000 m. (2,030 - 164,000 ft.)		24 and 12 times
	EM 4 m R (H) 34 (13.1 ft. base)	670 - 550,000 m. (2,200 - 164,000 ft.)		24 and 12 times
	EM 1.75 m R (5.83 ft. base)	500 - 8,000 m. (1,640 - 26,250 ft.)		15 times
	EM 1.25 m R (4.1 ft. base)	500 - 8,000 m. (1,640 - 26,250 ft.)		12 times
	EM 1 m 36 (3.28 ft. base)	500 - 10,000 m. (1,640 - 32,800 ft.)		6 times
	EM 1 m R (3.28 ft. base)	250 - 8,000 m. (820 - 26,250 ft.)		8 times
		Speed of Traverse	Target Height at Future Position	Ground Range
Fire control instruments (predictors)	Kdo Ger 40	300 m/s (985 f.s.)	12,000 m. (39,370 ft.)	14,500 m. (15,800 yds.)
	Kdo Ger 36	150 m/s (492 f.s.)	8,000 m. (26,250 ft.)	13,000 m. (14,200 yds.)
	Kdo Ger 36 (extended range)	180 m/s (590 f.s.)	8,000 m. (26,250 ft.)	15,600 m. (17,100 yds.)
	Kdo Ger 35	150 m/s (492 f.s.)	12,000 m. (39,370 ft.)	12,000 m. (13,120 yds.)
		Range		Speed of Target
A.A. Sights	Flakvisier 35	2,700 m. (8,900 ft.)		120 m/s (170 m/s with extended range)
	Flakvisier 36	3,500 m. (11,500 ft.)		120 m/s (170 m/s with extended range)
	Flakvisier 37 (mechanical clock-work sight only for 3.7 cm. Flak)	4,200 m. (13,800 ft.)		Greatest unlimited angle of deflection ± 30°

SHEET 2 OF APPENDIX C   PERFORMANCE DATA OF GERMAN A.A. EQUIPMENT

Equipment	Nomenclature	Performance		
		Range		Speed of Target
A.A. Sights (continued)	Flakvisier 40 (40a) (electrical sight for 2 cm. Flakvierling 38)	2,500 m. (8,200 ft.)		Greatest unlimited angle of deflection ± 22°
	Schwebekreisvisier 28, 30 and 38	1,200 m. (4,000 ft.)		180 m/s (590 f.s.)
	Schwebedornvisier 43	3,000 m. (9,850 ft.) or 4,000 m. (13,125 ft.)		200 m/s (650 f.s.)
			Power of Lamp	Range (Starry Moonless Night)
Searchlights	Flakscheinwerfer 60 cm.		135 million candlepower	Approximately 4 km.
	" 150 cm. (34 and 37)		1.0 milliard "	" 10 km.
	Flakscheinwerfer 200 cm. (40 A B and 43)		3.0 " "	" 15 "
	Flakscheinwerfer Vierling		4 x 1.0 milliard candlepower	" 20 "
			Normal Static Height (Gas Filled)	Height in Good Wind (Maximum Effective)
Balloons	Barrage Balloon 200 cu. m. with 3.6 mm. cable		1,500 m. (5,000 ft.)	1,900 m. (6,250 ft.)
	" 2.8 " "		2,050 m. (6,725 ft.)	2,600 (8,500 ft.)
	Barrage Balloon 77 cu. m. with 2.8 mm. cable		660 m. (2,160 ft.)	900 m. (2,950 ft.)
		Effect against Flying Targets with HE. Ammunition		Effect against Armoured Targets with Anti-Tank Ammunition
Ammunition	2 cm. Calibre	Single rounds only effective if vital parts or pilot have been hit		Penetration up to 12 mm. (.5 ins.)
	3.7 cm. Calibre	Single rounds have a good effect, but only if vital parts are hit. Several hits will force aircraft down. Best results are obtained with "MINEN GRANATEN"		" " " 25 " (1 in.)
	8.8 " "	Lethal zone within 7 m. (23 ft.) of point of burst - damaging zone up to 18 m. (59 ft.)		" of Flak 18, 36 and 37 up to 110 mm. (4.3 ins.). Flak 41 up to 200 mm. (7.8 ins.)
	10.5 cm. Calibre	Lethal zone up to 9 m. (30 ft.) - damaging zone up to 25 m. (82 ft.)		Penetration up to 128 mm. (5 ins.)
	12.8 cm. Calibre	Lethal zone up to 10 m. (33 ft.) - damaging zone up to 30 m. (98 ft.)		" " " 144 " (5½ ins.)

DATA FOR GERMAN ARTILLERY EQUIPMENTS

APPENDIX D

COAST DEFENCE GUNS

Nomenclature	Length (cals.)	Weight of Projectile (lbs.)		M.V. (f.s.)	Maximum Range (yds.)	Elevation	Traverse	Weight	Remarks
3.7 cm.S.K.C/30 in Einheitslafette C/34 (1.45 in.C.D/A.A.gun on dual purpose mounting C/34)	80 (2,962 mm.) (116.6 ins.)	HE	- 1.64	3,280	7,200	-10° +80°	360°	-	Static Naval dual purpose A.A/C.D. gun. Also fitted on twin pedestal mounting
3.7 cm. Abk. K (1.45 in. sub-calibre gun)	20 (740 mm.) (29.1 ins.)	HE	- 1 1/32		5,000	-4° +30°	360°	-	Sub-calibre gun for practice fire with the 8.8 cm.S.K.C/35
7.5 cm. Pak 40 in 7.5 cm.L.M.39/43 (2.95 in. A/Tk. gun on Naval pedestal mounting)	49 (3,700 mm.) (145.67 ins.)	HE APCBC	- 12.6 - 15	1,800 2,600	8,420 3,280	-10° +40°	360°	2 tons 12½ cwt.	Modified Pak 40 for C.D.use
8.8 cm.S.K.C/35 in Ubts. L.C/35 (3.46 in.Q.F.gun on submarine mounting)	45 (3,990 mm.) (157.1 ins.)	HE Star	- 20 - 20.7	2,295 1,970	13,500 --	-4° +30°	360°	-	Submarine gun emplaced ashore in C.D.role
10.5 cm.S.K.C/32 n.L in 8.8 cm. MPL C/30.D (4.14 in.Q.F.gun on modified 3.46 in. Naval mounting)	45 (4,740 mm.) (186.6 ins.)	HE Star	- 33.2 - 32.4	2,575 2,130	16,800 10,400	-3° +79°	360°	17 tons 3 cwt.	Dual purpose C.D/A.A.gun
10.5 cm.S.K.L/60 (4.14 in.Q.F.gun on coastal mounting)	60 (6,300 mm.) (248 ins.)		33	3,000	19,100	-10° +80°	360°	9 tons 12 cwt.	-
12.7 cm. Abk. K.L/35 (5 in. sub-calibre gun)	35 (4,445 mm.) (175 ins.)		61.6	1,968	15,300	-	-	-	This is a practice equipment fitted to the 38 cm.S.K.C/34 and is used for practice firing only. No particulars are available as to how it is attached to the parent gun
15 cm. (5.9 in.) twin barrel, turreted, C.D.gun.	60 (9,000 mm.) (354 ins.)	HE AP/HE Star	- 99.6 - 99.6 - 55	2,870	27,000	-7° +40°	350°	-	These twin mounted guns in turret possess all the features of a Naval mounting - elevation electric, traverse hydraulic, rammed and fired electrically
15 cm.S.K.C/28 Kst. M.P.L.C/36 (5.9 in. gun on coast mounting)	55 (8,291 mm.) (326.4 ins.)	HE AP Concrete	- 100 - 100 - 95.7	2,870	25,700	-5° +35°	360°	-	Manual laying - receiver dials. Ordnance same as 15 cm. K in Mrs. Laf.
15 cm. Tbts. C/36 (5.9 in. Torpedo boat gun)	47 (7,013 mm.) (276.4 ins.)	HE	- 100	2,740	21,350	-4° +40°	360°	-	Low pedestal mounting on holdfast
15 cm. Ubts. u Tbts.K.L/45 (5.9 in. Submarine and torpedo boat gun)	45 (6,820 mm.) (268.6 ins.)	HE (L/4.1) HE BO (Nose fuze)	- 100 - 114	2,230 2,155	17,500 15,000	-4° +45°	60°	-	Modern Naval design, primarily designed for ships but largely used in

SHEET 2 OF APPENDIX D

DATA FOR GERMAN ARTILLERY EQUIPMENTS
COAST DEFENCE GUNS

Nomenclature	Length (cals.)	Weight of Projectile (lbs.)	M.V. (f.s.)	Maximum Range (yds.)	Elevation	Traverse	Weight	Remarks
15 cm.S.K.L/40 (5.9 in.C.D.gun)	40 (5,960 mm.) (234.6 ins.)	HE (Fixed) - 100 HE (Separate) - Star	- 2,640	14,200 21,870 7,660	-10° +30°	360°	-	Old Krupp design used in CD role. Ordnance same as 15 cm. K.(E)
17 cm.S.K.L/40 (6.7 in.C.D.gun)	40 (6,900 mm.) (271.6 ins.)	HE - 138	2,870	30,620	-5° +45°	Up to 360°	-	Fixed pedestal mounting enclosed in casemate. Ordnance same as 17 cm. K in Mrs. Laf.
20.3 cm.S.K.C/34 (8 in.C.D.gun)	60 (approximately) (12,150 mm.) (478.34 ins.)	HE - 260.4 AP - 275	3,035	40,465	-5° +40°	Up to 360°	-	Ordnance same as 20.3 cm. K.(E)
24 cm.S.K.L/40 (9.4 in.C.D.gun)	40 (9,550 mm.) (31.3 ft.)	HE - 326.7 AP - 332.2	2,657	29,250	-5° +45°	Up to 360°	-	Ordnance same as 24 cm. Theodor K.(E)
24 cm.S.K.L/35 (9.4 in.C.D.gun)	35 (8,400 mm.) (27.5 ft.)	HE (L/4.5) - 333 HE (L/4.2) - 327	2,210	22,200	-5° +45°	Up to 360°	-	Ordnance same as 24 cm. Theodor Bruno.K.(E)
28 cm.S.K.L/40 (11 in.C.D.gun)	40 (11,200 mm.) (36.75 ft.)	HE - 528	2,690	32,250	-5° +45°	360°	-	Made by Krupp for Naval use in 1914 - later employed as railway and CD gun. Ordnance same as 28 cm. kurze Bruno.K.(E)
28 cm.S.K.L/45 (11 in.C.D.gun)	45 (12,735 mm.) (41.8 ft.)	HE - 624.8	2,870	39,500	-5° +45°	Up to 360°	-	Ordnance same as 28 cm. lange Bruno.K.(E)
28 cm.S.K.L/50 (11 in.C.D.gun)	50 (14,150 mm.) (46.4 ft.)	HE - 626 AP - 666	2,970 2,920	42,760 33,900	-4° +50°	Up to 360° Up to 360°	-	-
30.5 cm.S.K.L/50 (12 in.C.D.gun)	50 (1,525 mm.) (50 ft.)	HE - 551 AP - 893 Practice - 15½	3,674 2,805 1,434	56,210 35,540 9,100	-4° +45°	340°	177 tons	Mounting is supported on massive circular concrete pedestal having rails outside a dry moat round the pedestal to support rear portion of mounting. Casemate opening restricts the traverse from 360° to approximately 180°. Krupp built - electrically or manually operated
38 cm.S.K.C/34 (Siegfried) (15 in.Q.F.Model 34 gun)	52 (19,630 mm.) (64 ft.4½ ins.)	Si Gr - 1,091 Si Gr - 937 HE - 1,764 AP - 1,764 Practice - 882	3,444 3,018 2,690 2,460	61,000 50,850 46,040 26,360	-4° +60°	Limited by casemate	-	This turret gun is mounted within a massive casemate. Although of 1934 construction, the mounting, etc., are thoroughly modern. Electric ramming and laying and rapid rate of fire
40.6 cm.S.K.C/34 (Adolf) (16 in.Q.F.Model 34 gun)	50 (20,300 mm.) (66.6 ft.)	HE - 2,271 AP - 2,271 Ad Gr - 1,323	2,655 3,445	46,800 61,250	0° +60°	Limited by casemate	-	Gun was designed as main armament for battleships. Modified for CD role by increasing length of chamber. See also remarks on "Siegfried" gun above

TABLE OF COMPARATIVE DATA FOR "RAUPEN GERÄTE" AND OTHER MISCELLANEOUS HEAVY AND SUPER-HEAVY EQUIPMENTS AS AT JULY, 1942
(including Projects, Designs and Equipments in Service)

(N.B.   R = RAUPEN GERÄTE = Equipments on tracked carriages or transporters).

Nomenclature of Equipment	For which Service Developed	Calibre	Weight of Shell	Muzzle Velocity	Maximum Range	Weight in Action	Number of Travelling Loads	Number of Railway Loads	State of Development
	A = Army N = Navy	mm.	kg.	ms.	Km.	Metric Tons	T = Tracked WT = Wheeled Transporters		P = Project D = Design CP = In Production S = In Service
Krupp R.5 Gun	(N)	149	42	980	28.5	45	One T	1	D
Krupp 17 cm. S.P. Gun	(A)	172.5	68 / 62.8	860 / 925	28 / 31	40 / 50	One T	-	D
Krupp R.4 Gun	(N)	203	112	985	41	70	One T	1	P
Skoda K.39/40	(A)	210	135	800	29.9	38	Three WT	-	S
Krupp K.38	(A)	210.9	120	905	33.8	25	Two WT	-	S
Krupp R.5 Howitzer	(A)	211	113	580	16.7	45	One T	1	D
Krupp 21 cm. Howitzer	(A)	211	113	565	16.7	40.5	One T	-	D
Krupp R.4 Howitzer	(N)	238	175	740	26	60	1	1	P
Krupp R.3 Gun	(A)	238	160	1,030	43	80	1	1	P
Rheinmetall K.4	(A)	238	152.3 / 152	970 / 1,090	37.5 / 47	54 / 93	Five WT / Three T	-	S / CP
Krupp K.4	(A)	238	160	1,075	49	75	Two T	-	CP
Skoda 24 cm. Howitzer	(A)	240	166	600	18.3	27.1	Three WT	-	S
Skoda 24 cm. Gun	(A)	240	215	750	26.3	79.1	Four WT	-	C
Krupp K.4 Howitzer	(A)	283	300	760	30	75	Two T	-	D
Krupp R.2 Gun	(N)	283	330 / 195	890 / 1,100	43 / 53	110	1	1	D
Krupp K.5	(A)	283	255	1,120	61	160	Three T	-	D
Krupp R.3 Howitzer	(A)	305	370	665	25	80	1	1	P
Skoda 30.5 cm. Howitzer	(A)	305	289	450	12.3	23	Three WT	-	S
Rheinmetall M.1	(A)	355.6	575	570	21	78	Seven WT	1	S
Krupp R.2 Howitzer	(A)	380	1,000	500	20	100	1	1	P
Krupp R.1 Gun	(N)	380	500 / 800	1,135 / 960	65 / 55	190	2	3	P
Krupp "Siegfried" K	(A)	380	500 / 800	1,020 / 820	53 / 42	294	Nil	1	S
Krupp K.5 Howitzer	(A)	420	1,000	585	21	160	Three T	-	D
Skoda 42 cm. Howitzer	(A)	420	1,215 / 860	500 / 600	18 / 20.5	127	Six WT	-	D
Krupp 42 cm. Howitzer	(A)	420	1,020 / 860	- / -	22 / 25	-	Three T	-	P
Krupp R.1 Howitzer	(A)	520	1,950	590	25	220	1	3	P
Krupp "Siegfried" Howitzer	(A)	520	1,950	590	25	220	Nil	1	D
Rheinmetall Gerät 041	(A)	540	1,580 / 1,250	- / -	7 / 10	125	One T	1	S

APPENDIX F

DATA FOR GERMAN ARTILLERY EQUIPMENTS

RAILWAY GUNS

Nomenclature	Length of Barrel	Weight in Action	Weight of Standard Projectile	Maximum Horizontal Range	Maximum Muzzle Velocity	No. of Charges Fired	Elevation	Traverse	Remarks
15 cm. Kanone (E) (5.88 ins.)	40 cals. (19.55 ft.)	74 m tons (72.8 tons)	43 kg. (95 lbs.)	22,500 m (24,610 yds.)	805 m/s (2,640 f.s.)	3	10° to 45°	360°	4 equipments delivered in 1937
17 cm. Kanone (E) (6.8 ins.)	40 cals. (22.6 ft.)	80 m tons (78.47 tons)	62.8 kg. (138 lbs.)	26,800 m (29,300 yds.)	875 m/s (2,870 f.s.)	1	10° to 45°	360°	6 equipments delivered in 1937
20 cm. Kanone (E) (8 ins.)	60 cals. (39.86 ft.)	86 m tons (84.75 tons)	122 kg. (268 lbs.)	36,400 m (39,800 yds.)	925 m/s (3,035 f.s.)	1	10° to 47°	360° Turntable	Actual calibre 203 mm. 8 equipments delivered in 1940
21 cm. K.12.(E) (8.3 ins.)	158 cals. (109.25 ft.)	318 m tons (313 tons)	107.5 kg. (236.5 lbs.)	100/123 km. (71½ miles)	1,500 m/s (4,920 f.s.)	2	25° to 55°	360° Turntable	3 equipments produced in 1939
24 cm. Theodor Bruno Kanone (E) (9.4 ins.)	35 cals. (27.5 ft.)	94 m tons (92.5 tons)	148.5 kg. (326.7 lbs.)	20,200 m (22,100 yds.)	675 m/s (2,215 f.s.)	1	0° to 45°	±1°	6 equipments delivered in 1939
24 cm. Theodor Kanone (E) (9.4 ins.)	40 cals. (31.3 ft.)	95 m tons (93.5 tons)	148.5 kg. (326.7 lbs.)	26,750 m (29,250 yds.)	810 m/s (2,657 f.s.)	2	0° to 45°	±1°	3 equipments delivered in 1937
28.3 cm. kurze Bruno Kanone (E) (11.14 ins.)	40 cals. (36.75 ft.)	129 m tons (127 tons)	240 kg. (528 lbs.)	29,500 m (32,250 yds.)	820 m/s (2,690 f.s.)	1	0° to 45°	±1°	8 equipments delivered in 1938
28.3 cm. schwere Bruno Kanone (E) (11.14 ins.)	42 cals. (39.14 ft.)	118 m tons (116.13 tons)	284 kg. (625.8 lbs.)	35,700 m (39,050 yds.)	860 m/s (2,821 f.s.)	1	0° to 45°	±1°	2 equipments delivered in 1938
28.3 cm. lange Bruno Kanone (E) (11.14 ins.)	45 cals. (41.8 ft.)	123 m tons (121 tons)	284 kg. (625.8 lbs.)	36,100 m (39,500 yds.)	875 m/s (2,870 f.s.)	1	0° to 40°	±1°	3 equipments delivered in 1938
28.3 cm. Bruno neue Kanone (E) (11.14 ins.)	58 cals. (53.8 ft.)	150 m tons (147.6 tons)	255 kg. (561 lbs.)	46,600 m (51,000 yds.)	995 m/s (3,264 f.s.)	1	0° to 50°	±1° (360° Turntable)	4 equipments produced in 1943
28.3 cm. K.5.(E) (11.14 ins.)	76 cals. (70 ft. 8 ins.)	218 m tons (215 tons)	255 kg. (561 lbs.)	62,000 m (67,900 yds.)	1,120 m/s (3,675 f.s.)	2	0° to 55°	±1° (360° Turntable)	Different types of barrel for normal prerifled projectiles. Maximum Range with Rocket Assisted shell was 54 miles, with sub-calibre shell 100 miles approximately
38 cm. Siegfried Kanone (E) (16 ins.)	52 cals. (64 ft. 4⅞ins.)	294 m tons (289.3 tons)	495 kg. (1,091 lbs.)	55,700 m (61,000 yds.)	1,050 m/s (3,445 f.s.)	2	0° to 52°	360° Turntable	3 equipments completed out of order for 12
40.6 cm. Adolf Kanone (16 ins.)	50 cals. (66.6 ft.)	323 m tons (318 tons)	960 kg. (2,100 lbs.)	45,000 m (49,000 yds.)	850 m/s (2,790 f.s.)	1	0° to 40°	Spur or Turntable	Only a few equipments in service
52 cm. lange Gustav (20.47 ins.)	87 cals. (148.4 ft.)	1,500 m tons (1,476 tons)	1,580 kg. (1.55 tons)	150 mm. (93.25 miles)	1,240 m/s (4,070 f.s.)	1	0° to 65°	Spur	Project only - no equipments built
80 cm. schwere Gustav (31.5 ins.)	40.6 cals. (106.6 ft.)	1,350 m tons (1,329 tons)	7,100 kg. (7 tons) 4,800 kg. (4.72 tons)	38,000 m (41,560 yds.) 47,000 m (51,400 yds.)	700 m/s (2,296 f.s.) 820 m/s (2,690 f.s.)	3	65°	Spur	2 equipments completed - named Gustav and Dora

www.ingramcontent.com/pod-product-compliance
Lightning Source LLC
Chambersburg PA
CBHW080909230426

43664CB00017B/2761